LANGUAGE AND LITERACY SERIES

Dorothy S. Strickland, FOUNDING EDITOR
Celia Genishi and Donna E. Alvermann, SERIES EDITORS

ADVISORY BOARD: Richard Allington, Kathryn Au, Bernice Cullinan, Colette Daiute, Anne Haas Dyson, Carole Edelsky, Shirley Brice Heath, Connie Juel, Susan Lytle, Timothy Shanahan

(Continued)

For volumes in the NCRLL Collection (edited by JoBeth Allen and Donna E. Alvermann) and the Practitioners Bookshelf Series (edited by Celia Genishi and Donna E. Alvermann), please visit www.tcpress.com.

URBAN LITERACIES

Critical Perspectives on Language, Learning, and Community

EDITED BY

Valerie Kinloch

FOREWORD BY
Arnetha F. Ball and Carol D. Lee

AFTERWORD BY
JoBeth Allen

**TEACHERS
COLLEGE
PRESS**

Teachers College
Columbia University
New York and London

Published by Teachers College Press, 1234 Amsterdam Avenue, New York, NY 10027

"Poem for Anyone Who Thinks I'm Not African Enough" by Uchechi Kalu, from *Flowers Blooming Against a Bruised Gray Sky* (Whit Press, 2006), is published by permission of Whit Press (www.whitpress.org).

Library of Congress Cataloging-in-Publication Data

Urban literacies : critical perspectives on language, learning, and community / edited by Valerie Kinloch ; foreword by Carol D. Lee and Arnetha Ball ; afterword by JoBeth Allen.
     p. cm. — (Language and literacy series)
  Includes bibliographical references and index.
  ISBN 978-0-8077-5182-4 (pbk. : alk. paper) 1. Education, Urban—Social aspects—United States. 2. Literacy—Social aspects—United States. 3. Minorities—Education—United States. 4. Critical pedagogy—United States. I. Kinloch, Valerie, 1974–
  LC5131.U696 2011
  302.2'244—dc22

                                        2010054360

ISBN 978-0-8077-5182-4 (paperback)

Printed on acid-free paper

Manufactured in the United States of America

18 17 16 15 14 13 12 11   8 7 6 5 4 3 2 1

To all those brave, courageous teachers, teacher educators, and researchers,

and to the children, youth, and adults with whom you work,

this book is dedicated to you.

Contents

Foreword

This volume represents a handoff to a new generation of literacy scholars committed to use their scholarship to achieve social justice ends. They understand the ways that literacy (e.g., reading, writing, and speaking) is intimately tied to our most fundamental identities as individuals and members of communities. Their ascendance comes at an important historical moment when new forms of literate practices are expanding at unprecedented rates: forms of spoken word taken up by young people as poets and performers, who chronicle the conundrums of their times with creatively sculpted language and rhythms, acting on street corner stages, rooted deeply in communities; a massive array of digital tools, from powerhouse devices small enough to fit the palms of their young hands to communicative tools that situate users as producers, from Twitter to YouTube. This is an exciting communications era not only because of new tools and genres but because also—much like in the momentous 1960s when we were at the phoenix of our young development—this movement is being led largely by young people, including the new generation of literacy scholars featured in this historic volume.

Just as the historic 1974 declaration of the rights of the student to his own language emerged out of institutional social justice organizing within the professional ranks of CCCC, so an important cauldron for the development and nurturing of these young scholars is the Cultivating New Voices mentoring program of the National Council of Teachers of English, in which we and the other senior scholars who have written the afterwords have participated. Each generation stands on the shoulders of those who precede them. For us this includes great writers like Langston Hughes and Zora Neale Hurston, who shouted critically in the 1930s and 1940s that the language and rhythms of the everyday people were indeed a voice that the great narratives of what it means to be human should embody, as Alice Walker who heard Zora's expansive and proud spirit reflects on Celie's voice as that of her great-grandmother.

This celebration of the language and rhythms of everyday life has been embraced by our greatest writers and by today's young generation but has continued to elude our educational institutions. The scholars in this volume present us with guidance rooted in rigorous research, guidance for teachers and teacher education to be empowered to learn from and build upon the linguistic and creative energy bounding on street corners, in community bookstores, out of digital devices, and through Internet airwaves.

Just as the writers of the 1974 resolution on *Students' Rights To Their Own Language* served a wake-up call to scholars and researchers to take on the challenge of researching and expanding the understanding of knowledge and experiences that all teachers should have in order to meet the needs of culturally and linguistically diverse students, the new generation of literacy scholars in this volume are serving a wake-up call to 21st-century scholars to move beyond our old paradigms and create new spaces for knowledge that expands the application of research to practice. These new and emerging voices present theoretically rich and practically sound chapters that extend prior conversations on the literate lives, academic achievements, and social networking systems of students of color in urban environments, through rigorous research, various theoretical orientations, and diverse methodologies.

The work that we have forged in the areas of language, literacy, and teacher education over the last 2 decades afforded us numerous opportunities to reflect with great concern on the challenges facing urban education. Our reading of this volume, however, has proven to be a source of hope, for within the pages of this volume emanates our confidence that the next generation of research is in good hands. Indeed, the voices of these scholars have actually risen to the challenges that lie ahead. We are inspired by them in this historic volume. They have paved a new groundwork for empowering literacies in schools and communities.

Arnetha F. Ball
Carol D. Lee

Acknowledgments

Sometime in 2007, I was asked by members of the Research Foundation of the National Council of Teachers of English (NCTE) to become the next Director of the Cultivating New Voices Among Scholars of Color Program (CNV). As a fellow in the very first cohort (2000–2002) and—years later— as a mentor to new fellows (2006–2008; 2008–2010), I felt an obligation to "rise to the occasion." I accepted the invitation to direct the program and to work intimately with senior scholars who volunteered their time to mentor advanced doctoral students and junior scholars of color into the professoriate and beyond. In my opinion, CNV is an important mentoring program, one that prides itself on supporting the professional, intellectual, and activist activities of scholars of color by pairing each fellow with a senior scholar in the field (e.g., education/teacher research; literacy, language, cultural studies; English). Undoubtedly, CNV is committed to supporting the critical work and professional endeavors of scholars of color (for more information, see http://www.ncte.org/grants/cnv).

Therefore, I must first thank CNV—its founders, Carol D. Lee, Arnetha Ball, and Peter Smagorinsky; its former directors, Peter Smagorinsky and María Fránquiz; the dedicated mentors and fellows; and members of the NCTE Research Foundation. Your commitment to CNV (and to other mentoring programs for scholars of color) must be acknowledged.

Secondly, I thank the contributors to *Urban Literacies*. It was a pleasure working with you, reading your chapters, and attending presentations where you discussed aspects of your work. From the top to the bottom of my heart, I thank you for your participation and I thank your participants for inviting you into their literacy lives to document important elements of their lived conditions.

Anyone who has ever edited a book knows of the labor of love that goes into its creation. Many people, including the section introduction authors and external reviewers, supported this collection. I would be remiss if I do not publicly thank them. In no particular order, I thank the section introduction authors—Juan Guerra, Anne Haas Dyson, Celia Genishi, Colleen Fairbanks, and Detra Price-Dennis. I also thank the invited, external chapter reviewers for insightful, timely feedback: Sarah Freedman, Beverly

Moss, Susi Long, Maria Torres-Guzman, Adam Banks, Lalitha Vasudevan, Mollie Blackburn, Caroline Clark, David Bloome, and Peter Smagorinsky.

I thank Carole Saltz, director of Teachers College Press, for believing in this project, and my acquisitions editor, Meg Lemke, for helping me develop my initial ideas into a book. From the Language and Literacy Series Editors, the Production Team, to the anonymous external reviewers, I honor your hard work.

As director of CNV, I sought to build on the research foundation that was already in place. This book serves as one of my attempts to support the scholarship of CNV scholars *and* other scholars in the field who may not be directly involved with CNV, but whose work aligns with the mission of CNV—that is, to forge new paths and conduct critical, rigorous research that honors the lives and literacies of all children, youth, and adults, particularly, but not exclusively, those of color attending school and/or residing in urban settings. I thank you!

URBAN LITERACIES

On Critical Urban Education

An Introduction

Valerie Kinloch

Over the last 57 years, the landscape of American public schools—in urban, suburban, and in rural settings; from pre-K, elementary, middle, and high school, to college and beyond—has been affected by a number of key historical moments, such as *Brown v. Board of Education of Topeka*, the civil rights movement, the integration of the William Frantz Elementary School in New Orleans led by an African American student named Ruby Bridges, and the integration of Central High School in Arkansas by the Little Rock 9. Additionally, the reality of immigration, globalization, shifting community patterns, structures, and members, and the resulting changes in student demographics, have contributed to today's racially, ethnically, and linguistically diverse classrooms. The increasing diversity within schools and surrounding communities raises a number of challenges for educators. These challenges, among others, include: a) utilizing creative pedagogical strategies and tools in our work with students in order for them to enhance academic skills, critical literacies, and civic responsibilities as they prepare for participation in a multicultural democracy; b) employing culturally relevant methods/resources that encourage students to question multiple lines of differences in classrooms and communities; c) learning how to build on the accumulated knowledge(s) that students bring into classrooms from familial communities; and d) critiquing the growing racial, economic, and linguistic boundaries between students and teachers. Such challenges are important to discuss in the face of current demographic trends that predict by 2020, students of color will comprise 46% of our nation's students, many of whom, according to educational researchers Pallas, Natriello, and McDill (1989), will be poor.

The projected trends concerning students of color within American public schools reveal highly complicated national issues around community change (e.g., demographic shifts, land redevelopment, gentrification), identity (e.g., race, ethnicity, language, class, gender, sexual orientation, debates over a *singular* national identity), and the assertion of power (e.g., the Arizona immigration law, attacks on ethnic studies, the continued existence of English-only policies). Educational research and researchers must continue to question, critique, and propose alternative and just approaches to addressing these changes. A lot is at stake, especially, although not exclusively, for urban children, youth, and adults. Thus, *Urban Literacies* serves as one attempt to speak to the critical times in which we live as language and literacy educators.

In this collection of research on issues in urban education, new and emerging scholars of color in the field have authored theoretically rich and practically sound chapters that extend current conversations on the literate lives, academic achievements, and social networking systems of students of color in urban environments during and after school time. The primary focus of this book is to closely and carefully investigate—through rigorous research, various theoretical orientations, and diverse methodologies—meanings of and current concerns with urban education in the lives of children, youth, and adults of color across three intersecting spectrums. These include: 1) research on family and community literacies, 2) research in teaching and teacher education, and 3) research in popular culture, digital media, and forms of multimodality. I believe these three spectrums intersect in ways that reveal important narratives about *how* some children, youth, and adults of color produce extended meanings of schooling, including the ways they engage in "talking back" or critical talk (Kinloch, 2010b) by writing and performing powerful, personal, and politically driven spoken-word pieces (Fisher, 2007; Hill, 2009; Jocson, 2008), and how they refigure identities in schools, local communities, and online to assert agency (Blackburn, 2004; Staples, 2008; Kirkland, 2008). These three spectrums also contribute to *what* some children, youth, and adults of color are doing, such as adopting ethnographic stances (e.g., interviewing, surveying, analyzing data) to inquire into unfair school and community policies that appear to threaten their civil liberties (Darling-Hammond, 2006; Kinloch, 2010a; Vasudevan & Campano, 2009), and negotiating the different terrains of, relationships within, and competing identities involving home, school, and online communities. Extending the focus on literacy from school-sponsored practices and events, all of the chapters take as their individual cases urban education to situate and resituate literacy across political and educative conditions and situations that involve children, youth, and/or adults of color.

In extending the focus, contributors inquire into important questions: What does this (re)-situation mean and imply for education in urban settings?

What are examples of projects and practices that encapsulate linguistically and culturally rich identities of children, youth, and adults of color in urban settings and across contexts defined as schools, local and national communities, and online environments? How can critical educational research in urban settings account for dynamic interactions, practices, and literate engagements of children, youth, and adults in ways that critique popular and often unfounded notions that they are disengaged from learning?

THE THREE INTERSECTING SPECTRUMS

Contemporary accounts of the literacy experiences of children, youth, and adults of color have begun to critically investigate literacy practices and events within family, community, school, and online environments as well as in popular culture (Kirkland, 2008; Moje, 2002; Morrell, 2008; Morrell & Duncan-Andrade, 2002; Moss, 2003; Vasudevan, 2008). As the chapters in this book attest, studies on and about literacy have gradually shifted from a singular focus on school-sponsored learning to a more complex focus on the practices of children, youth, and adults across multiple sociopolitical contexts (Ball, 2006; Lee, 2007). This shift is important to note, especially as more and more children, youth, and adults of color are rewriting popular narratives that paint them as disconnected from active, participatory forms of learning (Ginwright, Noguera, & Cammarota 2006; Morrell, 2008; Vasudevan, 2009).

Many of us know all too well about the effects unjust educational mandates, standardized testing, and ongoing political and economic policies can have on the identities, literacy lives, and academic achievement of countless children and young adults. Therefore, *Urban Literacies* is intentionally organized by three intersecting spectrums—research on family and community literacies, in teaching and teacher education, and in popular culture, digital media, and forms of multimodality. In these ways, the chapters—all using pseudonyms to protect the identities of participants—are responsive to the visible gap in research that articulates new visions of literacy studies and teaching on the lived conditions and daily interactions of children, youth, and adults of color.

Chapters in the first section, "Research on Family and Community Literacies," inquire into a variety of questions: What are examples of critical research on family and community literacies in urban settings? How can involvement with family and community literacies create opportunities to bridge "sociological distances" (Cushman, 1996, p. 8; see also Kinloch, 2009) between literacy engagements in home and school? What lessons can we learn from research on family and community literacies as we reconceptualize the purposes and functions of education for children, youth, and adults across multiple, often competing contexts? What implications might this work have for additional research on family and community literacies, and what connections does it pose for studies in teaching and teacher education? The chapters assembled in this first section each present focused cases on family and/ or community literacies and offer practical implications for teachers and researchers in the "Critical Perspective" feature closing each piece.

In the second section, "Research in Teaching and Teacher Education," contributors consider a number of issues: In what ways does scholarship in teaching and teacher education demonstrate insightful practices on and ways to critically think about urban children, youth, and adults in relation to curricular goals? What are examples of research that is being done, and in what ways does this research provide insights into teaching practices, projects, and forms of collaborative work in and out of school learning communities? What does this work look like, mean, and suggest for research in teaching and teacher education? The three chapters in this section share a central concern, which is to locate innovative practices, approaches, and ways of thinking about/talking with urban children, youth, and teachers in light of cultural, political, and social conflicts. In their "Critical Perspective" feature, authors describe strategies to teach urban youth in a variety of contexts while confronting specific teaching and learning tensions.

Finally, in "Research in Popular Culture, Digital Media, and Forms of Multimodality," contributors address various questions: What is the significance of conducting research in popular culture, digital media, and forms of multimodality? How does this body of scholarship contribute to existing literature and current projects in urban education? Specifically, how does this body of scholarship challenge existing literature in accounting for the sophisticated practices and engagements of children, youth, and/or adults? What are examples of projects in popular culture and digital media, and what do they imply for what we know and need to know about urban education? The three chapters in this section are attentive to political and educational influences that forms of popular culture have on the academic lives of youth. In their "Critical Perspective" feature, authors present models, methods, and practices for teachers and researchers to use in their work with youth and popular culture.

OVERVIEW AND DESCRIPTION OF THE CHAPTERS

The first section opens with Juan Guerra's introduction, "In Consideration of Family and Community Literacies," which situates the chapters in existing scholarship on language, literacy, community, and culture. Guerra argues for additional research that contributes "new insights to a growing mosaic of understanding related to rhetorical and discursive agility children from disenfranchised communities demonstrate in- and out-of-school." Taking Guerra's assertion seriously can help us reaffirm our commitment to putting children and young adults first.

Chapter 1, "*Aprendiendo de sus Comunidades*/Learning from Their Communities: Bilingual Teachers Researching Urban Latino Neighborhoods," considers how educators experience the diversity of language and literacy practices within an urban community. Lucila Ek, Margarita Machado-Casas, Patricia Sánchez, and Howard Smith employ New Literacy Studies, sociocultural theories of language and literacy, and the language ideologies paradigm to investigate how 23 bilingual teacher candidates utilized research methods to explore local community language and literacy practices. While the authors acknowledge overall ambivalence towards bilingualism and bilingual education, their findings demonstrate that Latino/a communities are not monolithic with respect to language ideologies. In their critical perspective feature, they recommend that urban teacher preparation programs incorporate research methods as a strategy for teacher candidates to learn about local communities.

Chapter 2, "A Different World: Black Bookstores as Literacy Counterpublics," by Marc Lamont Hill, examines the role of Rasul's, a 40-year-old Black bookstore in West Philadelphia, in relation to local literacy practices and events. Rasul's operated as a *literacy counterpublic* that enabled a range of social practices and processes. This chapter focuses on how members of Rasul's community engaged in literacy practices that enabled them to acquire oppositional formations of knowledge, challenge majoritarian narratives about the canon, and reimagine the purposes and functions of literacy within their everyday lives. Such insights, as featured in this chapter, are critical not only for literacy researchers, but for teachers and teacher educators as they develop authentic, culturally responsive spaces for literacy instruction.

Chapter 3, "Identity Construction in the Borderlands: The Acosta Family," by Carmen Martínez-Roldán and Guillermo Malavé, offers narratives from immigrant Latino families in the U.S. Southwest as they mediate the tensions some families encounter after moving from small towns in Mexico to urban barrios in the U.S.-Mexico borderlands. The focus is on how—through narratives and conversations—parents and children negotiate identities in response to the demands of their new contexts. Examining the narratives that students and parents share about being immigrants can provide valuable information on the role of schools in this process. The authors feature ideas for creating meaningful curricula that utilize lessons from the narratives of immigrant families.

In Chapter 4, "Double Reading: Young Black Scholars Exploring Whiteness in a Community Literacy Program," Stephanie Power Carter and Kafi Kumasi partnered with African American high school students in a community literacy program to explore how youth draw on literacies from home and community settings to confront Whiteness. Employing a sociocultural framework allows them to theorize how participants enact double consciousness to challenge pathologies about Black identity that persist in mainstream discourses. In the critical perspective feature, they offer implications of this work on teaching and learning by discussing ways teachers and researchers can utilize the home and community literacies of young people. This chapter's emphasis on learning, identity, and race within communities leads into the chapters on teaching and teacher education presented in the next section.

In, "The Buzz on Teaching and Community," Anne Haas Dyson and Celia Genishi introduce the chapters in the second section by taking us into a science class in which students are enamored by "human bees," or human beings. Their introduction provides an important theoretical and practical shift from examinations into literacies within homes and communities to investigations into literacies, teaching, and teacher education within institutionally sanctioned settings.

This section opens with Chapter 5, "A Different Kind of Teaching: Culture Circles as Professional Development for Freedom." Mariana Souto-Manning documents situated representations of transformative teacher education by focusing on a critical teacher study group using Freirean culture circles. She explores how early childhood teachers engaged in dialogue through differences of perspective to reframe the role of teacher educator as ethnographer. She highlights perspectives of teachers who voiced the importance of dialogue for sharing daily struggles. The chapter features strategies for teachers and teacher educators to talk about tensions and cultural conflicts as these things impact multicultural work.

Chapter 6 "(Re)Framing Teaching in Urban Classrooms: A Poststructural (Re)Reading of Critical Literacy as Curricular and Pedagogical Practice" by Marcelle Haddix and Mary Rojas examines the role of critical literacy for educators who teach adolescent literature in urban school settings. Haddix and Rojas turn attention to publishers' suggestions (included in various textbooks) for teaching Latino/a literature, highlighting discussion questions and suggested literary analyses that shape curricular and pedagogical practices. They move beyond critical literacy toward poststructuralist perspectives to question power and contest static constructions of knowledge. In their feature section, they highlight strategies and practices to critically teach multicultural texts.

"Down for the Ride but not for the Die: Theatre as Language for Incarcerated Girls," is the title of Chapter 7 by Maisha T. Winn. This chapter begins with the premise that the work of language and literacy researchers and teacher educators must include scholarship on the school-to-prison pipeline. It examines how incarcerated and formerly incarcerated girls use writing and performance as acts of resistance to talk back to institutions of power. Winn demonstrates how this work is valuable for educators within traditional school settings who work with various students, but who may overlook incarcerated or formerly incarcerated girls transitioning back into schools. In her feature section, she highlights how teachers and teacher educators can acknowledge and work with this critical population of youth.

Colleen Fairbanks and Detra Price-Dennis invite us to reflect on sentiments by Heron-Hruby, Hagood, and Alvermann (2008) that young people can teach adults a lot about popular culture and literacy. Indeed, they can! And in their introduction to the final section, "Studies on Popular Culture and Forms of Multimodality," Fairbanks and Price-Dennis ask us to consider making space in the classroom for learners to "assert their agency and their humanity."

In Chapter 8, "Writing as a Site of Struggle: Popular Culture, Empowerment, and Politics of (In)Visibility," Korina Jocson and Jamal Cooks employ theories of empowerment and critical pedagogy to examine 21st-century writing and popular culture in secondary classrooms. In so doing, they refer to traditional and new media texts such as music videos, rap songs, documentaries, blogs, essays, and postings on MySpace and Facebook. These texts, part of empowering processes of learning, recognize how young people of color in English classrooms in northern California write about and critique relations of power. Jocson and Cooks feature curricular examples to demonstrate how teachers and teacher educators can do similar work in multicultural settings.

In the last few years, there has been growing interest around popular culture and youth. Undoubtedly, youth culture has been highly influenced by mass media and technology. Chapter 9, "Is It Bigger Than Hip-Hop? Examining the Problems and Potential of Hip-Hop in the Curriculum" by Jung Kim, investigates how a Chicago high school teacher creates curricula centered on hip-hop pedagogies to improve students' academic achievements. In her feature section, Kim provides teachers and teacher educators with methods by which to utilize hip-hop (and popular culture). She also describes dilemmas of using hip-hop to address student academic achievement, identity, and power constructs in meaningful, critical ways.

Considering arguments from the previous two chapters, Chapter 10, "'The Consciousness of the Verbal Artist': Understanding Vernacular Literacies in Digital and Embodied Spaces" by Django Paris and David Kirkland, conceptualizes the educational value of *vernacular literacies*. Such literacies are forms of multimodal, written communication that features vernacular languages and indigenous cultural understandings of urban youth. The authors draw on research with youth of color to illustrate vernacular literacies within social networking sites, multimedia texting, and messages found on cloth and skin. Paris and Kirkland push us to understand the complexities of vernacular literacies in various real and imagined contexts, and conclude by featuring pedagogical approaches and literacy practices for teachers and researchers.

Together, these insightful chapters get us onto our feet and invite us to take up powerful, transformative, and collaborative action-oriented research. Equally important is that these chapters are authored by new, emerging, and mid-career scholars of color who are committed to conducting critical, cutting-edge research in classrooms and communities of color. They help us rethink meanings of education in relation to the literacies and lives of children, youth, and adults of color from diverse linguistic, racial, ethnic, and cultural backgrounds who attend school and/or reside in urban communities. I invite you to join us as we reimagine what it means to work at the intersection of studies on language, literacy, and culture and as we debate critical perspectives on research in urban settings.

REFERENCES

Ball, A. (2006). *Multicultural strategies for education and social change: Carriers of the torch in the United States and South Africa.* New York: Teachers College Press.

Blackburn, M. V. (2004). Understanding agency beyond school-sanctioned activities. *Theory Into Practice, 43*(2), 102–110.

Cushman, E. (1996). The rhetorician as an agent of social change. *College Composition and Communication, 47,* 7–28.

Darling-Hammond, L. (2006). Securing the right to learn: Policy and practice for powerful teaching and learning. *Educational Researcher, 35*(7), 13–24.

Fisher, M. T. (2007). *Writing in rhythm: Spoken word poetry in urban classrooms.* New York: Teachers College Press.

Ginwright, S., Noguera, P., & Cammarota, J. (Eds.). (2006). *Beyond resistance! Youth activism and community change.* New York & London: Routledge.

Heron-Hruby, A., Hagood, M. A., & Alvermann, D. E. (2008). Switching places and looking to adolescents for the practices that shape school literacies. *Reading & Writing Quarterly, 24,* 311–314.

Hill, M. L. (2009). *Beats, rhymes, and classroom life: Hip-hop pedagogy and the politics of identity.* New York: Teachers College Press.

Jocson, K. (2008). *Youth poets: Empowering literacies in and out of schools.* New York: Peter Lang Publishers.

Kinloch, V. (2009). Suspicious spatial distinctions: Literacy research across school and community contexts with students. *Written Communication, 26*(2), 154–182.

Kinloch, V. (2010a). *Harlem on our minds: Place, race, and the literacies of urban youth.* New York: Teachers College Press.

Kinloch, V. (2010b). "To not be a traitor of Black English": Youth perceptions of language rights in and urban context. *Teachers College Record, 112*(1), 103–141.

Kirkland, D. (2008). "The rose that grew from concrete": Hip hop and the new English education. *English Journal, 97*(5), 69–75.

Lee, C. D. (2007). *Culture, literacy, and learning: Taking bloom in the midst of the whirlwind.* New York: Teachers College Press.

Moje, E. B. (2002). But where are the youth? On the value of integrating youth culture into literacy theory. *Educational Theory, 52*(1), 97–120.

Morrell, E. (2008). *Critical literacy and urban youth: Pedagogies of access, dissent, and liberation.* New York: Routledge.

Morrell, E., & Duncan-Andrade, J. M. R. (2002). Promoting academic literacy with urban youth through engaging hip-hop culture. *English Journal, 9*(6), 88–92.

Moss, B. (2003). *A community text arises: A literacy text and a literacy tradition in African American churches.* Cresskill, NJ: Hampton Press.

Pallas, A. M., Natriello, G., & McDill, E. L. (1989). The changing nature of the disadvantaged population: Current dimensions and future trends. *Educational Researcher, 18*(5), 16–22.

Staples, J. (2008). "Are we our brothers' keepers": Exploring the social functions of reading in the life of an African American urban adolescent. In M. L. Hill & L. Vasudevan (Eds.), *Media, learning, and sites of possibilities* (pp. 57–72). New York: Peter Lang.

Vasudevan, L. (2008). *Media and adolescent literacies.* NewLits.Org. Retrieved January 28, 2010, from http://www.newlits.org/index.php?title=Main_Page.

Vasudevan, L. (2009). Performing new geographies of literacy teaching and learning. *English Education, 41*(4), 356–374.

Vasudevan, L., & Campano, G. (2009). The social production of adolescent risk and the promise of adolescent literacies. *Review of Research in Education, 33,* 310–353.

PART I

In Consideration of Family and Community Literacies

Juan C. Guerra

Ever since Heath's groundbreaking *Ways with Words* was published (1983), we have benefited from book-length studies on family and community literacy that add to our understanding of "learning incomes" (Guerra, 2008, p. 296) students bring from homes and communities to K–12 and college classrooms. Philips's *The Invisible Culture* (1983), Taylor's *Family Literacy* (1983), Taylor and Dorsey-Gaines's *Growing Up Literate* (1988), Delgado-Gaitan's *Literacy for Empowerment* (1990), Vasquez, Pease-Alvarez, and Shannon's *Pushing Boundaries* (1994), Valdes's *Con Respeto* (1996), Cushman's *The Struggle and the Tools* (1998), Mahiri's *Shooting for Excellence* (1998), my own *Close to Home* (1998), Moss's *A Community Text Arises* (2003), Richardson's *African American Literacies* (2003), Orellana's *Translating Childhoods* (2009), Kinloch's *Harlem on Our Minds* (2010), and countless other texts provide nuanced analyses of the "funds of knowledge" (Moll, 1994, p. 202) educators must integrate into pedagogical and curricular practices. The chapters in this section contribute to that tradition. They add new insights to a growing mosaic of understanding related to rhetorical and discursive agility children from disenfranchised communities demonstrate in and out of school.

Ek, Machado-Casas, Sánchez, and Smith, in the opening chapter, highlight the importance of educators discovering students' learning incomes. They focus on surveys collected by bilingual teacher candidates from local community members in several neighborhoods and from parents, school staff, and teachers at different elementary schools. Findings signal the value of providing teacher candidates opportunities to conduct research in communities that cultivate children who will populate their classes.

Hill moves the conversation about literacy into a bookstore in Philadelphia to theorize meanings of *literacy* and *counterpublics*. He draws attention to how members in this community site, Rasul's bookstore, engaged in literacy practices that challenged "majoritarian narratives." In so doing, he challenges assumptions about community literacy and community sites.

Martínez-Roldán and Malavé's chapter shifts the conversation to focus on intimate details of a mother's storytelling in ethnographic interviews and her daughter's talk in literature discussions. The mother's stories and daughter's talk illustrate how "parents develop strategies to socialize their children into [particular] cultural beliefs, practices, and identities" and the role that schooling plays in challenging these efforts.

In Power Carter and Kumasi's chapter, they report on work with Black youth in the Community Literacy Intervention Program (CLIP) through an extension of Du Bois's idea of double consciousness. They develop a model that illustrates a "double read" that helps educators understand how a theory of double consciousness can enhance pedagogical practices "in ways that prompt truer and deeper expressions of ideals, particularly around sensitive issues of race."

In their closing features, "Critical Perspective," the authors take what they have learned from students, teachers, parents, and others and share strategies designed to provide educators with the tools they need to ensure that students' learning incomes are integrated into teachers' pedagogical and curricular practices. Despite the long history of research on connections among home, community, and school that I rehearsed in the opening paragraph, the chapters exemplify our need to probe these connections or risk losing another generation of children of color to an institutional apparatus that continues to practice assimilation rather than acknowledge the important role transculturation plays in the work of, as Lisa Delpit puts it, educating other people's children.

REFERENCES

Cushman, E. (1998). *The struggle and the tools: Oral and literate strategies in an inner city community*. Albany: SUNY Press.

Delgado-Gaitan, C. (1990). *Literacy for empowerment: The role of parents in children's education*. New York: The Falmer Press.

Delpit, L. (1996). *Other people's children: Cultural conflict in the classroom*. New York: New Press.

Guerra, J. C. (1998). *Close to home: Oral and literate practices in a transnational Mexicano community*. New York: Teachers College Press.

Guerra, J. C. (2008). Cultivating transcultural citizenship: A writing across communities model. *Language Arts 85*.4: 296–304.

Heath, S. B. (1983). *Ways with words: Language, life, and work in communities and classrooms.* New York: Cambridge University Press.

Kinloch, V. (2010). *Harlem on our minds: Place, race, and the literacies of urban youth.* New York: Teachers College Press.

Mahiri, J. (1998). *Shooting for excellence: African American and youth culture in new century schools.* Urbana: NCTE.

Moll, L. C. (1994). Literacy research in community and classrooms: A sociocultural approach. In B. Ruddell, M. Ruddell, & H. Singer (Eds.), *Theoretical models and processes of reading* (4th edition) (pp. 208–230). Newark, DE: IRA.

Moss, B. (2003). *A community text arises: A literacy text and a literacy tradition in African American churches.* Cresskill, NJ: Hampton Press.

Orellana, M. F. (2009). *Translating childhoods: Immigrant youth, language, and culture.* New Brunswick, NJ: Rutgers University Press.

Philips, S. U. (1983). *The invisible culture: Communication in classroom and community on the Warm Springs reservation.* New York: Longman.

Richardson, E. (2003). *African American literacies.* New York: Routledge.

Taylor, D. (1983). *Family literacy: Young children learning to read and write.* Exeter, NH: Heinemann.

Taylor, D., & C. Dorsey-Gaines. (1988). *Growing up literate: Learning from inner city families.* Portsmouth, NH: Heinemann.

Valdes, G. (1996). *Con respeto: Bridging the distances between culturally diverse families and schools.* New York: Teacher College Press.

Vásquez, O. A., Pease-Alvarez, P., & Shannon, S. M. (1994). *Pushing boundaries: Language and culture in a Mexicano community.* New York: Cambridge UP.

CHAPTER 1

Aprendiendo de Sus Comunidades/ Learning from Their Communities

Bilingual Teachers Researching Urban Latino Neighborhoods

*Lucila D. Ek, Margarita Machado-Casas,
Patricia Sánchez, and Howard L. Smith*

As the United States enters the second decade of the 21st century, the achievement gap for Latinos/as, the nation's fastest-growing minority population, continues to increase. Also on the rise are xenophobic ideologies and politics, such as anti-bilingual education policies, that are hostile to the languages and cultures of students of color. Moreover, the educational system continues to implement curricula, pedagogies, and practices that neglect the language and literacy needs of urban students of color, issues that we address in this chapter.

This chapter examines how bilingual teacher candidates utilized research methods to explore various communities within an urban South Texas setting. Equipped with qualitative research tools, teacher candidates documented local community members' perspectives on language and local print environments. They interviewed community members and business owners in predominantly Latino immigrant neighborhoods and conducted language attitude surveys at six elementary schools where they interviewed parents, school staff, and teachers. Our findings indicate that Latino/a communities are not monolithic with respect to language ideologies. Rather, there is ambivalence toward bilingualism and bilingual education, often couched in explanations of "Spanish as important" versus "Spanish as necessary," which reflect dominant ideologies. Undergirding our study is the notion that bilingual Latinos/as are not immune to dominant linguistic ideologies that reify the hegemony of English while stigmatizing Spanish. Such attitudes countered the teacher candidates' expectations that community members would have more vocal support for bilingualism and bilingual education. Thus, we seek to provide teacher candidates with an effective tool that can help them critically examine linguistic ideologies for the benefit of their future students.

SOCIOCULTURAL VIEWS OF LANGUAGE, LITERACY, AND IDEOLOGY

To shed light on the links among language, literacy, and ideology, our conceptual framework includes sociocultural theory, New Literacy Studies, and the language ideologies paradigm. From a sociocultural perspective, language and literacy are socially constructed tools that support cognitive processing (Vygotsky & Kozulin, 1986) and social interaction (Lovelace & Wheeler, 2006) while standing as cultural artifacts (Dyer & Friederich, 2002). Indeed, language is the preeminent meaning-making tool for learning as a socially mediated activity (Cole, 1996; Rogoff, 1990; Vygotsky, 1978). In addition to language and literacy, humans surround themselves with culturally embedded signs and symbols that evoke meaning (Cope, Kalantzis, & New London Group, 2000; Lynch, 2007). All communities and cultures have unique language and literacy knowledge and practices (Heath, 1996, p. 479).

Sociocultural theory provides a productive framework from which to study questions of language and literacy for Latino/a immigrant students because it highlights inextricable links between language and literacy. For bilingual Latino communities, families, and students, any discussion of literacy must include a treatment on language given that issues of language are at the center of literacy and biliteracy teaching and learning. To better understand the situation of Latino languages, including Spanish and its dialects, we use a language ideologies framework to explore historical and current attitudes, beliefs, and perspectives on Spanish.

Language Ideologies

Rooted in linguistic anthropology, the language ideologies framework (Schieffelin, Woolard, & Kroskrity, 1998; Wortham, 2001) is particularly productive for examining the complex linguistic situation of Latinos/as in the southwestern United States. Woolard (1998) observed that ideologies about language are never just about language alone: "Rather they envision and enact ties of language to identity, to aesthetics, to morality, and to epistemology" (p. 3).

Linguistic ideologies are about consciousness, subjective representations, beliefs, and ideas that are rooted in, reflective of, or responsive to the interests of a particular social position (Woolard, 1998). Because language ideologies can be tools in the contestation of power, they can legitimate asymmetrical relations of power (Woolard, 1998). This definition of language ideologies is useful for illuminating how in the United States, English is privileged over Spanish and how institutions uphold its status.

In the Southwest, the Spanish language existed long before the 1848 Mexican-American War, as these territories were part of Mexico. Upon signing the Treaty of Guadalupe-Hidalgo, Mexicans living on the north of the Rio Grande, which was now U.S. territory, faced tremendous discrimination that included hostility toward the use of Spanish, despite having been granted full U.S. citizenship. It was not long before overt discrimination became evident in public schools, as Mexican children were harshly disciplined for speaking Spanish. The hopes embedded in these acts were to eradicate the Spanish language completely: "In many ways, the campaign to remove Spanish from public schools in the Southwest was merely the regional expression of a national campaign" (San Miguel, 1999, p. 43).

The United States, with its longstanding Americanization project, has never accepted indigenous or immigrant languages of its people; in fact, "throughout the 20th century, until the 1960s, use of a language other than English was regarded as evidence of retardation and a major obstacle to success in U.S. society" (Hakuta & Díaz, 1985, as cited in Worthy, Rodríguez, Assaf, Martínez, & Cuero, 2003, p. 278). It was not surprising that "teachers [were] being told to speak only English to Spanish-speaking students, to punish the use of Spanish in school, and to encourage parents—many of them limited in English proficiency—to speak/teach their Spanish-speaking children English" (García, 1999, p. 144). The "No Spanish Rules" prohibited "the use of Spanish in the classrooms, at lunch time, and on the playgrounds" (Acuña, 1988, as cited in MacGregor-Mendoza, 2000, p. 356) and the violation of the rules was often punished physically with the use of switches, rulers, or kneeling (Guajardo, Sánchez, Fineman, & Scheurich, 1998).

This historical linguistic violence toward Spanish and its speakers continues today (Ek & Sánchez, 2008; Machado-Casas, 2009). Furthermore, language has become a proxy for race (Gutiérrez, Asato, Santos, & Gotanda, 2002), or as Urciouli (1996) explains, "Whenever English speakers complain about the 'unfairness' of hearing Spanish spoken in public spaces or in the workplace, they racialize Spanish by treating it as matter out of place" (p. 35). As evidenced by a slew of policies that our nation has witnessed—including laws that make English the official language, anti-bilingual education measures, and growing movements to make English-only constitutional—indigenous and immigrant populations, and their languages, continue to be targets of hostility.

Similar to how Spanish is stigmatized, literacies of working-class Latino communities are often denigrated because they do not map onto what are considered good literacy practices. Sociolinguistic studies show that within any society particular languages and literacies are privileged and others are devalued (Cooney & Akintude, 1999; Richardson & Lawrence-Brown, 2004). While schools readily value the literacy behaviors of mainstream, English-speaking families (Gee, 1996), this is not true of minority families (Purcell-Gates, 2007). Additionally, schools, despite empirical studies indicating the importance of local community literacy (Allen & Labbo, 2001), often deprecate the literacy knowledge of poor or working-class communities, especially when a minority language is used (Gee, 1996; Valencia & Black, 2002). This attitude is indicative of a "deficit ideology" (Sleeter, 2004) that devalues the capacities of minority parents and their communities. Bourdieu (1977) and Willis (1981) shed light on the cultural and linguistic differences between middle-class and working-class White people by highlighting how privileged youth have certain advantages over working-class youth. In addition, Heath (1983) demonstrates that middle-class White students' ways of speaking, learned as part of their home socialization, translate into higher teacher expectations for achievement. By upholding the value of White middle-class practices while devaluing minority and working-class ways, middle- to upper-class and White become synonymous with "correct" practices.

Undoubtedly, when teachers lack the appropriate cultural and linguistic awareness of the communities they serve, there can be devastating effects on learners (Delpit, 1995; Ladson-Billings, 2009; Nieto, 2004; Valdés, 1996; Valenzuela, 1999). The literature on diversity preparation for teacher candidates reports varying degrees of success in relation to multicultural education (e.g., language diversity, cultural diversity). Burstein and Cabello (1989) argue: "Teachers, as others, frequently try to achieve a 'cultural fit.' That is, they try to fit students into their own cultural system" (p. 9). Even when teachers are of the same ethnicity as their students, they may be unaware of their language or cultural ideologies (cf. Dee & Henkin, 2002; Flores & Smith, 2007; Flores, 2001). As Flores and Smith (2007) found, teachers of any ethnic background must engage in critical reflective practices that explore their preconceived notions about language-minority children and their communities.

The Home and School Language (and Literacy) Divide

Research on the importance of home and community educational experiences of culturally and linguistically diverse students highlights the rich language and literacy learning that takes place across various contexts (Baquedano-López, 1997; Ek, 2005, 2008, 2009; González, Moll, & Amanti, 2005; Orellana, 2009; Vásquez, Pease-Alvarez, & Shannon, 1994;

Zentella, 2005). Such research illuminates stark contrasts between students' school and non-school engagements, highlighting how home and community literacies are often more productive than school practices that may not adequately engage students (Ek, 2008; McMillon & Edwards, 2000). For example, McMillon and Edwards's (2000) study on the differences between church and school environments reported that an African American child was a "superstar" at church whereas his behavior was socially unacceptable in preschool. At church, the child engaged in language and literacy practices that were not shared by his preschool. This latter point demonstrates why a focus on multiplicity of literacies and literate behaviors across contexts is important in understanding young people's actions and development. Whereas McMillon and Edwards (2000) examine disconnects with how a child is represented in church in comparison to school, Cowan (2004) investigates a dialogic relationship between a "Latina/o visual discourse community" and dominant discourses. Such an investigation helps us further understand how teacher candidates may "read" the physical environment and material resources found in the communities they studied. It also illuminates how their views of working-class Latino communities may connect with dominant and often stigmatizing perceptions of these settings.

URBAN CONTEXT: A CITY IN SOUTH TEXAS

The study described in this chapter was located in San Antonio—the seventh-largest city in the United States. The city has a population of 1.3 million that is comprised of 61% Latino/a residents, with 13% of them foreign-born (U.S. Census Bureau, 2006–2008). Writing about this transnational city, Romo (2008, citing Alba, 2005) observed that it "blurs the boundaries between recent immigrants who have many connections with Mexico and second- and third-generation Mexican Americans who may have never been to Mexico." In addition, the 2000 Census identified 44% of the population in San Antonio as Spanish speakers (Romo, 2008). In this region of the state, it is not uncommon to hear residents speaking "a mixture of Spanish and English in their homes and communities" (Romo, 2008). This majority Latino/a population fosters a way of life, a culture, and a language that is not unlike those found along the U.S.-Mexico border, even though San Antonio is 150 miles from the border.

TEACHER CANDIDATES: INTRA-ETHNIC LATINAS/OS

Our participants, Latino/a bilingual teacher candidates—traditional and nontraditional college students—are seeking certification in grade levels pre-K to 6 from a Hispanic Serving Institution (HSI). Although they all speak English and Spanish, there are varying levels of oral and written bilingualism among the members. In addition, the overwhelmingly female participants come from different immigrant backgrounds: long-term Tejanas, bordertown second-generation Mexican Americans, Fronterizas who grew up on both sides of the Texas–Mexico border, Mexican nationals, Central Americans, and self-identified Chicanas. The 22 females and one male participant reflect a diversity of other characteristics. They ranged from early 20s to over 40 years of age, 17 spoke Spanish and 6 English as their native language, and the median were second-generation immigrants, with four foreign-born. The median income of their own families, in their childhood, was $20,000–$40,000. With these things in mind, this chapter focuses on their explorations of language views and literacy environments of urban Latino neighborhoods.

METHODS

Data were collected from two bilingual teacher candidate cohorts who progressed through the HSI's undergraduate certification program. All four authors regularly teach in the program's four capstone courses known as the "block." These block courses are taught primarily in Spanish and cover bilingual education theory and methodology.

We collected completed class assignments and demographic information from 23 bilingual teacher candidates across two semesters. Thus, the corpus of data is extensive and includes: 1) illustrated language history map projects written in Spanish (adapted from Olsen and Jaramillo, 1999), 2) essays written in Spanish on language and literacy learning trajectories (*trayectorias*), 3) community ethnographies exploring funds of knowledge, 4) field notes and/or audio- or video-recordings of in-class discussions, 5) student demographic surveys, and 6) reflective narratives compiled from their community language/literacy research projects. This last item is the focus of analysis in this chapter and will be explained in more detail below; however, the other collected assignments helped inform our analysis and findings.

During the block, the bilingual teacher candidates are expected to provide a critical description of the linguistic environment of the school and community where they are placed for field experiences. Using ethnographic methods, they are asked to pay attention to posters, advertisements, stores, businesses, signs, newspapers, music, and the communication style of the local community, and to seek out three individuals from the community to survey and interview. The candidates interviewed various community members including four restaurant managers/store owners; eight store/

dry cleaners/laundromat, bakery, and restaurant employees; a mechanic; a priest; and a librarian. However, 13 community members interviewed did not identify their occupation. Each teacher candidate also asked three individuals from the school to respond to a language attitude survey. Individuals from the school who were surveyed included bilingual teachers, paraprofessionals, and other school staff. In all, the teacher candidates conducted a total of 63 interviews.

Our chapter findings are based on a thematic analysis of 23 reflective narratives written in Spanish, where we looked specifically for instances in which students offered: interpretations of urban community landscapes and environmental print, language preference and use among urban community members, and features of language ideology. The narratives focus on six elementary schools located throughout four different school districts in San Antonio. Student quotes are taken directly from their reflective narratives and, thus, may contain grammar and/or punctuation *errors* in Spanish. However, their English translations do not reflect these *errors*. In the next sections, we detail the students' findings of these landscapes.

LANGUAGE AND LITERACY LANDSCAPE OF LATINO COMMUNITIES IN AN URBAN CENTER

The six urban schools studied by the bilingual teacher candidates are heavily Latino/a, bilingual in nature, and accorded Title I status. Each school has either a (Spanish/English) dual-language program or a traditional transitional bilingual education program. The schools share similar demographics in terms of size, ethnic makeup, and socioeconomic status, with an average of 640 students, 81–98% Latinos/as, and 78–98% qualifying for free/reduced lunch. (All names of schools and participants are pseudonyms.)

What follows is a translated summary of the rich descriptions written by the bilingual teacher candidates in conducting their projects. Each of the six schools had three to seven students collecting ethnographic and survey research on it and its local community; then each student composed reflective narratives based on her/his findings. At the end of the summaries compiled below, we provide a brief analysis of the community aspects students chose to highlight and write about, with a particular focus on language use.

Las Perlas Elementary

This school is located in the Westside of San Antonio—a Latino barrio over 100 years old. In front of the school are apartments and houses. Many of the houses do not have central air and instead use window units, and many have altars in their front yards dedicated to the Virgin Mary (*Vírgen de*

Guadalupe). One of these homes offers catechism to kids who are preparing for their first holy communion. Across the street from the school is a day-care for kids in an afterschool program. There is also a nearby baseball field. Grocery stores include HEB and La Fiesta. A few blocks from the school is a historical landmark: a city cemetery that attracts scores of visitors each week (almost exclusively Latinos/as paying homage to their deceased loved ones). There are several mom-and-pop shops that sell real and artificial floral arrangements for graves. Evidence of Spanish use includes store signs that indicate the week's shopping specials. Near the school, there is also a health clinic for low-income families; a used furniture and used cars lot; a beauty salon; flower shops; *elote* and *raspa* stands; and a public library. Tellez Tamales y Barbacoa is a local favorite. This community also boasts of a multi-service strip mall where families can pay utilities, bank, buy groceries, clothes shop, or receive services such as Planned Parenthood. The languages that predominate here are "Tex-Mex" and Spanish. Although the elementary school provides a dual-language program, the kids are nearly 100% Latino/a with varying levels of English fluency.

Cedar Hills Elementary

This school is located in the southern part of the city. Humble homes surround the school, and fences and businesses have graffiti on them. Most kids are dropped off and picked up at school by their families/parents, who walk. Next to the school is a community center where adults can take GED, computer, or citizenship classes. Next to this community center is a low-income medical clinic. There is a strong presence of Mexican culture within the local businesses: a *tortillería* (El Molino), a *botánica*, a *frutería*, a *pulga*. Several Catholic churches and many small Mexican restaurants abound. In the next tier of local establishments are many typical fast food chain restaurants such as Whataburger, Wendy's, Taco Bell—where English predominates (as well as in banks)—and mom-and-pop businesses such as Los Valles Frutería, Taquería Jalisco, La Panadería El Tapatío. The latter have bilingual signs written in English and Spanish. The majority of these mom-and-pop businesses address clients in Spanish, and music in these places is also in Spanish. Most families in this community are second- or third-generation Latinos/as. Thus, English dominates. However, there are hybrid practices such as a "washatería" and intergenerational language choices: youth speak in English and older adults in Spanish.

Riverside Elementary

Riverside is the only school in this study located "outside the 410 Loop." Historically, San Antonio residents have referred to places "inside" or "outside" the 410 Loop—a loop route of Interstate 10 around the city. Locally, it is often assumed that those businesses or communities inside the 410 Loop are more authentically Mexican or Mexican American whereas those communities outside the Loop are less so. Riverside Elementary is flanked on one side by an urban, commercial area and the other a residential zone with houses and apartments. Directly across the street is a Mexican restaurant called El Taco de Jalisco. Another nearby restaurant features a menu that includes "chicken fried steak," "seafood enchiladas," "grilled pork chops," and "Tampiqueña plate"—a hybrid of dishes. There is a dry cleaner, Laundromat, gas station, McDonald's, and pizza parlor two blocks from the school. Many of these establishments have signs in both English and Spanish.

Lockhill Elementary

Located inside the 410 Loop, this school is in the northwestern area of San Antonio and is in its second year of hosting a dual-language program. Previously, the school had a bilingual program. Its neighborhoods have both houses and apartments—some with hybrid names such as "Casablanca Apartments"; a funeral home; many churches; several grocery stores (Culebra Meat Market and La Fiesta), restaurants, and other businesses that cater to a Mexican clientele (e.g., selling barbacoa, tamales, and tortillas). There is also a nearby park with swings and slides that are deteriorating and a baseball field. The elementary school is close to a middle and high school as well as to 22 other schools (public, charter, private) within a 3-mile radius. Many police cars patrol the area. The majority of children and families walk to and from school. The nearby public library was named after a Mexican American leader from the community and it has books, announcements, and flyers in Spanish.

Domínguez Elementary and Espinoza Elementary

These two schools are located within one block of each other, in the same community, just north of Lockhill Elementary and inside the 410 Loop. Both schools feature dual-language and bilingual education programs. About three blocks from these schools is a major street that is home to a professional beauty school and stores such as La Fiesta, Blockbuster, Sonic, Dairy Queen, and McDonald's. These neighborhoods have several grocery stores, restaurants, pharmacies, gas stations, a health clinic, senior citizen apartments, churches, and service agencies; the majority of these places offer services in Spanish and English. This is evident by the many signs in both languages and the employees who are bilingual. Both Chase Bank and the grocery stores offer money-wiring services to Mexico and Latin

America. Also, there are Mexican bakeries, a shop that sells *quinceañera* items, another that sells piñatas and party items, and eateries such as Taquería Jalisco. Many "dollar stores" abound as well: Dollar General, Family Dollar, and Dollar Tree. One student noted the less wholesome presence of a discount cigarette store and a liquor shop. In this zip code area, 65% of the residents speak Spanish at home. Local, small-press newspapers are in Spanish, such as *El Mundo* and *El Continental,* and the more popular bilingual paper is called *La Prensa.*

Although the bilingual teacher candidates were expected to document evidence of the environmental print in their quest to research local language and literacy use, many spent a considerable portion of their analysis interpreting the overall landscape of each urban micro-community. "Markers" or "signs" of Latino/a culture were often mentioned (e.g., religious altars or images, eateries with Mexican food). Bilingual teacher candidates "read" the poverty depicted in these neighborhoods when they focused on homes with air-conditioned window units, for example, or empty lots with overgrown grass. Such analysis speaks to the presence of visual literacy within communities and how such signs are interpreted by outsiders or newcomers.

Many of the students noted the mixture of Spanish and English they encountered in the communities around the six schools they researched. As noted above, some communities were filled with "Tex-Mex" language varieties, or Spanglish (e.g., "washatería"), when residents carried out daily activities, personal interactions, or business transactions. This hybrid use of Spanish and English is representative of code switchers and is a strong marker of the historical use of these two languages in the southwestern United States.

CHALLENGING THE LANGUAGE AND LITERACY ASSUMPTIONS HELD BY LATINO/A TEACHER CANDIDATES: HOW A WALK IN THE COMMUNITY CAN GO A LONG WAY

When we asked students to visit the communities and interview their members, we anticipated that they would be confronted with cultural and language ideologies that would cause them to reflect on their personal beliefs and ideologies. Their written reflections revealed their assumptions around language and literacy in the communities that surrounded their assigned school. Some assumptions were confirmed and others contradicted. One issue was the value placed on bilingualism. Gloriana, one of the block students, was surprised that people gave equal importance to English and Spanish. She stated, *"Me sorprendió que la gente le diera la misma importancia a los dos idiomas."* [It surprised me that people gave the same importance to both languages.] Although not officially diglossic, most of the neighborhoods represented in the present study were home to large numbers of bilinguals. This view presupposes a positive use for Spanish, which may extend (perhaps) beyond the household.

At the same time, there were other members of the same neighborhood who expressed little or no regard for bilingualism. Even while living in an urban bilingual community, one of Gloriana's respondents advocated for English monolingualism in schools: "*También me sorprendió que algunos dijeran que las escuelas no deberían tener clases en español porque en este país de los Estados Unidos, no es necesario que hablen dos idiomas.*" [I was also surprised that some said schools should not have classes in Spanish because in this country, the United States, it is not necessary to speak two languages.] This perspective could be seen as a *language-as-problem* (Ruiz, 1995) orientation that argues that the United States should strive for the goal of monolingualism and monoculturalism to ensure unity and prosperity. This monolithic view of the United States argues against the need for two languages (Hornberger, 2003).

It is important to point out that Gloriana was raised in northern San Antonio where she did not have much contact with the Mexican American community. Gloriana wrote:

> *Mi experiencia sobre esta investigación me sorprendió por que yo fui creada en el norte de San Antonio y no tuve mucho contacto con la comunidad méxico-americana. Siempre estuve al margen del los racismo y los malos tratos que los méxico-americanos sufrieron en esta ciudad.*

> [My experience with this research surprised me because I was raised on the north side of San Antonio and I did not have too much contact with the Mexican American community. I'm always at the margin of racism and the bad treatment that the Mexican Americans suffered in this city.]

Another student, Yolanda, was surprised by people's positive views of bilingualism:

> *Al analizar todas mis observaciones de la comunidad y entrevistas de residentes de la comunidad, concluí que el bilingüismo en esta comunidad es valorado e importante. En mi opinion yo pensaba que iba a ver más opiniones negativas acerca del bilingüismo y del idioma español.*

> [While analyzing my community observations and surveys I conducted of community members, I concluded that bilingualism in this community is valued and important. In my opinion, I thought I was

going to see more negative opinions regarding bilingualism and the Spanish language.]

She contrasted interviewees' positive views toward Spanish with her previous experience working in a Mexican restaurant where she says, "*a mucha gente hispana no le gusta hablar español. . . . Creo que se sienten incómodos y avergonzados de hablar español.*" [A lot of Hispanics do not like to speak in Spanish. . . . I think they feel uncomfortable and ashamed of speaking Spanish.] Yolanda interpreted people's positive views toward bilingualism and Spanish as a sign that they appreciate their culture and language (*"aprecian su cultura y su idioma a mucha honra"*).

Some teacher candidates were surprised by the ubiquity of Spanish in the communities. For example, Lolita wrote:

> *Lo que me sorprendió un poco era que en esta comunidad el español si es más fuerte porque hay muchos lugares que ofrecen servicios en español pero lo que descrubrí es que la gente de la comunidad que habla español frecuenta a ciertos lugares para hacer sus mandados.*

> [What surprised me a little was that in this community Spanish is in fact stronger because there are many places that offer services in Spanish, but what I discovered is that people from the community who speak Spanish use it at specific places to run their errands.]

She saw that there are many places that offer their services in Spanish but noticed, too, that people who spoke Spanish went to certain places for their errands. The places she mentions include Mexican restaurants, grocery stores, and fruit and meat markets. In contrast, places where English dominates include the bank, post office, and department stores.

The ubiquity of Spanish in these communities, however, did not translate into the dominance of the language. For instance, one of the teacher candidates, Julie, wrote:

> *Al terminar la encuesta me di cuenta que aunque el español domina mucho en esta comunidad, la gente suele a preferir el inglés. El simple dicho que responden de una manera no apasionada me dice esto. Fueron sorprendentes algunas respuestas que recibí, mas me di cuenta que uno no puede entrar a una encuesta o un trabajo esperando ciertos resultados. Siempre he tenido la ilusion que todos los latinos compartían la misma creencia que el español debe de practicarse y oírse lo mas que se pueda. Esta encuesta me ayudo descubrir la magnitud de diferencia que hay entre una comunidad.*

[When I finished the survey, I noticed that although Spanish is dominant in the community, people prefer English. The simple fact that
people responded in a dispassionate manner made me believe this.
Some answers I received were surprising; I noticed one cannot conduct a survey expecting specific results. I always had the illusion that
all Latinos shared the same belief that Spanish should be practiced
and heard as much as possible. This survey helped me discover the
magnitude of differences that exist within one community.]

Like many other Latino/a bilinguals in the United States, the people in the
community Julie studied defaulted to English. Julie interpreted the interviewees' dispassionate ways of speaking about Spanish as a sign of their
preference for English. In addition, Julie reflected on the importance of not
making assumptions about a community's language ideologies based on shared
ethnicity. Conducting this project has taught her that not all Latinos/as share
the belief that Spanish should be spoken more than English and that one
community can have widely diverging views.

COMMUNITY AMBIVALENCE TOWARD SPANISH

Several bilingual teacher candidates mentioned that they noticed diverse
perspectives and beliefs about bilingualism and bilingual education within
their school communities. They reported that most community members
held positive views about the importance of Spanish and bilingualism. Upon
analysis, however, the community members' comments did not reflect total
commitment for or support of bilingual education. There seemed to be ambivalence in how community members expressed support for the maintenance of the Spanish language, which signaled more of an alignment with
dominant ideologies of language than initially proposed.

Several of the interviewees said Spanish was important but not necessary. Roxana interviewed the father of a student who she described as
"medio confundido" (somewhat confused). She wrote:

*Note que se cree que es importante hablar y saber español pero a la
misma vez piensa que no es una necesidad. Por sus respuestas en-
tiende que quiere lo mejor para sus hijos y por eso piensa que ser
bilingüe no tiene sus ventajas.*

[I noticed that he believed that it is important to speak and understand Spanish but at the same time he believes that (Spanish) is not a
necessity. By his answers, I understood that he wants the best for his

children and that's why he thinks that being bilingual does not have its advantages.]

Roxana noted that this father believed it was *important* to speak and know Spanish but could not see any advantages to being bilingual. Another community member interviewed believed that Spanish is important, particularly for a person who lives on the south side of the city, but stated that English should still be the priority.

Roxana interviewed another parent, a school volunteer, with a school-age child. She agreed that it was important for her daughter to learn Spanish but she did not have her in a developmental bilingual program (i.e., a model that develops both English and Spanish). About this mother, Roxana wrote, *"Aunque ella cree que es importante saber español piensa que con el español que aprende (su hija) por sus abuelos maternos es suficiente."* [Although she thinks that it is important to know Spanish, she thinks that the Spanish that her daughter learns with her maternal grandparents is sufficient.] Hence, this mother did not see the need for bilingual education at school because her daughter was learning Spanish from her grandparents.

Interestingly, some community members realized that there were advantages to being bilingual, although they did not privilege Spanish bilingualism. Roxana wrote this about a community member: *"Ella sabe que una persona bilingüe tiene más capacidad que una persona monolingüe pero no cree que sea necesario hablar español."* [She knows that a bilingual person has more capacity than a monolingual, but she does not think that it is necessary to speak Spanish.] Thus, some people did not link the ability to speak Spanish with greater mental function, a point that led Roxana to conclude that people in the community around Riverside Elementary need more information about bilingualism.

Other interviews suggested possible sources of some community members' ambivalent attitudes or frustration toward the teaching and learning of Spanish. For example, commenting on an interview with a young man who considers himself Latino and whose parents are from Mexico and Guatemala, Julie wrote:

> *El me dijo que le gusta escuchar el español que se habla correctamente. Me comentó que no le gusta cuando oye que la gente habla el español mal. . . . [M]e explico que no cree que el español deba ser forzado en el aprendizaje de un estudiante. Piensa que deberían ser los padres del estudiante que digan si el niño/a debe aprender el español.*

[He told me that he likes to hear Spanish that is correctly spoken. He told me that he does not like to hear people speak Spanish badly. . . . He explained that he does not think that Spanish should be forced on any student. He thinks that the parents are the ones who should decide if the child should learn Spanish.]

Another community member who Gloriana interviewed—a school secretary—echoed this sentiment. *"La secretaria expresó que no estaba muy segura que deberían obligar a los estudiantes a hablar el idioma [Spanish] si no quieren."* [The secretary expressed that she was not sure that students should be forced to speak Spanish if they do not want to.] Both the young man and the secretary seem to value the Spanish language. The young man wants people to speak a standard Spanish and the secretary agrees that Spanish should be maintained, but they both question acts of "forcing" people to learn the language.

INSIDE THE SCHOOLS: COMPETING IDEOLOGIES OF SPANISH AND ENGLISH

Although the majority of communities around the six urban schools were clearly bilingual, students found ambivalence toward full Spanish support within several of the school environments. Many noted that although the landscape of the community was in Spanish and English, the landscape of certain schools catered to a monolingual English population. Claudia elaborates:

Aunque casi todos los estudiantes, o por lo menos la gran mayoría hablan español, ya sea porque están en el programa bilingüe, o porque sus padres lo hablan en la casa, la escuela no usa el español como el idioma predominante. Al pasar por los pasillos de la escuela, pude ver muchos informes de cada clase en los boletines asignados, pero casi ninguno eran en español.

[Although almost all the students, or at least a majority, speak Spanish, because they're in a bilingual program, or because their parents speak it to them at home, the school does not use Spanish as the dominant language. While walking the school's hallways, I could see many announcements on classroom bulletins, but almost none were in Spanish.]

The ambivalence toward the use of Spanish in school was not consistent with the commitment to promoting it academically and socially. In many cases, the use of Spanish in school was at odds with how many children and families actually depend on it for "daily utility" (Machado-Casas, 2006) in the community. Many bilingual teacher candidates felt that although they were conducting their field hours in a bilingual school, Spanish was lacking and in most cases was there only for "aesthetic" and not "authentic" purposes. This practice demonstrates the hegemony of English and how it is perpetuated even among bilingual programs and schools serving urban immigrant Latino/a populations.

Another student noted that although the school where she was completing her hours had bilingual signs, the administrators who ran the bilingual and dual-language programs did not connect with urban Latino/a parents because they omitted doing the most basic tenet of school-family partnerships with immigrant families: engage with caregivers in their native language. Roberta provides an example:

> *La directora de la escuela Riverside es Ms. Martinez; ella no habla español y creo que algunos padres de familia que son monolingües en español quisieran tener una principal bilingüe porque ha sucedido que en las juntas nada mas se dan en ingles y algunos padres no asisten por esta razón. En la ultima junta para los padres en el lenguaje dual quien tiene hijos en el programa asistieron y muchos de ellos decidieron irse ya que no se les estaba dando la información en español. Algunos de ellos fueron valientes y dejaron algunas mensajes por escrito, diciendo cual fue la razón de salirse del cuarto de junta.*

> [The principal of Riverside Elementary is Ms. Martinez; she does not speak Spanish and I think some parents that are monolingual Spanish speakers would like to have a bilingual principal because meetings are only held in English, and some parents don't attend for that reason. In the last parent meeting for parents who have children in the dual-language program, many who went to the meeting decided to leave because they were not receiving any information in Spanish. Some of them were brave and left written messages, stating the reason why they left the meeting room.]

The schools' ambivalence inadvertently produces competing ideologies about the use of Spanish, and in many cases locates Spanish inside classrooms and not in interactions with children's families. This linguistic contradiction contributes to mixed messages that bilingual children often receive about language expectations and increases communication gaps that widen school–home divides.

BILINGUAL TEACHER CANDIDATES' SHIFTS IN ATTITUDES

The research projects and reflective narratives of the 23 bilingual teacher candidates reveal attitudinal shifts in three areas: 1) bilingualism, 2) biliteracy, and 3) beliefs about language ideologies in local communities. Transformative types of activities like the ones explored in this study are important for understanding the role(s) of the bilingual teacher and her/his connection with the community—particularly urban communities. Because of these potential attitudinal shifts, the community is a great, untapped resource in the preparation of future educators. Next, we discuss in more detail the shifts experienced by our study's participants in these three areas, based on their writings.

Bilingualism

The narrative reflections revealed students' growing awareness about bilingualism, biliteracy, and language ideologies. Although all are bilingual Latinos/as, out of the 23 bilingual teacher candidates, at least 17 were unaware of the Spanish language varieties that existed within their local communities (even among their professional cohorts at the HSI). Twenty stated that they were surprised there were so many language variations, including sounds and lexicon (vocabulary), within bilingual communities. All 23 expressed an increased understanding of the complexities of language use within bilingual contexts. In their narratives, they demonstrated an awareness of linguistic traits (e.g., pronunciation, verb forms, meaning, and use) within individual bilingual communities.

Biliteracy

This project shifted 15 teacher candidates' views from a lack of value for language diversity to an appreciation of the benefits of biliteracy and linguistic diversity. Eighteen bilingual teacher candidates expressed that this experience now helps them to consider various language varieties in order to better teach biliteracy—that is, to be more inclusive of different ways words are written and to accept these as legitimate. Nineteen bilingual teacher candidates noted that communities' language variations are not taken into account even within their own communities—that is, some feel that their language use is "correct" without considering regional differences within the same neighborhoods.

Language Ideologies

Twenty-one bilingual teacher candidates expressed disappointment that academic student success—often defined by student performance on standardized tests—was highly dependent on the ways schools and exams privileged particular language varieties while castigating those that use local varieties of language. Furthermore, all 23 bilingual teacher candidates expressed doubt that school officials were aware of language varieties and ideologies that exist within school and community contexts and felt it was critical for them to become better informed about this discrepancy. All 23 bilingual teacher candidates gained an awareness of the importance of using Spanish as a vehicle that guides professional discourse and preparation.

TOWARD GREATER LINGUISTIC AWARENESS

The research projects that the bilingual teacher candidates carried out reveal various issues related to bilingual Latino communities in urban settings. One of the findings confirms the nature of language learning and use and its "continuum" (Hornberger, 2003) regardless of age. Students only captured one moment in this continuum when they conducted their investigations; each of the micro-communities they studied is in transition from either using a great deal of Spanish, having a preference for English, or developing a combined local variety of the two. There are many factors that influence these language shifts, including recent immigrant arrivals, hegemonic English policies, and local schools promoting or dismissing bilingualism. Thus, students often found language preferences that confirmed or dismissed their initial perceptions of the communities they were assigned to work in for one semester.

Although the teacher candidates set out to document environmental print, residents' and businesses' use of Spanish and English, they also captured cultural markers of Latinidad and ascribed meaning to visual representations of poverty or working-class realities. They "read" the community landscape of the schoolchildren they work with each week with the intent of putting into context a fuller meaning of being raised in an urban Latino setting. More important, they were armed with research tools such as observations, surveys, interviews, analysis, and reflection to accomplish this task. This differs from an informal or casual assessment of an impoverished urban setting, which may have the onlooker overlook community assets, important cultural markers of identity, or the complexity of daily economic struggle.

As the Latino/a students sought to understand their assigned communities' use and attitude toward Spanish, many discovered the range of ideologies present in a seemingly monolithic barrio. Indeed, students' beliefs were challenged—despite all 23 of them being Latino/a themselves. Just as Latino/a communities are not homogeneous in history, culture, or political orientation, neither are their language ideologies. This is an important consideration because we often assume that teacher candidates with ethnic and language backgrounds similar to those of their future students will "know" and understand each other well. However, ideologies about language—in particular hegemonic ones—have a way of embedding themselves even in those who have encountered racial and linguistic discrimination. By having teacher candidates engage in this kind of activity, they develop linguistic *concientización* (Smith, Sánchez, Ek, & Machado-Casas, forthcoming) about the ideologies and varieties present in Latino/a communities that may share the same geographic space.

In their reflections, the bilingual teacher candidates began to problematize long-held beliefs about Spanish and its local varieties. With their new awarenesses, they suggested that school administrators would benefit from similar ethnographic experiences and would make better decisions for language minority children. Though still in training, the opportunity for community language study afforded the bilingual teacher candidates a chance to explore and expand their understandings of language, literacy, and culture. In our critical perspective feature, we present recommendations for urban teacher preparation programs and educational stakeholders to bridge community and school language/literacy contexts.

CRITICAL PERSPECTIVE

Although classroom and text-based experiences are valuable in the preparation of teacher candidates, there is power in having university students experience firsthand the neighborhoods, businesses, and services of an urban community as well as interact with its residents. Doing so reduces their lack of familiarity with communities they will be serving in their future placements and increases their knowledge of the vast cultural and linguistic norms present in dynamic urban settings. Carrying out their investigations gave them the tools to access members of a community while providing them with a legitimate reason for community engagement. Research of this type creates a mini-collegiate presence in some barrios that are far removed from institutions of higher education.

The preparation of bilingual teachers requires teacher educators to problematize how languages are ideologized in theory and reality. One of the greatest "Aha!" moments we saw in this endeavor was when our students discovered that public urban schools with bilingual education programs do not always espouse an ideology that is "bilingual"—instead, it is often a pervasively monolingual one. Research experiences like the one examined in this chapter helped our students problematize language beliefs and couched them in the larger community context. For teacher education purposes, we believe that research can become a critical pedagogical tool in the preparation of all teachers working with students of color, particularly those in urban city centers, and it demystifies the notion of research as useful to more than PhDs, social scientists, or other elite groups. We found that the majority, if not all, of our students saw its value in coming to terms with social phenomena.

Ultimately, we propose that students training to become teachers of urban students of color prepare to serve as advocates and not just educators. In particular, we encourage teacher candidates of color toward advocacy and activism by taking a firmer grasp of the communities in which they will serve. However, we do not want to mislead readers. Incorporating a research project in a teacher preparation program is demanding—for teacher candidates and university professors. There is a good deal of scaffolding necessary for students to refine their interviewing/observation skills and a good deal of class time needed to process their ongoing field experiences and findings. Many students are unsure why they must learn to be researchers/ethnographers/anthropologists when they signed up to be educators. We found that once the final projects were turned in and presented in class, many came to appreciate the power of research and the long-term skills they had gained in this endeavor. This understanding gave us the impetus to encourage them to continue the journey they had embarked of seeing themselves in multiple roles—learner, teacher, researcher, and advocate—because the stakes are high in navigating difficult urban public school systems, but even higher if we send out unprepared and uninformed teachers.

REFERENCES

Acuña, R. (1988). *Occupied America: A history of Chicanos.* New York: HarperCollins.

Alba, R. (2005). Bright vs. blurred boundaries: Second-generation assimilation and exclusion in France, Germany, and the United States. *Ethnic and Racial Studies, 28*(1), 20–49.

Allen, J., & Labbo, L. (2001). Giving it a second thought: Making culturally engaged teaching culturally engaging. *Language Arts, 79*(1), 40.

Baquedano-López, P. (1997). Creating social identities through doctrina narratives. *Issues in Applied Linguistics, 8*(1), 27–45.

Bourdieu, P. (1977). *Outline of a Theory of Practice.* Cambridge: Cambridge University Press.

Burstein, N. D., & Cabello, B. (1989). Preparing teachers to work with culturally diverse students: A teacher education model. *Journal of Teacher Education, 40*(5), 9.

Cole, M. (1996). *Cultural psychology: A once and future discipline.* Cambridge, MA: The Belnap Press of Harvard University Press.

Cooney, M. H., & Akintude, O. (1999). Confronting white privilege and the "color blind" paradigm in a teacher education program. *Multicultural Education, 7*(2), 9–15.

Cope, B., Kalantzis, M., & New London Group. (2000). *Multiliteracies: literacy learning and the design of social futures.* London & New York: Routledge.

Cowan, P. (2004). Devils or angels: Literacy and discourse in lowrider culture. In J. Mahiri (Ed.), *What they don't learn in school: Literacy in the lives of urban youth* (pp. 47–74). New York: Peter Lang.

Dee, J., & Henkin, A. (2002). Assessing dispositions toward cultural diversity among preservice teachers. *Urban Education, 37*(1), 22.

Dyer, B., & Friederich, L. (2002). The personal narrative as cultural artifact: Teaching autobiography in Japan. *Written Communication, 19*(2), 265–296.

Ek, L. D. (2005). Staying on God's path: Socializing Latino immigrant youth to a Christian Pentecostal identity in southern California. In A.C. Zentella (Ed.), *Building on strength: Language and literacy in Latino families and communities* (pp. 77–92). New York/Covina, CA: Teachers College Press/California Association for Bilingual Education.

Ek, L. D. (2008). Language and literacy in the Pentecostal Church and the public high school: A Case Study of a Mexican ESL Student. *The High School Journal, 92*(2), 1–13.

Ek, L. D. (2009). "It's Different Lives": A Guatemalan-American adolescent's construction of ethnic and gender identities across educational contexts. *Anthropology and Education Quarterly, 40*(4), 413–430.

Ek, L. D., & Sánchez, P. (2008, June). *Latina/o Preservice Bilingual Teachers in Texas: Narratives of Bilingualism and Biliteracy.* "Raising Voices: U.S. Latino/ as for Linguistic, Educational, and Political Rights," Conference proceedings of the 8° Congreso de Lingüística General. Madrid, Spain.

Delpit, L. D. (1995). *Other people's children: Cultural conflict in the classroom.* New York: New York Press.

Flores, B., & Smith, H. (2007). Teachers' Characteristics and Attitudinal Beliefs About Linguistic and Cultural Diversity. *Bilingual Research Journal, 31*(1/2), 323.

Flores, B. B. (2001). Bilingual education teachers' beliefs and their relation to self-reported practices. *Bilingual Research Journal, 25*(3), 275.

Flores, B. B., & Smith, H. L. (2007). Teachers' characteristics and attitudinal beliefs about linguistic and cultural diversity. *Bilingual Research Journal, 31*(1/2), 323.

García, E. (1999). *Student cultural diversity: Understanding and meeting the challenge* (2nd ed.). Boston: Houghton Mifflin.

Gee, J. P. (1996). *Social linguistics and literacies: ideology in discourses* (2nd ed.). London: Taylor & Francis.

Gee, J. P. (1996). *Social linguistics and literacies: Ideology in discourses.* New York: RoutledgeFalmer.

González, N., Moll, L., & Amanti, C. (2005). *Funds of knowledge: Theorizing practices in households and classrooms.* Mahwah, NJ: Erlbaum.

Guajardo, M. A., Sánchez, P., Fineman, E., & Scheurich, J. J. (Producers). (1998). *The labors of life/Labores de la vida: Voices of Tejano migrant farm workers.* [Videotape]. Austin, TX: Department of Educational Administration at the University of Texas at Austin.

Gutiérrez, K. D., Asato, J., Santos, M., & Gotanda, N. (2002). Backlash pedagogy: Language and culture and the politics of reform. *Review of Education, Pedagogy & Cultural Studies, 24*(4), 335–351.

Heath, S. B. (1996). *Ways with words: language, life, and work in communities and classrooms.* Cambridge England; New York: Cambridge University Press.

Heath, S. B. (1983). What no bedtime story means: Narrative skills at home and school. *Language in Society, 11*(1), 49–76.

Hornberger, N. (2003). *Continua of biliteracy: an ecological framework for educational policy.* UK: Multicultural Matters, Ltd.

Ladson-Billings, G. (2009). *The Dreamkeepers: Successful teachers of African American children.* San Francisco, CA: Jossey-Bass.

Lovelace, S., & Wheeler, T. (2006). Cultural discontinuity between home and school language socialization patterns: Implications for teachers. *Education, 127*(2), 303.

Lynch, P. (2007). Making meaning many ways: an exploratory look at integrating the arts with classroom curriculum. *Art Education, 60*(4), 33.

Machado-Casas, M. (2006). *Narrating Education of New Indigenous/Latino Transnational Communities in the South.* Unpublished dissertation. Chapel Hill, University of North Carolina at Chapel Hill.

Machado-Casas, M. (2009). The Politics of Organic Phylogeny: The Art of Parenting and Surviving as Transnational Multilingual Latino Indigenous Immigrants in the U.S. *High School Journal. 92*(4), 82–99.

MacGregor-Mendoza, P. (2000). Aquí no se habla Español: Stories of linguistic repression in southwest schools. *Bilingual Research Journal, 24*(4), 333–345.

McMillon, G. T., & Edwards, P. A. (2000). Why does Joshua "hate" school . . . but love Sunday school. *Language Arts, 78*(2), 111–120.

Nieto, S. (2004). *Affirming diversity: The sociopolitical context of multicultural education* (4th Ed.). New York: Pearson Education.

Olsen, L., & Jaramillo, A. (1999). *Turning the tides of exclusion: A guide for educators and advocates for immigrant students.* Oakland, CA: California Tomorrow.

Orellana, M. F. (2009). *Translating childhoods: Immigrant youth, language, and culture.* New Brunswick, NJ: Rutgers University Press.

Purcell-Gates, V. (2007). *Cultural practices of literacy : case studies of language, literacy, social practice, and power.* Mahwah, NJ: Lawrence Erlbaum Associates.

Richardson, G. S., & Lawrence-Brown, D. (2004). Rejecting Pygmalion: The social and cultural capital of working-class women Ph.D. students. *Race, Gender & Class, 11*(3), 36.

Rogoff, B. (1990). *Apprenticeship in thinking: Cognitive development in social context.* New York: Oxford University Press.

Romo, H. (2008). The extended border: A case study of San Antonio as a transnational city. In R. Márquez & H. Romo (Eds.), *Transformations of la familia on the US-México border.* Notre Dame, IN: Notre Dame Press.

Ruiz, R. (1995). Language Planning Considerations in Indigenous Communities. *The Bilingual Research Journal. 19*(1), 71-81.

San Miguel, Jr., G. (1999). The schooling of Mexicanos in the Southwest, 1848–1891. In J. F. Moreno (Ed.), *The elusive quest for equality: 150 years of Chicano/Chicana education.* Cambridge: Harvard Education Press.

Schieffelin, B. B., Woolard, K. A., & Kroskrity, P. V. (Eds.). (1998). *Language Ideologies: Practice and Theory.* Oxford: Oxford University Press.

Sleeter, C. (2004). Context-conscious portraits and context-blind policy. *Anthropology and Education Quarterly, 35*(1), 132.

Smith, H., Sánchez, P., Ek, L. D., & Machado-Casas, M. (forthcoming). From linguistic imperialism to linguistic *conscientización:* Learning from heritage language speakers. In D. Schwarzer, M. Petrón, & C. Luke, (Eds.), *Practice Informing Research—Research Informing Practice: Innovative Teaching Methodologies for World Language Educators (Vol. VII).* Greenwich, CT: Information Age Publishing, Inc.

Urciouli, B. (1996). *Exposing Prejudice: Puerto Rican Experiences of Language, Race, and Class.* Boulder, CO: Westview Press.

U.S. Census Bureau, 2006–2008 American Community Survey. Retrieved from http://factfinder.census.gov/ on October 6, 2010.

Valdés, G. (1996). *Con respeto: Bridging the distances between culturally diverse families and schools.* New York: Teachers College Press.

Valencia, R. R., & Black, M. S. (2002). "Mexican Americans Don't Value Education!"—On the Basis of the Myth, Mythmaking, and Debunking. *Journal of Latinos & Education, 1*(2), 81.

Valenzuela, A. (1999). *Subtractive schooling: U.S.-Mexican youth and the politics of caring.* Albany: State University of New York Press.

Vásquez, O. A., Pease-Alvarez, P., & Shannon, S. M. (1994). *Pushing boundaries: Language and culture in a Mexicano community.* New York: Cambridge University Press.

Vygotsky, L. S., & Kozulin, A. (1986). *Thought and language* (Version Translation newly rev. and edited). Cambridge: MIT Press.

Vygotsky, L. (1978). *Mind in society.* Cambridge, MA: Harvard University Press.

Willis, P. (1981). *Learning to Labor: How Working Class Kids Get Working Class Jobs.* New York: Columbia University Press.

Woolard, K. (1998). Language Ideology as a Field of Inquiry. In B. B. Schieffelin, K. A. Woolard, & P. V. Kroskrity,. (Eds.). *Language Ideologies: Practice and Theory.* Oxford: Oxford University Press.

Wortham, S. (2001). Language ideology and educational research. *Linguistics and Education 12*(3), 253–259.

Worthy, J., Rodríguez, A., Assaf, L., Martínez, L., & Cuero, K. (2003). Fifth grade bilingual students and the precursors to "subtractive" schooling. *Bilingual Research Journal, 27,* 275–294.

Zentella, A. C. (2005). *Building on strength: Language and literacy in Latino families and communities.* New York: Teachers College Press.

CHAPTER 2

A Different World

Black Bookstores as Literacy Counterpublics

Marc Lamont Hill

This chapter takes a sociocultural approach, which stands in sharp relief to traditional literacy scholarship. Historically, literacy has been framed as a set of acquirable (and neutral) skills that have a universally ameliorative impact on a range of cognitive, epistemological, and social processes, irrespective of the contexts in which people acquire literacy skills (e.g., Goody, 1977; Goody & Watt, 1968; Ong, 1982). Such approaches, which Street (1984) refers to as "autonomous models" of literacy, have dominated social policy, as well as many public and academic discourses.

LITERACY IN SOCIOCULTURAL CONTEXT

By taking a sociocultural approach to the study of literacy, scholars can examine the ways in which literacy operates not merely as an autonomous process, but as a political and socially contingent set of practices and ideologies within a range of formal and informal contexts (e.g., Brandt, 2001; Gee, 1996; Street, 1984). This approach has been buttressed by three decades of cross-cultural ethnographic studies that examine literacy within local settings. Through these studies, scholars have highlighted a wide range of identities, practices, ideologies, and texts (i.e., "literacies" rather than "Literacy") that are constituted within particular social, cultural, political, and geographic contexts.

Although useful, the current body of sociocultural literature suffers from two key conceptual tensions that are addressed in this chapter. First, as Brandt and Clinton (2002) argue, much of the current research "exaggerat[es] the power of local contexts to set or reveal the forms and meanings that literacy takes" (p. 1). As a result of this overemphasis on the local, we lose sight of the broader processes, discourses, and arrangements of power that inform local literacy practices. Second, as both Street (2003) and Collins and Blot (2003) argue, the expansion of sociocultural research literature has resulted in a series of studies that add descriptive textures of particular local contexts, but fail to address more general theoretical and practical issues. These two concerns are particularly problematic with regard to the study of the literacy practices of Black people.

Despite an ever-expanding body of sociocultural literacy research, there remains a dearth of scholarship on the literacy practices of Black people. Although historical research has provided insight into the role of literacy within Black communities (e.g., Gaines, 1996; McHenry, 2002; McHenry & Heath, 1994; Richardson, 2003), there are few contemporary ethnographic studies on the local literacy practices of Black people in light of broader discourses, institutions, and arrangements of power, particularly within out-of-school contexts. Although a new generation of literature on sociocultural literacy is appearing in the field (e.g., Fisher, 2009; Kinloch, 2010; Kirkland, 2009), there remains a considerable lacuna of research that examines how Black people conceptualize, obtain, and deploy literacy within formal and informal settings. In this chapter, I aim to contribute to the theoretical and empirical sectors of the literature by exploring the relationships among Black people, literacy, and counterpublicity.

LITERACY AND THE PUBLIC SPHERE

In developing my notion of *counterpublic literacies*, I draw upon the deep, growing body of interdisciplinary scholarship on "public sphere." Introduced by Habermas (1962) as a historical phenomenon and normative framework for democratic dialogue, the bourgeois public sphere was imagined as an inclusive, transparent, and egalitarian space in which private citizens could come together within public spaces (e.g., coffee houses, Masonic lodges) to discuss and debate problems of common concern. Through these dialogues, citizens were able to offer critiques of the state and create discursive spaces for spotlighting and resisting oppressive or arbitrary formations of power. According to Habermas, the public sphere flourished in 18th- and 19th-century Europe, but was ultimately undermined by the expansion of mass media, which transformed the public into passive consumers. It also led to the emergence of the welfare state, which insinuated the state into society in ways that eroded the autonomy of the public sphere.

A central, though underexamined, dimension of public sphere theory is its implicit beliefs about the salience of literacy in the development of democracy. Historical analyses of the public sphere suggest that its expansion was directly connected to growing literacy rates, increased access to a range of printed texts (e.g., books, pamphlets), and the emergence of critical (i.e., uncensored) print journalism (Habermas, 1962; Schudson, 1992). Scholars situate interactions of the public sphere within literacy institutions like salons, book clubs, and philosophical societies. Within such contexts, citizens engaged in critical discussions about particular literary and artistic texts, using them as springboards into broader conversations about the government, politics, and public policy.

Implicit in this stance are several noteworthy yet problematic claims about literacy. First, by viewing the expansion of a literate citizenry and the increased availability of printed texts as the predicate for a fully realized democracy, scholars appeal to what Graff (1979) refers to as the "literacy myth." This model ascribes universal, transformative, and emancipatory power to traditional (e.g., Western, alphabetic) conceptions of literacy without attending to the particular social, cultural, and economic circumstances in which they are produced. Also, by framing these forms of literacy proficiency as the pre-condition for participation in the public sphere, scholars reify an elitist and ethnocentric oral/literate divide that privileges Western alphabetic literacy, thereby legitimating the exclusion of "non-literate" individuals from full democratic citizenship. In addition to prioritizing particular literacy practices, such an approach privileges certain texts, including mainstream newspapers and books, at the expense of other textual traditions, genres, and modalities.

LITERATE COUNTERPUBLICS
AND COUNTERPUBLIC LITERACIES

In response to Habermas, an interdisciplinary cadre of scholars has offered a range of critical rejoinders. At the core of many of their critiques is the assertion that Habermas's conception of the public sphere appeals to an ahistorical and largely nostalgic narrative of history that obscures its exclusionary nature. In response, many scholars have offered revisionist historiographies that spotlight various ways the bourgeois public sphere failed to accommodate historically marginalized groups such as women, people of color, gays and lesbians, and working-class citizens. (I use the phrase *revisionist history* not in pejorative terms, but in the manner used by academic historians to describe intellectual projects that challenge orthodox or hegemonic narratives of historical events.) Also, in addition, scholars have challenged the notion of "common concern" that underpins the democratic ethos of the bourgeois public sphere. Specifically, they have shown how notions of commonality and consensus are tethered to the interests of dominant groups, thereby designating particular concerns central to public discourse while simultaneously rendering others marginal or invisible.

In addition to critiquing the fundamental premises of Habermas's public sphere, many scholars have also spotlighted the ways marginalized groups have responded to the exclusionary dimensions of the bourgeois public sphere. Fraser (1990) argues that marginalized groups respond by creating "alternate public" or "counterpublic" spheres, which she defines as "[p]arallel discursive arenas where members of subordinated social groups invent and circulate counterdiscourses to formulate oppositional interpretations of their identities, interests, and needs" (p. 123). Subsequent scholarship (e.g., Asen & Brouwer, 2001; Calhoun, 1993; Harris-Lacewell, 2004) has demonstrated how a range of counterpublics has crafted spaces that respond to the "exclusionary violence" (Black Public Sphere Collective, 1995) of the bourgeois public sphere.

Although the current literature on counterpublic spheres has produced useful theoretical and empirical insights, it has largely ignored the literacy issues that undergird notions of publicity and counterpublicity. Although this is partly due to the diminished role of literacy within many conceptualizations of the counterpublic sphere, there remains a need to consider: a) the ways in which literacy institutions serve as counterpublic spaces; b) the ways particular literacy practices and ideologies enable the constitution of counterpublic space; and c) how particular counterpublic spaces enable new conceptions and practices of literacy.

To provide analytic room for these ideas, I offer the terms *literacy counterpublics* and *counterpublic literacies*. By literacy counterpublics, I refer to spaces in which written texts are central to the engagement of social practices that enable participants to challenge the authority of the state, develop oppositional politics, reinterpret dominant social narratives, and counternarrate their own lived experiences. By counterpublic literacies, I refer to any literacy practice that functions in the service of counterpublicity, irrespective where such practices are engaged. This chapter provides texture to these concepts through my ethnographic examination of Rasul's, a Black bookstore in West Philadelphia.

RESEARCHING RASUL'S

From 2005 until 2009, I conducted a multi-sited ethnographic study of Black book vendors in Philadelphia. One of the three primary sites for the study was Rasul's, a popular West Philadelphia bookstore that was considered a cultural staple of the city's Black community. As a teenager growing up in Philadelphia, I had spent a great deal of time in the bookstore and had developed a relatively close relationship with Rasul, the owner, prior to his death in 1997. It was this relationship (and my promise to volunteer 4 hours per week) that I leveraged in convincing Sister Jamilah, Rasul's daughter and current manager of the store, to allow me to spend large amounts of time hanging out in the bookstore, observing the reading and purchasing practices of customers, examining thousands of books, and talking to hundreds of customers.

Over time, I became more fully integrated into the community, which was nearly all Black but extremely diverse with respect to age, income, education level, religion, and political ideology. As a result, I developed relationships with regular customers that extended beyond the store. These relationships provided me with hundreds of hours of formal and informal interview data, fieldnotes from other contexts, and mounds of documents and projects created by research participants. Although the bulk of data is not explicitly referenced in this chapter, it nonetheless informs the conceptual and analytic frames that underpin the research.

A Different Curriculum

Although incense, calendars, soaps, and urban fiction novels accounted for the majority of the store's sales revenue, Rasul's was known around the city for its selection of "hard-to-find" Black books. It was these books, and the community's engagement with them, that built Rasul's reputation as a site for alternative, oppositional, and political texts about people of African descent. As Baba Shanjay, an elder in the community who worked part-time in the bookstore, explained:

> People come here to get stuff they can't get anywhere else. Books on Freemasonry, Black religion, *real* African history. . . . Whatever you want that *they* don't have, you can get it here. [laughing] We got a whole different curriculum going on around here. [emphasis added]

Baba Shanjay's notion of a "different curriculum," which was routinely articulated in a variety of ways by Rasul's customers, reflects how the store privileged different intellectual, cultural, and political traditions than the ones typically found within mainstream literacy publics.

Among the most popular books at Rasul's were Black nationalist texts, conspiracy theory books, prison memoirs, and revisionist historiographies about human civilization. At nearly any moment during the day, customers could be seen holding, purchasing, or reading books such as *The Isis Papers* by Frances Cress Welsing (1991), a collection of essays that advances "melanin theory," or the belief in the inherent superiority of humans with darker (i.e., more melanin-filled) skin; *Message to the Black Man in America* by The Honorable Elijah Muhammad (1965), a canonical text of the Nation of

Islam and a foundational text for 20th-century Black Nationalism; *Soledad Brother* by George Jackson, an epistolary narrative from an incarcerated Black Panther; and *Behold a Pale Horse* (1991) by William Cooper, a text filled with conspiracy theories regarding secret societies, UFOs, and government plots against Black and Brown people. In addition to political books, the store contained a range of cultural nationalist texts. Books about natural hair, African art, and naming ceremonies, none of which could be regularly found within mainstream literacy publics, filled the shelves of Rasul's and were purchased with great regularity. These texts embodied the notion of a "different curriculum" and helped constitute Rasul's institutional identity as a counterpublic literacy space that challenged mainstream discourses, ideologies, identities, and texts.

Rasul's reputation for offering "a different curriculum" was not only linked to its content, but to the store's perceived relationship to mainstream literacy publics, particularly large commercial booksellers, public libraries, and White-owned independent bookstores. As Sister Jamilah would often say, this contrast shaped Rasul's counterpublic identity in the eyes of store patrons and the broader community:

> The big bookstores won't ever carry a book like *The Isis Papers* or *Message to the Black Man*. No, not because it don't sell. . . . How many books they got in those stores that don't sell any copies? Many of our books sell a hundred times more copies than some of those books they got over there. No, it's because they don't want the *kind* of people that buy those books in the store. Plus, they don't want their customers being exposed to that kind of knowledge. With us, though, people know that they can come in here and get everything they want, and stuff they don't even know they want, will be right here on the shelf. This is a place where they can get *real knowledge* [emphasis added].

Sister Jamilah's comment reflected a general sense among customers that the store's texts were being deliberately excluded from mainstream bookstores for deleterious reasons. Such beliefs were not entirely implausible, given the exclusion of many of Rasul's most popular texts from mainstream stores. For example, although all of the aforementioned books were bestsellers, each having sold hundreds of thousands of copies nationwide, only George Jackson's *Soledad Brother* could be found at any of the Borders or Barnes and Noble bookstores and public libraries within a 40-mile radius. Although there are numerous explanations for this decision—for example, the fact that many of Rasul's bestsellers were primarily sold to prison inmates—the belief that there was a widespread conspiracy against "real knowledge" books only enhanced Rasul's reputation as a precious site for counterpublic literacy engagement.

The notion of a "different curriculum" not only reflects the range of intellectual traditions found within Rasul's, but also the quite literal ways books diverged from the local public school curriculum. As explained by Sean, a 10th-grade student at a neighboring high school who would routinely come to the bookstore after school, Rasul's offered a powerful and necessary complement to the books he was reading at school. According to Sean: "When I go to school, I read a lot of stuff that's good for getting in college and being able to talk to White people and rich people and stuff. But in here I get the real stuff that I need to understand what's going on in the world, and to talk to *my* people."

In many ways, Sean reiterates Fisher's (2006) notion that Black bookstores offer patrons a "dual degree," or an opportunity to supplement school-sanctioned knowledge with information from other intellectual traditions. It was this belief that prompted many customers to bring or send their children to Rasul's after school and on weekends to purchase books. As one parent told me, "Sending my kids here is like an afterschool program. They get the kind of information they need to be a whole Black person."

Although this notion of a "dual degree" was often expressed, it was equally common for customers to describe Rasul's as a space for supplanting rather than supplementing school-sanctioned knowledge. For instance, Richard and Kamal, both high school seniors, would regularly leave school at noon and spend the rest of the day at Rasul's reading books such as *Stolen Legacy* and *They Came Before Columbus*, which challenged traditional historiographies by spotlighting the impact of African people prior to the arrival of Europeans. Rashad, another youth who visited the store several times per week, explained, "The books in here teach me the truth. Why go to school and hear lies when the real [stuff] is someplace else?" Although Rashad's arguments against going to school were regularly challenged by elders in the store—they emphasized the practical and intellectual value of graduating high school—it was generally expressed that Rasul's offered a corrective to the misinformation offered in school. In both cases, the bookstore was a counterpublic space whose "different curriculum" challenged narrow conceptions of "official knowledge" (Apple, 1990), thereby highlighting alternative bodies of knowledge, worldviews, and traditions.

A Different Tradition

At first glance, there is little difference between Rasul's and most mainstream bookstores. Against the walls of the store are signs that marked the disciplinary divisions that exist in most bookstores: literature, history, psychology, and social science. Upon closer examination, however, customers notice that the books stocked under the signs are markedly different from those found in mainstream bookstores. In the place of books from major publishing houses such as Random House, Penguin, or Simon and Schuster are texts from independent Black presses such as Third World Press and Africa World Press, which exclusively publish books on topics related to Black people. Although virtually invisible within mainstream literacy publics, these books were extremely popular and profitable within Rasul's, as well as other counterpublic literacy spaces throughout the city.

Through the promotion of alternative publishers and publishing traditions, Rasul's also spotlighted alternate traditions of book authorship. In addition to featuring new and local authors, the store also heavily promoted bestselling authors such as Frances Cress Welsing, Ben Jochannan, Haki Madhubuti, and Jawanza Kunjufu. Although these authors were not big sellers in mainstream circles, they were very popular at Rasul's and other Black bookstores, as customers would regularly request them by name. According to Sister Jamilah, the presence of these texts and authors were central to the store's functionality as a counterpublic space:

> The books here come from different people, different authors, different publishers. Therefore, when you come in here and read these books, you gonna have what? That's right, a different conversation. A lot of the books we read and discuss in here are from brilliant brothers and sisters who can't get a shot with the big White publishers and they end up publishing with a Black company or putting it out themselves. That may not be good enough for some places, but around here it's the brilliance of the ideas that matter. We read them and we use them!

In many ways, Sister Jamilah overstates the democratic nature of the bookstore. For example, despite providing a wide range of texts, there were no books in the store written by Black conservatives and few by gay and lesbian authors. Also, the very process of book publishing privileges particular literacy practices, genres, and modalities that are inevitably exclusionary. Still, she accurately speaks to the ways Rasul's exposed customers to alternate intellectual traditions that promoted new ideas, new authorial voices, and new possibilities for critical democratic exchange. The significance of the bookstore, however, is not exhausted at the level of individual book content. Rather, the store also represented a tradition of counterpublic authorship and publishing that enabled customers to challenge dominant notions of canonicity that are normalized within dominant literacy publics.

Prior to entering Rasul's, many customers, even those who identified as lifelong readers, were unaware of the authors and genres that were featured in the store. For example, Mary, a graduate student in psychology at a local research university, had not encountered the tradition of African-centered psychology until she became a regular customer at Rasul's. After several months of coming into the bookstore, she had read numerous African-centered psychology texts from authors such as Na'im Akbar, Amos Wilson, and Wade Nobles, none of which were included in her graduate school courses. Although she appreciated the insights provided by the texts themselves, she also recognized the broader significance of engaging marginalized traditions within her field:

> I go to one of the best schools in the country. I'm supposed to be getting the best education in the world, right? And I guess I am in a certain kind of way. But there's a whole other stream of knowledge that they won't even acknowledge. That is, if they know about it themselves! [laughs] . . . Bottom line, I'm just glad to be reminded that *we* have ideas too! [emphasis added]

For Mary, Rasul's served not only as a site for questioning dominant perspectives within the discipline of psychology, but also for challenging tacit narratives about who has the intellectual capacity to possess and disseminate academic knowledge. In this case, Mary's reading of the African-centered tradition of psychology reinforced the idea that "we" (i.e., Black people) had contributed to the intellectual canon of psychology.

For many other customers, the books in Rasul's served as their first exposure to Black nonfiction authors. As Sister Jamilah explained, "Our store is like a meetinghouse for Black people and Black ideas." This point was made clear by Basil, an 18-year-old high school senior who had been frequenting the store for 2 years. When he first came into the store, he was interested in books about the history of Black people throughout the African Diaspora, but did not expect the authors of the books to be Black. He explained:

> When I first came into the store, I didn't know that Black people had written books about real stuff like history and science. In school, we only read books by White people that talk about that kind of stuff. Now I know that whatever I'm reading about, there's a Black person that probably wrote something important about it. Even if they don't talk about it in school, I know it's here or somewhere else.

These sentiments were not exclusive to youth, as many adult customers privately confessed that they were not aware of nonfiction Black intellectual traditions until they entered the store. As one customer told me, "I knew we wrote books but I didn't realize that we had written so much until I came here!"

A Different Identity

When Rashad began visiting Rasul's, he was already an avid reader. In both formal and casual conversations, he would routinely use terms such as *bookworm*, *nerd*, or *lifelong* student to describe himself. As he spent more time reading books from the store, Rashad started using terms such as *scholar*, *scientist*, and *researcher* to describe his engagement with books. When I pointed out this descriptive shift to him, he explained:

> I been reading books my whole life, but I was doing it in a "school" kinda way. In school, we write to pass tests and do what teachers want you to do. It wasn't until I started readin' real knowledge that I realized that some books got the truth in them. You can use that truth to grow, to school other people in the community, to, like, make the world better. Now I'm not just a student, I'm like a young scholar in training.

Like many members of the Rasul's community, Rashad's engagement with counterpublic traditions within the bookstore allowed him to discard a technocratic vision of reading in favor of one that viewed literacy as a vehicle for personal and community development. In doing so, Rashad and others eschewed instrumentalist notions of literacy, which frame it as a "competency-based skill-banking approach" (Macedo, 1994, p. xvi), in favor of ones that were more complex, critical, and functional within their daily lives. Through this fundamental shift in understanding, he and other members of the community were able to identify or develop literacy practices that informed new individual and social identities. The two most prominent identities that emerged over time were that of the "intellectual" and the "writer."

For a large number of customers, all of whom were male, their changing understanding of literacy caused a shift in their readerly identities, as they went from passive consumers of knowledge to engaged intellectuals for whom the practice of reading was the seedbed of individual transformation and social activism. To them, the practice of reading was not merely about individual enlightenment and pleasure, but the predicate for intellectual leadership and social change within the Black community. As Ali, a 25-year-old construction worker who regularly purchased books on Freemasonry and ancient Egyptian astrology, explained: "I used to read just 'cause I liked it. But now I'm reading for my people 'cause we still in the dark." Such comments were common among these readers, as they came to view the practice of reading as the primary means by which to discover obscured "truths" and disseminate them to unenlightened members of the community.

Although the notion of reading as an urgent political practice prompted many men in the store to read a wide range of books pertaining to the social, cultural, spiritual, and economic conditions of Black people, it also severely circumscribed their understanding of legitimate and socially acceptable reading practices. For example, male customers routinely rejected nearly all works of fiction as "unscientific" and "pointless." These critiques were explicitly gendered and subtly homophobic, as male customers would often dismiss fiction texts as "female shit" or playfully mock male purchasers of fiction by using stereotypically gay gestures and voice registers. These behaviors speak to the ways Rasul's, like all counterpublic spaces, simultaneously nurtured hegemonic and counterhegemonic political identities and discourses. Within the bookstore, fiction texts—as well as accompanying notions of escape, pleasure, desire, and playfulness—were largely imagined as effeminate, anti-intellectual and self-indulgent. Such beliefs not only reinforced hetero-patriarchal narratives about the relationship between literacy and masculinity, but delimited possibilities for how intellectual labor was imagined, articulated, and performed.

Although most customers described themselves as active readers, few identified themselves as writers. After spending time in Rasul's, however, many became more comfortable acknowledging and nurturing a writerly identity. Sean noted:

> I had been writing for a long time. Ever since I can remember. But I didn't think of myself as a *real* writer until I started reading a lot of the books in here. It was like I realized there are writers just like me. If they can write books and [stuff], why can't I? Matter of fact, I already am!

As Sean states, one of the biggest reasons for not initially seeing himself as a writer was his lack of identification with the authors to whom he had been exposed. This point was echoed and further nuanced by Tameka, a high school senior who regularly came into Rasul's to purchase fiction novels. In addition to reading two to three books per week, Taneka had written a short play and was in the process of completing her first novel. Despite these activities, she was reluctant to view herself as a "real writer." She explained:

> In school, we read books and most of the authors are White. The ones that are Black still don't seem like *us,* know what I mean? They weren't from where we from. When I started reading the books in here, I started feeling like regular people, who aren't rich or got all them degrees, could write books.

Tameka's sentiments were common among people in the bookstore, as many of them acknowledged that their initial conception of being a writer involved more than engaging in the literal act of writing. Such notions were not particular to Rasul's, as scholars have noted the common practice within Western society of assigning unique social and intellectual value to the practice of writing. Within the logic of this stance, reading is imagined as the mere passive absorption of information, while writing is framed as a more intellectually authentic activity that demands greater scrutiny, surveillance, regulation, and even repression within "modern" societies (Collins & Blot, 2003; Fernandez, 2001; Gates, 2003).

For many customers, the notion of being an authentic writer was linked to a set of ideologies that lay at the intersection of race and class. For example, Tameka had been exposed to (and enjoyed) the writing of highly celebrated Black authors such as Toni Morrison, James Baldwin, and Zora Neale Hurston at her high school prior to becoming a regular at the bookstore. Despite (or perhaps because of) their highly visible, celebrated, and even canonized status within mainstream literary circles, these authors were regarded by Tameka and others as being representatives of a different tradition of Black authorship than the ones in Rasul's. As such, their investment in their own identities as writers was not enhanced by engaging a racially diversified Western bourgeois literary canon, but through an engagement with the more racially and economically democratic traditions of authorship and publishing that were prominent within Rasul's. After engaging these traditions, they were able to begin challenging their previously held notions of authorship as a highbrow practice reserved for Whites and bourgeois Blacks. Instead, they began to reimagine the "literacies of authorship" in ways that were as diverse, democratic, and accessible to them as the ideas, authors, and traditions represented in the store.

A DIFFERENT DIRECTION

Rasul's provides a powerful counternarrative to public and academic conversations about political disengagement, anti-intellectualism, and cultural pathology among Black people. By examining the everyday practices of the store, we are able to spotlight how some Black people continue to deploy literacy in ways that defy the logic, aspirations, and expectations of the state and the bourgeois public sphere. Through counterpublic spaces like Rasul's, Black people are able to sustain the tradition of resistance, self-empowerment, and self-determination. Although these spaces are not without contradiction, as I have demonstrated throughout this chapter, they enable us to expand our scholarly gaze when locating sites of educational, political, and social possibility.

By analyzing spaces like Rasul's, we are also better able to understand the role of out-of-school contexts in providing educational experiences for communities, particularly those that have been historically marginalized within formal schooling institutions. In addition to providing necessary complements to school-based curriculum, these spaces are fecund sites for critical literacy, oppositional politics, and transgressive identity work. Such insights should not only deepen our appreciation for out-of-school contexts, but also inform our vision for producing more desirable learning environments within formal educational spaces.

CRITICAL PERSPECTIVE

The range and nature of the textual engagements within Rasul's speak to the need for linking the literacy curriculum to the lived experiences of Black students. Rather than relying purely on racial or ethnic affiliation, which has traditionally been the predicate for crafting multicultural, culturally relevant pedagogy and other progressive educational interventions, we must consider issues of class, ideology, and worldview. These and countless other factors enable us to move beyond essentialist understandings of students in favor of ones that are more complex, dynamic, and context-specific. In practical terms, this suggests that the school curriculum be expanded not only to accommodate more Black bodies, but to account for the wide range of experiences, identities, and ideologies that fall under the broad canopy of Blackness. Doing this can take on multiple and various forms such as a revision of school curriculum to include community resources (e.g., people, businesses, historical artifacts) and a rethinking of meanings of reading as a social practice to account for the community settings where people, particularly Black youth, read and the available resources within such settings.

Within Rasul's, individuals were able to negotiate a range of literacy identities that were unavailable to them within formal schooling contexts. In many cases, the same students who were assigned labels such as "disengaged" or "struggling" at school were becoming "intellectuals" and "writers" at the bookstore. This reality prompts us not only to locate new texts to engage students, but also new possibilities for whom and how students can be during their classroom time.

REFERENCES

Apple, M. (1990). The politics of official knowledge in the United States. *Journal of Curriculum Studies, 22*(4), 377–400.

Asen, R., & Brouwer, D. (2001). *Counterpublics and the state.* New York: SUNY Press.

The Black Public Sphere Collective. (1995). *The Black public sphere*. Chicago: University of Chicago Press.

Brandt, D. (2001). *Literacy in American* lives. New York: Cambridge University Press.

Brandt, D., & Clinton, K. (2002). Limits of the local: Expanding perspectives of literacies as social practice. *Journal of Literacy Research, 34*(3), 337–356.

Calhoun, C. (1993). (Ed.) *Habermas and the public sphere: Studies in contemporary German thought*. Cambridge, MA: MIT Press.

Collins, J., & Blot, R. (2003). *Literacy and literacies: Texts, power, and identity*. New York: Cambridge University Press.

Cooper, W. (1991). *Behold a pale horse*. Flagstaff, AZ: Light Horse Technologies Publication.

Fernandez, R. (2001). *Imagining literacy: rhizomes of knowledge in American culture and literature*. Austin: University of Texas Press.

Fisher, M. (2006). Earning "dual degrees": Black bookstores as alternative knowledge spaces. *Anthropology and Education Quarterly, 37*(1), 83–99.

Fisher, M. (2009). *Black literate lives: Historical and contemporary perspectives*. New York: Routledge.

Fraser, N. (1990). Rethinking the public sphere: A contribution to the critique of actually existing democracy. *Social Text*. No. 25/26, pp. 56–80.

Gaines, K. (1996). *Uplifting the race: Black leadership, politics, and culture in the twentieth century*. Chapel Hill: University of North Carolina Press.

Gates, H. L. (2003). *The trials of Phillis Wheatley: America's first Black poet and her encounters with the founding fathers*. New York: Black Civitas Books.

Gee, J. P. (1996). *Social linguistics and literacy: Ideology and discourses*. New York: Routledge.

Goody, J. (1977). *The domestication of the savage mind*. New York: Cambridge University Press.

Goody, J., & Watt, I. (1968). The consequences of literacy. In J. Goody (Ed.), *Literacy in traditional societies* (pp. 27–68). New York: Cambridge University Press.

Graff, H. J. (1979). *The literacy myth: Literacy and social structure in the nineteenth century city*. New York: Academic Press, Inc.

Habermas, J. (1991). *The structural transformation of the public sphere: An inquiry into a category of bourgeois society*. Cambridge: MIT. (Original work published 1962)

Harris-Lacewell, M. V. (2004). *Barbershops, bibles, and BET: everyday talk and Black political thought*. Princeton, NJ: Princeton University Press.

Kinloch, V. (2010). *Harlem on our minds: Place, race and the literacies of urban youth*. New York: Teachers College Press.

Kirkland, D. (2009). We real cool: Toward a theory of Black masculine literacies. Reading Research Quarterly, 44(3), 278–297.

Macedo, D. (1994). *Literacies of power: What Americans are not allowed to know*. Boulder, CO: Westview Press.

McHenry, E., & Heath, S. (1994). The literate and the literary: African Americans as writers and readers 1830–1940. *Written Communication. 11*(4). 419–444.

McHenry, E. (2002). *Forgotten readers: recovering the lost history of African American literary societies*. Durham, NC: Duke University Press.

Muhammad, E. (1965). *Message to the Blackman in America.* Chicago: The Final Call Publishers.

Ong, W. J. (1982). *Orality and literacy: The technologizing of the word.* New York: Methuen.

Richardson, E. (2003*).* African American literacies. New York: Routledge.

Schudson, M. (1993). Was there ever a public sphere? If so, when? Reflections on the American case. In C. Calhoun (Ed)., *Habermas and the public sphere* (pp. 143–163). Cambridge: MIT Press.

Street, B. (1984). *Literacy in theory and practice.* New York: Cambridge University Press.

Street, B. (2003). What's "new" in new literacy studies? Critical approaches to literacy in theory and practice. *Current Issues in Comparative Education, 5*(2), 77–91.

Welsing, F. C. (1991*). The Isis papers: The keys to the colors.* Chicago: Third World Press.

CHAPTER 3

Identity Construction in the Borderlands

The Acosta Family

Carmen M. Martínez-Roldán and Guillermo Malavé

Immigrant parents are aware of the importance of education, and while some are concerned about the Americanization of their children at school (Suárez-Orozco & Suárez-Orozco, 2001), they use different strategies for helping their children attain academic success and maintain their cultural identities. Parents often take their children to public libraries, buy them books, or engage in narratives to offer them *consejos* (giving advice), which involves inculcating the value of education and teaching children to show *respeto* (respect) to older people, teachers, and other figures of authority (Delgado-Gaitán, 1994; Pease-Alvarez, 1993; Valdés, 1996). Other immigrant parents support their children's success at school by encouraging them to learn English while keeping their cultural roots, first language, and the traditions that are considered part of their family values and beliefs (Malavé, 2006). As we illustrate in this chapter, parents develop strategies to socialize their children so that they learn these cultural beliefs, practices, and identities. Children, however, are not passive recipients of information provided by parents during socialization practices. Rather, they are actively trying to make sense of competing discourses while negotiating identities and becoming bicultural individuals in the borderlands.

We illustrate these negotiations of meanings and identities by focusing on a family living in Tucson, Arizona. Tucson, located in the southwestern United States about 60 miles from Nogales, Mexico, has been described as a border city, according to the classificatory schema proposed by Oscar Martínez (Martínez, 1994). He defines borderlands as border zones of two adjacent countries that stand out from interior zones because of the international climate and other unique characteristics such as transnational interaction, including economic and cultural interactions as well as ethnic conflict and accommodation (p. 10). Although separated by a physical border, both Tucson and Nogales are located within the cultural subregion of Sonora, within the broader region called the U.S.-Mexico borderlands.

The data presented in this chapter come from transcriptions of interviews and literature discussions that were the focus of two separate qualitative studies that shared some participants as case studies. Martínez-Roldán (2000) documented and analyzed the responses to literature of a group of 21 bilingual 2nd-grade students in a neighborhood school in Tucson, Arizona, while Malavé (2006) visited the homes of some of the children in that school and of other children attending primary grades in public schools in Arizona and Iowa. Ethnographic interviews and critical discourse analysis were used to examine narratives, discourses, and parental strategies that were used in the socialization of children. Ethnographic interviewing enabled us to elicit "the cognitive structures guiding participants' worldviews" (Rossman & Rallis, 1998, p. 132) and resembled informal conversations.

We present the experience of the members in the Acosta family (pseudonym) as narrated by both mother and daughter. The focus child in this common case study was one of the children, Diana, a 9-year-old girl enrolled in a bilingual 2nd-grade class. All children in this family were born in Tucson, Arizona. Mrs. and Mr. Acosta were born in Magdalena, a small town in Sonora on the Mexican side of the U.S.-Mexico border. At the time of the interview (2000), Mrs. Acosta had lived in the United States for 12 years and Mr. Acosta for 7. Mr. Acosta had a white-collar job in Mexico and decided to leave his country for family reunification and better job opportunities.

A CRITICAL-SOCIOCULTURAL APPROACH TO NARRATIVES AND IDENTITY DEVELOPMENT

Theories of learning and socialization, as well as theories of language, discourse, and ideology are needed for inquiries into the role of narrative in children's learning of cultural models and their cultural identity development. The analysis of narratives in this study was guided by theories of discourse provided by critical discourse analysis (CDA) and constructivist and sociocultural approaches to learning (Vygotsky, 1934/1986). The authors both share a critical-sociocultural perspective on socialization practices, in which social interactions and social construction of meanings affect the child's development of "commonsense" assumptions, cultural models, and cultural identity, while at the same time, meaning construction is affected by other factors at the macrosocial level of analysis, such as ethnic conflicts, power relations, and ideologies.

Fairclough (1992) points out the ideological character of discourse when he describes "the ideological work of discourse as simultaneously generating representations and organizing people into communities" (p. 134). Attempting to reconcile the structuralist and interactionist perspectives in language studies, Chouliaraki and Fairclough (1999) propose an approach to discourse that is based on a dialectical theory of language, describing discursive interaction as "an active, reflexive, interpretative and collaborative process of representing the world while simultaneously negotiating social relations with others and one's own identity, as one moment in social practice" (p. 46).

Ideology is not merely a set of beliefs but is the "socially shared beliefs of groups" (van Dijk, 1998, p. 135) and as such, implies the notion of group interests. Dominant groups use ideologies to legitimize their power over subordinated groups and to manipulate members of the oppressed groups to prevent insurgence. At the same time, subordinated groups may develop ideologies that respond to their own group interests. Thus, ideological discourses would play a role in people's identity development. From this critical-sociocultural perspective, we argue that cultural identity would develop as a result of the negotiation of meanings in different social contexts. It would be influenced, among other things, by the child's interpretations and understandings of a variety of narratives about social situations and personal experiences.

Cultural identities also develop, especially in the case of children of immigrants who are developing a "dual frame of reference," as they learn about cultural models on both sides of the border—"here" and "there" (Suárez-Orozco & Suárez-Orozco, 2001, p. 88). Spanish-speaking immigrants living in border cities who have migrated from small towns in Mexico to urban barrios in the United States sometimes find new job opportunities and new social circumstances that may be regarded as positive, but they may also face social problems, social constrains, and stressful situations, including acculturation stress (Suárez-Orozco & Suárez-Orozco, 2001, p. 73). These situations present dilemmas that become an object of reflection in their narratives and language socialization practices.

Narratives, or stories, as we use these terms, refer to personal accounts of experiences that may be told in informal storytelling events in everyday life or in informal conversations, as with the conversations that took place in the ethnographic interviews at home and in the literature discussions at school in this study. We incorporate the concept of "conversational narrative" as Fairclough (1992) describes it, highlighting the inherent historicity of texts through the dimension of intertextuality. That is, texts "are inherently intertextual, constituted by elements of other texts" (p. 102). A narrative could also be a "jointly-produced story" (Fairclough, 1992; Ochs & Capps, 2001).

The concept of socialization that we refer to differs from its common use by scholars in sociology and other disciplines, where it is influenced by a functionalist sociological approach. In this traditional approach, socialization is defined as a process through which children internalize social norms and develop conformism or obedience to rules. This explanation assumes that a social system can maintain its own equilibrium and social order, but overlooks issues of human agency and social change (Corcuff, 1995). The traditional approach to socialization is challenged by the Vygotskian constructivist view of learning.

Vygotsky (1934/1986; 1978) proposes a constructivist view of learning that emphasizes the role of social interactions in the social construction of knowledge and the social origins of higher psychological functions. A Vygotskian version of the constructivist view of learning acknowledges that the child is an active participant in the meaning-making process, who is engaged in the interpretation of the social events, regarded as intra-psychological (or intra-subjective) processes. However, this version also emphasizes inter-psychological (or inter-subjective) aspects, such as the social interactions and collaboration in the social construction of knowledge. Researchers associated with a sociocultural approach, especially those influenced by Vygotsky, have investigated a variety of issues and have used diverse terms related to cultural aspects of education and learning, such as "cultural mediation" and "cultural tools." The latter refer to "cultural artifacts" (psychological or material) that "mediate interaction with the world" (Cole, 1990, p. 91). The role of cultural resources in the formation and development of thinking is a fundamental principle in the sociocultural tradition (Moll, 1990).

Narratives are one such cultural tool people use for representing past experiences (Vygotsky, 1978; Wertsch, 1985). While we tell our stories, however, we are not only making sense of past events, but our narratives become a means by which the individual self is defined or re-created (Miller, 1994). People's personal narratives and stories provide an important basis for the social construction of self. In her study on language socialization, specifically on storytelling, Miller (1994) argues that personal storytelling is an important means by which young children, together with family members, (re)experience self in relation to others. That is, narrators understand themselves differently by representing their lives through narratives.

METHODS AND ANALYSIS

We used critical discourse analysis (CDA) to examine collected narratives as we sought to better understand the interplay between parents' socialization efforts and the Mexicano/Latino children's learning and meaning-making processes. Critical discourse analysis provides a theory of discourse and a method for examining narratives and storytelling events, as important aspects of discursive practices. Our version of CDA was influenced by several scholars, especially Fairclough (1992), Gee (2005), and van Dijk (1998). These scholars have in common a view of narratives as produced and used within the context of social practices, emphasizing the role of social interactions and other social aspects, including the social structure (e.g., social status, power issues) that affect people's interpretations and learning about the social world. In the analysis of narratives, it is also necessary to take into consideration the role of ideologies, especially when using a critical perspective, as we propose here. The role of parents in the reproduction of ideologies is acknowledged by van Dijk (1998) when he says that "families and their socialization practices are partly ideological, because of their role in the socialization of norms, values, and fragments of ideology" (p. 186).

A critical approach to discourse analysis allowed us to develop a detailed analysis of participants' discourses and narratives. This analysis demonstrated how parents and children engaged in informal conversations that helped children reflect upon different cultural models. Ogbu (1991) defines a cultural model as people's "understandings of how their society or any particular domain or institution works" (p. 7), which guides their interpretations of specific social events and society. Ogbu applies his notion of a cultural model to education and states that the cultural model of minority and majority groups exists "to provide group members with the framework for interpreting educational events, situations and experiences and to guide behavior in the schooling contexts and processes" (p. 7).

In the discourse analysis presented here, we concentrated on specific features of narratives such as the wording (and the situated meanings of words, according to Gee, 2005), analysis of content, topics, reported speech, strategies for persuasion, and rhetorical moves (Fairclough, 1992). We searched for cues to understand participants' beliefs, cultural models, and situated identities, the latter defined as "the ways we use language to get recognized as taking on a certain identity or role here and now" (Gee, 2005, p. 99). Next, we discuss the discursive practices used by Mrs. Acosta to socialize her daughter into the learning of some cultural models and into an identity rooted in their Spanish language, and the girl's responses to those efforts. Later, we do a content analysis of the girl's narratives and the cultural models she was negotiating through her narratives in literature discussions.

MOTHER'S USE OF SOCIALIZATION PRACTICES: IDEOLOGICAL TEACHING

Immigrant parents of Mexican descent use different strategies in their discursive practices to socialize their children into learning about Mexican culture and to motivate them to learn and use Spanish language. One strategy parents use in socialization practices is what the second author calls *inculcation of cultural beliefs* of the social-cultural group to which the parent belongs (Malavé, 2006). In this family, Diana's mother attempted to persuade her children to accept particular beliefs that, according to her, are essential for developing a sense of identity as Mexicans. These attempts to inculcate beliefs in socialization practices can be characterized as a type of "ideological teaching" (van Dijk, 1998, p. 91). Children are influenced not only by ideological teaching from their parents, but also by diverse narratives and discourses as they learn about their world at home and in school. Sometimes they receive competing or contradictory messages from diverse sources. These contradictions and conflicts became apparent in the narratives Diana produced as she participated in literature discussions at home and in conversations with her mother at home.

Mis Raíces Son Mejicanas/My Roots Are Mexican

In an interview with Diana's parents in which Diana was also present, participating occasionally in the conversation, the parents argued that Mexican-origin parents should teach their children about Mexican culture and should try to prevent language loss. In the following excerpt, Mrs. Acosta, the child's mother, presented an example of how she tried to educate their children about Mexican culture and identity. This informal education was part of her effort to socialize their children by inculcating certain cultural beliefs, such as the cultural model of a Mexican identity and the belief that they should feel proud of their Mexican identity. Below is an excerpt from the interview in Spanish, the language used in this family, and its translation showing Mrs. Acosta's perspectives on language and culture. To provide an example of how parents should teach their children about preserving their cultural roots and Spanish language, she told a short story about how she had attempted to educate on this matter at home:

> *Uno les debe ir fomentando desde chiquitos, irles fomentando que las raíces de uno son de español, son en español. Por ejemplo, mis raíces son Mexicanas y nosotros, por ejemplo ella, y lo digo y lo digo con orgullo, ella nació el 20 de noviembre, [cuando] en México se celebra la revolución mexicana. Y mi otra niña, la más chiquita, nació el 16 de septiembre y en México se celebra la independencia de México. Mis hijos son patriotas, porque . . . le trae a uno lo mexicano. Más por eso yo digo que todo depende de los papás porque uno tiene que irles, como se dice, empujándoles a que no pierdan sus raíces.*

[One should be promoting, starting when they are young, be promoting that one's roots are Spanish, are in Spanish. For example, my roots are Mexican and we, for example she (Diana), and I say this, I say this with pride, she was born on November the 20th, when Mexico celebrates the Mexican Revolution and my other girl, the youngest, was born on September 16th and in Mexico we celebrate the Mexican independence. My children are patriots because . . . it brings you the Mexican (Mexican culture). That is why I say that it depends on the parents because one has to be, like one says, pushing them to avoid that they lose their roots.]

In this excerpt, which contains part of a conversation in which the parents were answering a question about the cause of Spanish language loss in some Mexican families, Mrs. Acosta said "that it all depends on the parents." The implication is that children's language loss is largely a result of the failure of some Mexican immigrant parents who do not teach their children to learn/maintain their mother tongue. Although she supported bilingual education, Mrs. Acosta believed that parents play important roles in their children's language acquisition. Her use of the expressions "*irles fomentando que las raíces son de español*" (promoting, teaching them that one's roots are Spanish) and "*empujándoles a que no pierdan sus raíces*" (pushing them to avoid losing their roots) signals her preferred strategy in socialization practices: inculcating in her children certain beliefs, or cultural models, that insist on Spanish language remaining central to Mexican cultural heritage or *raíces* (roots) and identity.

Mrs. Acosta provided an example of the inculcation-of-beliefs strategy she had used to promote Spanish and Mexican identity within her family. This consisted of talking to her children about how her two daughters' birthdays coincided with particular Mexican patriotic celebrations or holidays, such as the Mexican Revolution and Mexican Independence Day. Analysis of this particular narrative reveals that this immigrant mother is taking for granted that Diana self-identifies as Mexican because she is learning about Mexican cultural roots. Diana, who was present at this interview, seemed very attentive during the conversation; she participated and answered questions posed by the interviewer or her mother, and she added comments, as illustrated in the following section.

Yo Soy Americana/I Am American

After Mrs. Acosta shared the above short story on how she tried to teach her children at home about the preservation of language and culture, the interviewer (GM) turned to Diana and asked her questions as a way to encourage her participation. Below, is an excerpt of the conversation presented in three parts to represent three moments in the exchange. The last moment (#3) includes a short narrative that Diana produced during our discussion on language loss.

Moment 1

GM: *Diana, tú sabes que a veces hay unas personas que tú les preguntas ¿qué tú eres? Y dicen "yo soy americano." Otros dicen "yo soy Chinese o chino." ¿Y qué tú eres?*

MRS. ACOSTA: *¿Qué tú eres, americana o mexicana?*

DIANA: *Americana.*

MRS. ACOSTA: *¿Americana?*

DIANA: *Yo nací aquí.*

MRS. ACOSTA: *Pues sí, pero tu descendencia ¿qué es?*

DIANA: *Mexicana.*

MRS. ACOSTA: *Mexicana, pues dilo (. . .)*

DIANA: *Mexicana.*

MRS. ACOSTA: *Pero como le digo, estoy bien orgullosa que de los tres de mis hijos, dos son que han nacido en días patrióticos mexicanos.*

DIANA: *Hijas.*

MRS. ACOSTA: *Hijas, sí, pues pero son mis hijos.*

GM: Diana, you know that sometimes there are people who you ask them "what are you?" And they say, "I'm an American." Others say, "I'm Chinese." So, what are you?

MRS. ACOSTA: What are you, American or Mexican?

DIANA: American.

MRS. ACOSTA: American?

DIANA: I was born here.

MRS. ACOSTA: Yes, but your ancestry, what is it?

DIANA: Mexican.

MRS. ACOSTA: Mexican, so say it (. . .)

DIANA: Mexican.

MRS. ACOSTA: But as I say, I'm very proud that out of three of my [male] children, two of them have been born on Mexican patriotic days.

DIANA: Daughters.

MRS. ACOSTA: Daughters, yes, well but they are my children.

Mrs. Acosta paraphrased the interviewer's question by presenting a more directive question. This prompted Diana to choose between two alternatives of cultural identity: American or Mexican. Diana self-identified as *Americana* soon after listening to her mother's discourse on Mexican culture and patriotism, and despite her mother's leading question.

Diana's mother reacted with surprise and followed up with another directive question, which could be a strategy for suggesting that Diana reconsider her answer: "*¿Americana?*" Despite this second directive question, Mrs. Acosta was surprised that her daughter did not change her stance. Contrary to her mother's expectations, Diana explained her argument for her self-identification as Americana: she was born in the United States. Her mother then used a third directive question that led Diana to self-identify as a person of Mexican descent, prompting the expected answer: "*Mexicana.*" The mother continued with a sort of lesson, asking the student to repeat the word once more: "*Mexicana.*" At the end of the narrative, Mrs. Acosta used repetition as a rhetorical strategy to demonstrate her pride in having children who were born on patriotic days.

As Mrs. Acosta complained about how Mexican youth are abandoning Spanish, Diana said something softly, which appeared to be a strategy to participate in the conversation, of which the researcher encouraged.

Moment 2

GM: *Ella quería decir algo allá ¿qué es?*

DIANA: *Que un chamaquito de aquí, vecino, viene todos los días, cuando él estaba chiquito, cuando estaba en kinder él sabía mucho español pero perdió el español y supo inglés y él no sabe leer en español. Todo lo supo en la escuela y ya no volvió a hablar español más nunca en la vida.*

GM: *¿Y qué tú crees de eso? ¿O sea cuál es tu opinión? ¿Tú crees que eso está bien?*

DIANA: *No.*

GM: *¿Por qué?*

NIÑA: *¿Y cómo le van a hablar a sus padres si es que no saben inglés?*

GM: She wanted to say something there, what is it?

DIANA: That a little kid, a neighbor, he comes around everyday, when he was little, when he was in kindergarten, he knew a lot of Spanish but he lost the Spanish and learned English and he doesn't know how to read Spanish. He learned everything at school, and he never spoke Spanish again ever in his life.

GM: And what do you think of that? I mean, what is your opinion? Do you think it is right?

DIANA: No.

GM: Why?

DIANA: So how he is going to talk to his parents if they don't know English?

The interactions between the child and her mother at different moments across the conversation show two things. First, during moment #1,

Mrs. Acosta is consistent in her strategy of encouraging the child to embrace a Mexican identity, repeating statements and narratives over and over again, such as the story about her children being born on Mexican patriotic days. Second, moment #2 shows that Diana does not passively accept whatever her mother says, but negotiates meaning and identity. After facing her daughter's unexpected responses, Mrs. Acosta made comments that demonstrate her socialization practices. She continued using the same strategies of persuasion, expressing her feelings and displaying her pride in being Mexican. At the end, Diana shared a story about a child who had lost his Spanish, which could be interpreted as a moment in which she was the one providing an example that supported her mother's argument about the need to keep the Spanish language.

Spanish Is My First Language . . . I Prefer English

The interviewer posed another question to Diana to explore her sense of identification with a particular language and to determine whether she understood the notion of language as a symbol of cultural identity, a point her mother had been trying to teach her throughout the conversation.

Moment 3

> GM: *¿Y cuál es tu idioma, Diana?*
> DIANA: *Es español mi primer idioma.*
> GM: *¿Y cuál prefieres?*
> DIANA: *Inglés.*
> GM: *Inglés, ¿prefieres el inglés? Y ¿por qué?*
> DIANA: *Porque hay muchos niños que hablan inglés, si no sé hablarlo, no puedo hablar.*
> GM: *O sea, porque muchos niños hablan inglés y tú quieres hablar inglés para poderlo hablar con ellos. Umm, entiendo.*
> MRS. ACOSTA: *¿Cuál es el idioma que hablas aquí en la casa?*
> DIANA: *Español.*

> GM: And what is your language, Diana?
> DIANA: Spanish is my first language.
> GM: And which one do you prefer?
> DIANA: English.
> GM: English, you prefer English? And why?
> DIANA: Because there are a lot of kids who speak English, if I don't know how to speak it, I can't talk.
> GM: So, because there are many kids who speak English and you want to speak English so that you can talk to them. Umm, I see.

MRS. ACOSTA: What is the language you speak here at home?
DIANA: Spanish.

Despite Mrs. Acosta's efforts to inculcate her beliefs and cultural values to her daughter, Diana said in Spanish that English was her preferred language. Diana mentioned that many children spoke English and that she could not talk to them if she did not know English, which is evidence of peer influence. Diana's mother asked her which language Diana spoke at home to remind her of their rule to speak Spanish at home. This conversation demonstrates, again, that Diana is not a passive learner. She freely expressed her ideas, notwithstanding her mother's attempt to use different strategies to provide guidance (advice) and to influence Diana's thinking, sense of cultural identity, and language use.

Language and identity were not the only aspects of the social world Diana was trying to understand. Literature discussions also provided opportunities to observe Diana and collect narratives about her family history. In the following section, we present Diana's participation in small group literature discussions or *pláticas literarias* at school, when students come together to think and talk about a book they read.

NEGOTIATING CULTURAL MODELS AND IDENTITIES THROUGH NARRATIVES

Diana frequently told stories about her family in literature discussions, stories that situated her identity as Mexican and American. The literature discussions were bilingual—that is, she could use Spanish or English. Diana always chose to tell her stories in Spanish, and translated in English if a group member was English dominant. The analysis of Diana's narratives shows the presence of intertextuality (Fairclough, 1992), instances in which she was not talking about her particular experiences, but rather retelling stories heard from her parents. Her stories seemed to be collective family memories that she was re-authoring as she shared them in the literature discussion groups. It seemed as if the stories and the group helped her to reach a collective understanding of her experiences and to negotiate her sense of place and belonging, as is shown in her responses below to *Baseball Saved Us* (Mochizuki, 1993). Although Diana, like her siblings, was born in Tucson, Arizona, "here" in the United States, she recalled experiences that happened "*allá*" ("there") in Mexico while visiting or living for short periods in her parents' country of origin. Diana constructed these narratives using several conversational turns, allowing her peers to ask questions that helped her to further develop her narrative (they were edited for reasons of space, omitting the co-construction aspect of the narratives):

Yo—ah—cuando fui yo, cuando yo estaba chiquita, yo vivía en Tasí-cori y allá en Tasícori no más había una tiendita, y esa tiendita estaba bien cerquita de nuestra casa y para cruzar era muy, muy, muy batal-loso, así que nosotros teníamos que ir hasta Magdalena a comprar comida . . . Porque—"Mami, mejor", le dije, le dije yo: "mejor nos movemos a Magdalena en vez de aquí." Entonces mi mamá: "No, nosotros nos vamos a mover hasta Tucsón." Entonces venimos, veni-mos, vivimos con mi nana y después nos cambiamos a unos aparta-mentos . . . luego otros departamentos. Cuando vivíamos en Tasícori fue nuestra primera casa, pero de todos modos, nosotros nacimos aquí. Después aquí hemos estado viviendo, y mi mama, pero dice mi mamá: "Ya no nos vamos a mover nunca," [Diana reports next what she said to her mother:] "Pero mamá, pero ya no sabemos si nos vamos a mover." . . . Entonces mi mamá me dijo: "¿Tú te quieres mover de aquí?" "Sí, sí, yo porque quiero estar cerquita de mi nana Fina" y después le decía: "No, porque, porque aquí está bien."

[I, when I went, when I was a little girl I lived in Tasícori, and there in Tasícori there was only one small market, and that market was very close to our house and it was very, very, very difficult to cross, so we had to go to Magdalena to buy food . . . (She continues describing the kinds of products they could find in Magdalena). Because—"Mom, we better,"—I told her: "we better move to Magdalena instead of (staying) here." Then, my mother said: "No, we are going to move to Tucson." Then we came [to live] with my grandmother, and later we moved to some apartments . . . later in other apartments. When we lived in Tasícori that was our first house, but anyway, we were born here. After that, we have been living here, and my mom, my mom says: "We won't ever move from here." [Diana reports next what she said to her mother.] "But mom, we don't know if we are going to move." . . . Then my mom asked me: "Do you want to move from here?"—"Yes, yes, I, because I want to be close to my nana Fina" and later I said to her; "No, because, because here it's fine."]

In the interview with her mother at home, Diana clarified that she was born in the United States and self-identified as *"Americana."* When she told her stories about the places she lived and where she was born—"When we lived in Tasícori, it was our first home, but anyway, we were born here [in Tucson]"—the connections between these narratives provide a clearer un-derstanding of Diana's processes of identity negotiation in different social contexts: home, school, "here" in the United States, and "there" in Mexico.

Diana's search for sense of place and belonging had been developing while her family moved from one place to another. The end of the excerpt, though, reflects her ambivalence regarding where she would like to live. She expressed the dilemma of wanting to live with her grandma in Mexico, but also wanting to stay in Arizona, where things had improved for them. She expressed this improvement in terms of their home, the new tiles in the kitchen, and remembering that when relatives visited the home they exclaimed, "*Tu casa huele a Magdalena*" [Your house smell like Magdalena (Mexico)], an experience that her mother proudly retold in another interview using exactly the same words as her daughter. Diana was learning that being connected to Magdalena, Mexico, was a source of pride. Through her narratives she seemed to be summoning different situated identities, as a Mexican who is frequently remembering her past experiences or her family's experiences in Mexico. Yet she maintains a bicultural identity as someone who was born "here" but speaks Spanish and, as her mother reminds her, is *Mexicana* and *Americana*. This affirmation contributes to the development of her bicultural identity.

The experience of moving back and forth between places, which represented a source of stress for the Acosta family, was not the only dilemma Diana faced during her infancy and as a child living in the borderlands, as she was trying to make sense of stories about her family experiences on both sides of the U.S.-Mexico border. In particular, Diana reflected on stories about her father's experiences.

MAKING SENSE OF THE AMERICAN DREAM

The picture book *Amazing Grace* by Hoffman (1991) deals with gender and racial issues that an African American girl faces when she wants to play the role of Peter Pan in a school play. The way the book solves the situation is by instilling in the girl the American cultural model of "success." The American dream—that you can be whatever you want to be if you put your mind to it and work hard—is a cultural model accepted by various members of different social groups. It is also a recurrent theme in children's literature about immigrants, in spite of the evidence that cultural and structural factors play a critical role in maintaining inequality or in helping individuals "get ahead" in life (MacLeod, 1995). The picture book was included as a choice for the literature discussions mostly for its potential to generate discussion about gender inequalities, responding to students' questions about gender issues, but a great part of the children's discussion was devoted to trying to make sense of the cultural model of the American dream. The children agreed that people can do whatever they want, whether they are boys or girls. However, at some point in the discussion, Diana told a story that at first glance seemed to support the message of the story, but that eventually contradicted and

challenged the ideological message of the book about the freedom we
have to do whatever we want:

> *Como todos, ellos pueden hacer lo que ellos quieran porque mi papá*
> *antes era—él no trabajaba en los techos, era el jefe allá en México,*
> *un . . . ¿cómo se llama? Era el jefe (group members try to help her*
> *with the word) . . . No sé, no sé pero él era otra cosa, y él quería hacer*
> *eso siempre, pero porque—yo tenía, como tres o cuatro años, no,*
> *digo, dos años—y él no venía sucio del trabajo (. . .) Porque vivíamos*
> *allá en con mi nana. El estaba—no venía sucio, venia con corbata, y*
> *todo, pero, mi papá cambió, cambió, porque ahora rezonga y en veces*
> *nosotros nos ponemos a llorar porque rezonga.*

Like everybody, they can do whatever they want because my dad (he)
was before—he did not work on the roofs, he was the boss, there in
Mexico, a . . . how is it called? He was the boss, he was something,
how is it called? (group members try to help her with the word) . . .
I don't know, I don't know, and he always wanted to do that, but
because—I was like three or four years old, no, I mean, two years
old—and he came dirty from the work. (. . .) Because we lived there
with my grandmother. He was—he was not coming dirty, he was
coming with a necktie and all that, but my dad changed, he changed
because now he grumbles and sometimes we begin to cry because he
grumbles.

In the first part of her story, Diana introduced her father as doing what
he wanted in Mexico. She recalled that he had a higher-status job and did
not come home dirty from work. She said that *there* in Mexico he was
(*antes*/before) "the boss," while *here* (*ahora*/now) in the United States, he
is working "on roofs." Although this 9-year-old child may be too young to
fully understand the situation, her use of linguistic parallelism, comparing
her father's previous job in Mexico with his current job, mentioning that
"*he comes dirty*" from work, indicates her awareness of family tensions related to her father's current job in comparison to his former job in Mexico.
In fact, Diana's father shared this experience in an interview one day when
Diana was not present. He talked about the hardship of his experience after
migrating to Tucson, where he found a working-class job in a construction
company installing roof tiles in houses, which was much harder work than
the white-collar job he had in Mexico. Diana seemed to be aware that he
did not like his current job, and from her perspective, this problem seemed
to have affected her father emotionally, describing him as a person who
"*rezonga*" (grumbles). In a different literature discussion, Diana elaborated
on this issue:

My father wants to go back to Magdalena, but my mother, she grumbles to him (*le rezonga*) a lot because he wants to go back to live with them, and Daniel, my brother, he wants to go back, when he grows up he wants to live there and my mother is—she will get very angry. (Translation from Spanish)

Diana was aware that her parents had different opinions about returning to Mexico. Her participation in literature discussions reveals that she was learning about the difficulties her family faced as immigrants and she was trying to make sense of those experiences vis-à-vis commonsense assumptions and the cultural model of the American dream promoted in the book. She was experiencing firsthand that it is not always true that you can be whatever you want, given often surmountable obstacles. She also talked about dilemmas between wanting to return to live with her nana in Mexico and staying "here" where the house is better than the one they had before. Diana was also negotiating a bicultural identity that led her to affirm that she was an American who needed to preserve her Spanish language and the memories of life in Mexico.

CHILDREN AS ACTIVE MEANING MAKERS OF IDEOLOGICAL DISCOURSES

This case study demonstrates that processes of language socialization and identity development of children living in urban communities in border cities are mediated not only by parents' narratives and discourses on identity, but by children's interpretations of the world, their experiences, and the narratives learned in their interactions with diverse people, particularly in the culturally diverse schools of their urban communities and in their families. As a child of immigrants living in borderlands, Diana was making sense of two realities: the role of her birthplace and her family's place of origin in her development of situated meanings and identities. She had heard and re-created a variety of narratives of the family's experiences on both sides of the border and narratives told in school and other contexts. The complex interplay of diverse narratives and discourses that are part of immigrant children's experiences are manifestations of cultural and ideological struggles in homes, schools, and communities and these multiple narratives and experiences are mediating children's sense of self.

However, children appropriate aspects of those narratives and identities and reject others. They are not simply learning norms and following rules established by their parents or adults who are attempting to teach them such rules and values. They may exercise some degree of agency and may sometimes even question what their parents say while trying to be respectful, as

Diana did in this case study. In trying to reconcile their parents' *consejos* with their new realities, many immigrant children begin to negotiate two worlds, two or more languages, multiple narratives, and contradictory cultural models (e.g., learned in schools' texts, from family's experiences, experiences at school, and in their neighborhoods).

Many immigrant children from Latin American backgrounds draw from different narratives about what it means to be Latino/a (Mexican, Puerto Rican, Cuban, and so on) and American as they negotiate identities. Although some children may appropriate more assimilationist discourses and narratives, many others, such as Diana, negotiate the emergence of a bicultural identity that allows them to keep a sense of belonging to their parents' homeland while engaging in a process of acculturation to their new country. Listening to and analyzing immigrant children's narratives helps us understand some of the dilemmas children face as they are developing a bicultural identity and appropriating narratives from different sources. Immigrant children would benefit from schools that understand these processes and support children's meaning making and bicultural identities, instead of pushing them into processes of assimilation.

CRITICAL PERSPECTIVE

In this section, we offer recommendations to develop curricula where narratives are considered cultural resources used to support students who are children of immigrants in the process of negotiating meanings in their new urban contexts in the borderlands where they live. The first recommendation highlights the benefits of creating opportunities in the classroom for conversational storytelling. When the lack of connection and relevance of curricula to the lives of urban and immigrant students defines a classroom, opening spaces in the curriculum where students and parents can bring in their experiences and narratives may offer children opportunities to not only make sense of academic content, but to reinvent themselves. This may require broadening the definition of what counts as narrative and storytelling in the classroom (Dyson & Genishi, 1994; Martínez-Roldán, 2003).

Broadening the definition of narratives and bringing students' voices into the curriculum do not mean ignoring issues of power. Children's stories can actually reproduce dominant cultural storylines that alienate some; thus as Dyson and Genishi (1994) point out, stories have the potential for empowering unheard voices—but stories can also constrain voices. Either way, creating a classroom context where all children can tell their stories offers an opportunity for teachers and peers to offer counterstories and/or challenge dominant cultural storylines that constrain instead of empower children.

Our second recommendation derives from the importance of using literature that allows students to learn narratives and stories told by authors that reflect some of the experiences within their own communities. In schools with large Spanish-speaking populations, students may benefit from having access to literature that is culturally specific to the Latino/a culture and dual language texts that incorporate Spanish and English. Latino/a authors' narratives and experiences may inspire many children from various backgrounds to tell and write their own stories while adding to the repertoire of narratives children are drawing on to negotiate meanings and identities. For example, *literatura fronteriza* (Benito & Manzanas, 2002; Castillo & Tabuenca-Córdoba, 2002; Trujillo, 1998) produced by some Latino/a authors, has the potential to mediate students' meaning-making process as children living within borderlands. *Literatura fronteriza* (border literature) deals with border crossing experiences such as the explicit act of crossing the U.S.–Mexico border, but also other forms of border crossings, such as cultural, linguistic, and identity crossings. Examples of this literature can be found in the work of Amada I. Pérez, Gloria Anzaldúa, Julia Alvarez, Viola Canales, Judith Ortiz Cófer, and the poetry of Alberto Ríos, to mention just a few. The work of these authors has prompted powerful responses from Latino/a children, parents, and teachers with whom we have worked.

Our third recommendation acknowledges the important role of language as a cultural tool that mediates thinking and identity development. Children who are learning two languages and developing bicultural identities may face dilemmas concerning language loyalty. Their ability to maintain their home language while learning a second language can have implications for children's sense of identification with particular social groups to which their parents and some of their friends belong. Bilingual students should be invited, whenever possible, to draw on their linguistic resources to participate in classroom discussions, especially when they are sharing narratives of personal experiences in which they may negotiate identities. Taken together, these three recommendations represent an approach to curriculum development that honors children's bilingualism, biliteracy, and identity development.

REFERENCES

Benito, J., & Manzanas, A. M. (2002). *Literature and ethnicity in the cultural borderlands*. Amsterdam: Rodopi.

Chouliaraki, L., & Fairclough, N. (1999). *Discourse in late modernity. Rethinking critical discourse analysis*. Edinburgh, UK: Edinburgh University Press.

Castillo, D., & Tabuenca-Córdoba, M. S. (2002). *Border women: Writing la frontera*. Minneapolis: University of Minnesota Press.

Cole, M. (1990). Cognitive development and formal schooling: The evidence from cross-cultural research. In L. C. Moll (Ed.), *Vygotsky and education:*

Instructional implications and applications of sociohistorical psychology (pp. 89–110). New York: Cambridge University Press.

Corcuff, P. (1995). *Las nuevas sociologías* [The new sociologies]. (B. Urrutia, Trans., 1998). Madrid: Alianza Editorial.

Delgado-Gaitán, C. (1994). Consejos: The power of cultural narratives. *Anthropology and Education Quarterly, 25,* 298–316.

Dyson, A. H., & Genishi, C. (Eds.). (1994). *The need for story: Cultural diversity in classroom and community.* Urbana, IL: National Council of Teachers of English.

Fairclough, N. (1992). *Discourse and social change.* Cambridge, UK: Polity Press.

Gee, J. P. (2005). *An introduction to discourse analysis: Theory and method* (2nd ed). New York: Routledge.

Hoffman, M. (1991). *Amazing grace.* New York: Scholastic.

MacLeod, J. (1995). *Ain't no makin' it: Aspirations in a low-income neighborhood.* Boulder, CO: Westview Press.

Malavé, G. (2006). *Hispanic parents: A sociocultural perspective on family, ideology, and identity.* The University of Arizona. Unpublished doctoral dissertation.

Martínez, O. J. (1994). *Border people: Life and society in the U.S.–Mexico borderlands.* Tucson: The University of Arizona Press.

Martínez-Roldán, C. M. (2000). *The power of children's dialogue: The discourse of Latino students in small group literature discussions.* The University of Arizona. Unpublished doctoral dissertation.

Martínez-Roldán, C. M. (2003). Building worlds and identities: A case study of the role of narratives in bilingual literature discussions. *Research in the Teaching of English, 37,* 491–526.

Miller, P. J. (1994). Narrative practices: Their role in socialization and self-construction. In U. Neisser & R. Fivush (Eds.), *The remembering self: Construction and accuracy in self-narrative* (pp. 158–179). New York: Cambridge University Press.

Mochizuki, K. (1993). *Baseball saved us.* New York: Lee & Low Books.

Moll, L. C. (Ed.) (1990). *Vygotsky and education: Instructional implications and applications of sociohistorical psychology.* Cambridge, UK: Cambridge University.

Ochs, E., & Capps, L. (2001). *Living narrative: Creating lives in everyday storytelling.* Cambridge, MA: Harvard University Press.

Ogbu, J. U. (1991). Immigrant and involuntary minorities in comparative perspective. In J. U. Ogbu & M. A. Gibson (Eds.), *Minority status and schooling: A comparative study of immigrant and involuntary minorities* (pp. 3–33). New York & London: Garland Publishing.

Pease-Alvarez, L. (1993). *Moving in and out of bilingualism: Investigating native language maintenance and shift in Mexican-descent children.* (Research Report 6: National Center for Research on Cultural Diversity and Second Language Learning, Santa Cruz, CA.) (ERIC No. ED 354-779).

Rossman, G. B., & Rallis, S. F. (1998). *Learning in the field: An introduction to qualitative research.* London: Sage.

Suárez-Orozco, C., & Suárez-Orozco, M. (2001). *Children of immigration.* Cambridge, MA: Harvard University Press.

Trujillo, C. (1998). *Living Chicana theory.* Berkeley, CA: Third Woman Press.

Valdés, G. (1996). *Con respeto: Bridging the distances between culturally diverse families and schools: An ethnographic portrait.* New York: Teachers College Press.

van Dijk, T. A. (1998). *Ideology: A multidisciplinary approach.* London: Sage.

Vygotsky, L. S. (1986). *Thought and language.* Cambridge, MA: The MIT Press. (Originally work published 1934)

Vygotsky, L. S. (1978). *Mind in society: The development of higher psychological processes.* (Michael Cole, Vera John-Steiner, Silvia Scribner & Ellen Souberman, Eds.). Cambridge, MA: Harvard University Press.

Wertsch, J. V. (1985). *Vygotsky and the social formation of mind.* Cambridge, MA: Harvard University Press.

CHAPTER 4

Double Reading

Young Black Scholars Responding to Whiteness in a Community Literacy Program

Stephanie Power Carter and Kafi D. Kumasi

In a society where Black youth are characterized as academically failing, anti-intellectual, violent, and materialistic (Richardson, 2003; Taylor, 1995), a group of community members—comprised of parents, church members, pastors, African American youth, as well as teachers and administrators— believed that the African American youth in their predominantly White community needed a space that would embrace their culture and support them academically. They created Closing the Gap Literacy Intervention Program (CLIP), a pre-college afterschool literacy program for middle and high school youth. One main goal of CLIP is to acknowledge the strengths and possibilities of Black youth and the challenges they face from their own perspective and in their own words. CLIP has two main academic components: a writers' club and a book club. The program meets every Tuesday and Thursday for 2 hours and includes three primary components: tutoring, academic enrichment activities, and leadership skills. Academic enrichment is foregrounded as an opportunity to "re-search" and "re-examine" issues that CLIP students, whom we will refer to as CLIP scholars, feel strongly about and want to educate themselves and the larger community.

As a result of our collaboration with 13 CLIP scholars, we have begun to examine more closely how W.E.B. Du Bois's concept of double consciousness influenced their interactions during our academic enrichment sessions. Du Bois, a preeminent 20th-century Black sociologist, used double consciousness as a lens to help explain social and psychological tensions that African Americans encountered while negotiating their experiences in a societal context structured mainly by dominant linguistic and cultural norms (Fanon, 1967;

Goodings-Williams, 2009; Lee, 2001; Kumasi, 2008). In his classic work, *Souls of Black Folk* (1903), Du Bois described double consciousness as:

> A peculiar sensation, this double-consciousness, this sense of always looking at one's self through the eyes of others, of measuring one's soul by the tape of a world that looks on in amused contempt and pity. One ever feels his two-ness,—an American, a Negro; two souls, two thoughts, two un-reconciled strivings; two warring ideals in one dark body, whose dogged strength alone keeps it from being torn asunder. (p. 3)

We suggest that Du Bois's scholarship on double consciousness provides a lens to better understand how some Black youth interact, negotiate their identities, and engage intellectually in academic settings (Aldridge, 2008). Given that some educational data characterize Black youth as failing and/or lacking intellectual acuity (e.g., Spencer, 2005), using Du Bois's notion of double consciousness helps us "re-search" and "re-see" how a group of Black youth negotiate their identities as they navigate two sets of norms: dominant White and Afrocultural ways of knowing and speaking during the book club activities and discussions. This chapter addresses the following questions:

- In what ways does using Du Bois's concept of double consciousness make more visible how a group of Black youth in a community literacy program confront and respond to Whiteness in a book club?
- How does using Du Bois's concept of double consciousness as a lens to "re-see" provide insight to better support and understand how a group of Black youth in a community literacy program act and interact while reading and discussing literature by and about Black people?

To address the above questions, we provide a brief literature review, followed by relevant CLIP data that extend Du Bois's notion of double consciousness to the field of language and to a of a double reading model as a means to better understand how some students of color engage in reading. This data will help illuminate conceptual understandings of intersections between literacy and racial identity development among Black youth. We close with a discussion of the implications of how this model might be helpful in affirming and supporting Black youth's intellect, identity, and literacy learning.

BLACK ADOLESCENT IDENTITY DEVELOPMENT

Tatum (1992) writes that African American youth are more likely to be engaged in identity issues than their White counterparts and that their identities are often informed by race and ethnicity. She notes that because those around us influence identity—and this influence serves as a coping mechanism in racially mixed environments—African American adolescents often sit together for support and comfort. Some scholars suggest that many African American youth have a heightened sensitivity to the ways in which Black people have been "othered," or positioned as culturally deviant and/or deficient by mainstream (aka White) society and media. Fordham and Ogbu (1986) contend that African American youth develop oppositional collective identity and cultural frames of reference in response to their growing awareness of the systematic exclusion of Black people from full participation in U.S. society. Similarly, Cross (1991) articulates some of the identity challenges that Black youth might face. In his model of racial identity development, Cross argues that there are five stages of racial identity development for African Americans: 1) pre-encounter, 2) encounter, 3) immersion/emersion, 4) internalization, and 5) internalization commitment. He suggests that the first two stages usually occur during adolescence. During the first stage of pre-encounter, "African-American students absorb beliefs and values about the dominant culture, including the idea that it is better to be White" (Tatum, 1997, p. 55). The encounter stage "is usually precipitated by an event or series of events that force the young person to acknowledge the personal impact of racism" (Tatum, 1997, p. 55).

Tatum (1997) asserts that African American students in predominantly White environments have a heightened sense of their racial identities as they constantly have to resist stereotypes and affirm other definitions of Blackness. Such negotiations can also inform students' educational experiences and ultimately have implications on their success in various academic settings, particularly school and classroom settings. According to Gadsden (1995), because the American educational system is based on Eurocentric norms, academic success is made even more challenging for Black students. Woodson (1933), an early 20th-century Black scholar, foreshadowed the educational challenges that currently plague the experiences of many Black students in the U.S. school system. He argued that American education had been used to teach Black people of their own inferiority. For Woodson: "When a Negro has finished his education in our schools, then, he has been equipped to begin the life of an Americanized or Europeanized white man" (Woodson, 1933, p. 5). Woodson's scholarship on Black education continues to be timely as it not only makes visible challenges that Black students continue to face, but it illustrates how racism and discrimination have forced Black youth to develop an often unarticulated way of surviving their education (see Carter, 2007b).

WHITENESS

Woodson's early work not only helps us to better understand Du Bois's concept of double consciousness, but it also begins to make visible that double consciousness can be seen as a response to Whiteness. Whiteness research is important as it helps to make explicit how White cultural norms inform and shape current educational experiences. It also works to illuminate how racism and discrimination have become systematically reproduced in the current U.S. educational system. In this light, McLaren (1998) describes Whiteness as a "sociohistorical form of consciousness," in that it has done the following:

> Given birth at the nexus of capitalism, colonial rule, and the emergent relationships among dominant and subordinate groups, Whiteness constitutes and demarcates ideas, feelings, knowledge, social practices, cultural formations and systems of intelligibility that are identified with or attributed to white people and that are invested in by white people as white. Whiteness is also a refusal to acknowledge how white people are implicated in certain social relations of privilege and relations of domination and subordination. (p. 67)

Issues of Whiteness are especially problematic for many Black students whose home and community literacy practices differ from those of the dominant group. Thus, viewing double consciousness as a response to Whiteness can further help make visible the negotiation process in which some Black youth engage (Greene & Abt-Perkins, 2003).

TOWARD A MODEL OF DOUBLE CONSCIOUSNESS: UNPACKING BLACK YOUTH INTERACTIONS

As we made sense of CLIP scholars' interactions through the lens of Whiteness, a model emerged that extends Du Bois's notion of double consciousness. We call this a *Double Read* model (see Figure 4.1). We define Double Reading as one's ability to understand and be aware of the consequences of knowing both dominant White ways and Afrocultural ways of knowing and speaking. We suggest that tension is central to Double Reading. Du Bois hinted at this tension by stating ". . . two thoughts, two un-reconciled strivings" (Du Bois, 1903, p. 3). Thus, we argue that a Double Read is about being able to articulate dominant and nondominant ways of knowing and an awareness of tensions and consequences in a given context. It is also about an awareness of what articulating those consequences might have on one's own identity in and across various contexts. We recognize that Double Reading involves cognitive processes and might be characterized as a conscious and/or unconscious unfolding of racialized perspectives, views, and ideas across contexts.

In this chapter, we focus more on the social and interactional aspects of Double Reading that center around language. We view language as central to providing material evidence for double reading. According to Voloshinov (1929/1973), "the actual reality of language-speech is not the abstract system

Figure 4.1. Double Reading Model

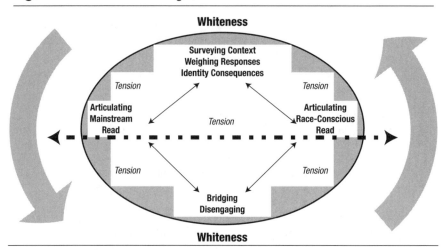

of linguistic forms, not the isolated monologic utterance, and not the psycho-physiological act of its implementation." It is, according to Voloshinov, "the social event of verbal interaction implemented in an utterance or utterances. Thus verbal interaction is the basic reality of language" (pp. 94–95).

We view language as a highly contextualized action, and something that people do to and with each other and themselves in a particular context. Although there is an abundance of scholarship on double consciousness in areas such as African American studies and multicultural education, there are few people in the field of literacy education who discuss double consciousness with regard to literacy (e.g., Willis, 1998). We see our work continuing to build on the scholarship of other language and literacy scholars whose work supports the literacy learning of African American youth (c.f., Kirkland, 2009; Kinloch, 2010; Fisher, 2007; Mahiri & Sablo, 1996; Morrell & Duncan-Andrade, 2002; Williams, 2007). In our work with CLIP scholars, we have come to understand double consciousness as several different things, but most importantly as strategic moves across particular kinds of situations and contexts. We see these moves as situated in a larger interaction we call Double Reading, and we see Double Reading as situated in Du Bois's theoretical construct of double consciousness. As stated earlier, we see double consciousness as complex and Double Reading as one way of capturing and articulating how the theoretical double consciousness can be used in the field of literacy to "re-see" how African American youth engage in literacy learning. In our attempt to represent the complexities of reading for some students of color, we have designed a double reading model. Given the constraints with writing a chapter, it might appear that we are discussing this Double Reading model in a linear fashion; however, we do not see the model as linear, but as fluid, layered, and complex. In Figure 4.2, we attempt to illustrate various strategic moves that we view as central to the Double Reading model as well as material evidence for this model. It is important to note that our understanding of the strategic moves emerged during our interactions with CLIP scholars as they engaged in the CLIP book club. The CLIP scholars were central to our emergent understanding of "Double Reading."

In the Double Reading model, we attempt to capture the complex interplay between Whiteness and Double Reading. Whiteness is the background to which the CLIP scholars were responding. In such a context, tension occurs at almost every level. The CLIP scholars we observed appeared to enter the conversation surveying the context for how Whiteness was being constructed in the immediate environment. The reading that occurred was not fixed, but complex, fluid, and contextual. Thus, the data we draw on provide material evidence for the value of employing such a model in relation to how CLIP scholars confronted Whiteness. We believe this model might provide insight into how teachers and educational researchers can better support the literacy learning of some Black youth as we seek to critically understand how some of them engage in reading.

METHODOLOGY

This study was part of a larger ethnographic study that took place in CLIP, which examined ways to bridge students' home and school cultures to facilitate academic success. Data were collected during CLIP book club sessions, coined *Circle of Voices* (COV) by Kumasi (2008), to validate the experiences that each young scholar brought to the book club discussions. The main goal for the book club was to engage in discussions and "re-search" around issues of Black culture while reading young adult novels. COV met during CLIP on Tuesdays at the local public library. All 13 CLIP scholars participated in COV. Due to space limitations, however, only those CLIP scholars whose voices appear in the COV book club transcript are highlighted below.

CLIP Scholar Profiles

Monique is a freshman. She happens to be one of the youngest scholars in the group. Despite her youth, Monique is one of the most vocal participants. She readily offers her opinion and has strong reactions to a lot of the issues that are discussed. Monique enjoys shopping and hanging out with her friends.

Anthony is like a big brother to Monique. He is a sophomore who recently moved from an urban city approximately 3 hours north

Figure 4.2. Strategic Moves of Double Reading

I. Surveying Context/Weighing Response/Assessing Risks

This aspect of Double Reading is complicated and often appears cognitive in nature. Material evidence for these strategic moves with regard to language is often revealed from interactions across multiple contexts (e.g., 3 months later, the student references what he or she was doing or why he or she was doing this).

Examples of Material Evidence:

- When a person of color articulates an awareness of perceptions about Blackness that exist in mainstream society and or being "othered" and possible consequences of Whiteness.
- When a person of color articulates risks that may accompany taking certain positions on racially sensitive subject matter. Actions that might suggest risk include hand raising or being called on and refusing to provide an answer.

Tension: Du Bois describes as two warring ideas—when one's identity and his/her community and cultural values and ideals are inconsistent or different from the identity that is being constructed in a given context.

Examples of Material Evidence:

- When a person of color articulates an alternative perspective about race and power that is counter to one that has already been articulated.
- When two or more alternative perspectives on race and power have been articulated in a given context.

Identity Consequences: The cost associated with constant struggle and contestation with mainstream culture about one's own racial identity, culture, and/or community.

Examples of Material Evidence:

- When a person of color articulates tension around how he/she might be positioned by others with regard to racial issues. When a person of color articulates the costs of how one's own racial identity, culture, and/or community are implicated and associated with constant struggle and contestation with mainstream culture.

II. Articulating Race Conscious Read

When one acknowledges the challenges of racial groups but also the possibilities, potential, and agency that are not often made visible in mainstream and Whiteness discourse.

Examples of Material Evidence:

- When a person of color verbally critiques issues of Whiteness with regard to issues of race and power regardless of consequences.
- When a person of color articulates the struggles and tensions around issues of race and power in mainstream society.

III. Articulating Mainstream Conscious Read (Race Neutral Read)

When a person of color does not acknowledge the possibilities and potential of people of color; instead, he or she consciously and/or unconsciously acknowledges their failures.

Examples of Material Evidence:

- When a person of color does not articulate the struggles and tensions around issues of race and power in mainstream society.
- When a person of color dismisses issues of race and/or power that exist in mainstream society.
- When a person of color devalues and generalizes the experiences of people of color in a particular context without taking into consideration the complexities of those experiences (e.g., Black kids are underperforming in school).

IV. Bridging

The ability to use the tensions that arise due to opposing perspectives to engage more deeply and educate and challenge around issues of race and power.

Example of Material Evidence:

- Two or more people articulating different race conscious reads, but instead of shutting down the conversation, they engage in the discussion more deeply. The end result might be a new emerging thought or some idea made more "visible" as a result of that interaction.
- Opposing mainstream and race conscious read(s) have been articulated and challenged, but instead of shutting down, people begin to engage more deeply and an issue is made "visible" as a result of that interaction.

V. Disengaging

One's ability to choose not to engage on a subject that may be perceived to have negative identity consequences. It is important to note that disengaging is not fixed and could mean different things in different contexts. Similar to Surveying Context/ Weighing Response/Assessing Risk, unless articulated, there is no real evidence and a person might not voice concerns immediately, but across time and context.

Example of Material Evidence:

- A student of color who declines to speak or does not raise hand or participate.

of this Midwest university town. He is involved in extracurricular activities such as the student chapter of the National Association for the Advancement of Colored People (NAACP) and holds leadership positions in the community.

Ayanna is an 8th-grade student whose favorite subjects are math and family and consumer sciences. Ayanna enjoys cheerleading, attending church, and running track. Her mother is pursuing her teaching credentials at a local college. Ayanna's grandmother plays a large role in her life and is an active member of a local Baptist church.

Merriel is a freshman who talks fast and is very creative. Whether writing poetry or essays on timely issues, Merriel keeps her fingers on the pulse of what is happening in the world. She enjoys reading novels by and about Black people, and frequents the library in her spare time.

Erica is a sophomore who entered the program in its second year. Erica has a very strong personality. Beneath her tough exterior, Erica is warm and sensitive. She has aspirations to become a cosmetologist and to own her own beauty salon.

Mike is a senior originally from Detroit who entered the program in its 2nd year. He worked at one of the local television stations as an editing assistant. One of the major contributions Mike brought to the program was producing the video montage for one of the program's culminating community literacy events. Mike has aspirations to establish a career in the music video industry.

Data Collection

Book club sessions were audio taped and videotaped over a 4-month period. Transcriptions were coded for instances where participants articulated Black racial identity through "identity statements" (see Kumasi, 2008), or claims participants made about what it means to be Black based on how they believe Black people view (or do not view) the world; speak (or do not speak); and behave (or do not behave). Data were also coded for instances where participants articulated what it means to be Black by linking Black identity to the consequences of Whiteness. As an example, there are statements where participants linked Black racial identity to experiences with racial oppression and marginalization in a dominant White context.

Data Analysis

We conducted a microethnographic discourse analysis of the transcript highlighted below. We drew from Bloome et al.'s (2004) description of microethnographic discourse analysis which is an approach to discourse analysis that examines human actions and interactions around language and theorizes the use of language in social contexts. A microethnographic discourse analysis approach lends itself to addressing the questions central to this study, questions that deal with tensions and struggles around race that inform how African American youth act and interact in the book club.

Moreover, a microethnographic approach is rooted in the theoretical precepts of sociolinguistic ethnography. Sociolinguistic ethnographers maintain that the processes through which social identities are named and constituted are essentially language processes (Gauker, 1994). A microethnographic analysis of discourse can make visible certain macro and micro power dynamics. By illustrating this negotiation process up close, the reader can better see the complex layers of interactions that might otherwise be invisible (Carter, 2007a; 2007b).

STRATEGIC MOVES: CAPTURING DOUBLE CONSCIOUSNESS INTERACTIONS

The following section utilizes excerpts from CLIP data to provide examples of various strategic moves as well as the ways scholars negotiated their racial identity in these two contexts. In Figure 4.3 we provide two single transcript segments from different CLIP sessions to help articulate the Double Reading model. In the following transcript segments, scholars are reading Angela Johnson's novel *First Part Last*. It is a coming-of-age story that deals with the trials of Bobbi, an African American teenage male, who is expecting a child with his high school girlfriend, Nia. Each chapter is written in alternating tenses of past and present. This format helps make a strong contrast between Bobbi's thoughts and habits before and after his daughter, Feather, is born. As the story ends, the reader is kept wondering whether or not Bobbi will succumb to family and peer pressures and give Feather up for adoption or decide to keep her and raise her himself. Prior to this segment, CLIP scholars had been discussing the aforementioned book and what it means to be a Black man in our society.

CAPTURING DOUBLE READING AMONG BLACK YOUTH INTERACTIONS

In this section, we use book club transcripts to provide material evidence of how Double Reading played out in the interactions of CLIP scholars as they discussed the novel *First Part Last*. It is important to reiterate that we view language as central to understanding and capturing Double Reading.

Figure 4.3. Transcripts of Class Discussion

Transcription Key

/ = Conversational pauses within the message unit

[ ] = Inaudible due to speech overlap in conversation or other interference

(*italics*) = Additional information inserted for clarity

CAPITALS = Emphasis or accentuation on syllables

! = Increase in voice pitch or tone

J = Group laughter

. . . = Brief pause

CLIP Scholars

AH: Anthony Houghes, African American male student

AS: Ayanna Scott, African American female student

Dr. C.: Dr. Carter, African American female researcher/ co-facilitator

ES: Erica Smith, African American female student

KK: Kafi Kumasi, African American female researcher/ co-facilitator

MB: Merriel Broddick, African American female student

MW: Monique Williams, African American female student

Transcript Segment 1 of Book Club Discussion on *First Part Last* by Angela Johnson. September 19, 2006

34. Dr. C.: Okay so what did you think about the novel so far? What are your initial impressions of the book?
35. AH: I didn't think it was realistic how the mother wasn't really involved once he had the baby. I mean most grandmother I see grandmothers help raise their grandkids. So that part was unrealistic for me.
36. MB: No but she did that on purpose. I think she was trying to teach him how to be a man.
37. Dr. C.: Okay/ So I mean—man/ everybody has a concept or a notion about what it means to be a man/ a Black man/ and I say Black man/is that what y'all were saying?
38. ES: [Right I] Huh? . . . No!
39. Dr. C.: No?
40. ES: What is/ What is that! / How you gon say/ what the? . . . Ne'mind
41. Dr. C.: No tell me Erica!
42. ES: You just don't say what's a Black man/ like/ you actin like you have to be like/ you have to act a certain a way to be a Black man or sumthin like that
43. Dr. C.: Okay/ So you don't?
44. ES: What are you talkin about?
45. J: Group laughter
46. Dr. C.: Somebody help me out!

47. ES: Anyway/well/like/I was just sayin
48. Dr. C.: Okay so I guess I was just sayin/ Erica raises another point cause I said/ What does it mean to be a man and then I said Black man/ and she was like hold up, hold up you know/ you know/ you know like you tryna single Black men out like their different/ that's what I get
49. ES: Right, yeah
50. Dr. C.: So
51. AH: But they are different! That's the thing.
52. Dr. C.: Are they?
53. AH: Yeah
54. AS: Some of them are different
55. ES: No/I don't know
56. Dr. C.: Some of them? Some of who?
57. KK   Elaborate
58. Dr. C.: Yeah elaborate
59. MB: But no, but I didn't say it Ayanna said it/ so elaborate over there
60. Dr. C.: Oh, Ayanna elaborate/ I mean like / okay cause I/ Erica was challenging me in terms of the fact when I said
61. ES: Yes, I shol was!
62. AS: Some Black people act White/ some people
63. AH: What is acting White?
64. MW: What's actin White? It's just cause you talk like you suppose to
65. ES: It's just talkin proper/ we supposed to talk proper/ even though we 't talk pro

Transcript Segment 2 Excerpt "But We are different" Book Club Segment on Black Males Continued on Thursday, September 21, 2006

5. Dr. C.: Black men. Okay. And I just wanna clarify something. Um there were several different notions going on about Black men. One was/ one, it was don't stereotype/that they're no different. I'm not sure different from who or different from what. I wanna believe/ was it Anthony that said, "Can't explain it, it's kinds like a swagger"? Was it you Barack that said that?
6. Barack: Actually it was Anthony.
7. Dr. C.: Okay. So what/ what is this/ I just wanna I understand you/ so/ Black man/ when you hear Black man/ do you think different from any other group? Or do you think similar or do you see it terms of difference? Or how DO you think/ when you think Black man?
8. MW: Difference.
9. Dr. C.: When you say difference, tell me what you mean when you say different.
10. MW: We gotta explain ourselves?
11. Dr. C.: You always have to explain yourself.
12. MW: Well then ne'mind they ain't got no difference
13. J: Group laughter

(continued)

14. AH: A whole different perspective on life
15. DR. C.: A whole different perspective on life
16. AH: A hustle [inaudible]
17. DR. C.: Like for example?
18. AH: Like them White boys—difference
19. DR. C.: I mean like when you say perspective/ what kind of different perspective?
20. AH: Like they have more of a struggle.
21. MW: You be makin the questions hard.
22. AH: What they just supposed to be easy?
23. KK: Remember you all are scholars.
24. DR. C.: Yeah scholars elaborate, we talk. You said because, you said about struggle right? Okay so it's about struggle. So you think
25. MB: Yeah
26. DR. C.: Is that what you were saying Monique or you were saying something different?
27. MW: No I was saying that
28. DR. C.: Would anyone disagree? I mean you can. We don't all have to agree. Scholars don't have to think alike. So let me say this. Let me ask you this, it was interesting, at the library what happened? Why, why was it, what happened that? And you know I need you all to be real—with me. I need you to always to be real—with me. What happened? You know cause you all couldn't articulate/ you all seemed to not want to articulate/ that at the library. I just seemed that way. What happened?
29. MW: We ain't want to offend nobody.
30. DR. C.: Okay so you were concerned that you would offend someone
31. MW: If I did I mean I would say sorry, but [inaudible]

Informed by sociolinguistics, we see language use as shaped by individual (micro) and societal (macro) forces and that one can theorize human interactions by studying language. Thus, we assert that by analyzing transcriptions of language in use we can capture Double Reading. Selected transcripts help show the dynamic, fluid nature of Double Readings across time and space. Again, the subsequent analysis involves data from two transcripts taken from two separate book discussions that occurred over a 3-day time period (Tuesday and Thursday). We draw from additional interviews with CLIP scholars that occurred outside the book session to bolster our analysis of double consciousness.

Double Reading: Disengaging, Weighing, Assessing, and Identity Consequences

As we looked across data, we noticed instances where CLIP scholars appeared to be pondering something or instances where some CLIP scholars who were very vocal might be unusually quiet or abruptly disengaged from a conversation. Of course, such processes were always complex. We selected the above transcripts because they seemed to articulate some of the complexities of Double Reading. This portion of the analysis focuses on surveying the context, weighing responses, assessing risk, and identity consequences. In Transcript 1, we see Monique speaking for the first time. In line 63, she poses a question: *What's actin White? It's just cause you talk like you suppose to.* As stated earlier, Monique is one of the most vocal students in the group, and it was customary for her to engage in debate about controversial issues, particularly issues of race. However, during this session, Monique barely speaks. It is never fully made clear during this session why she is not vocal, as usual. However, it is important to note that during this session, there is a White librarian and a couple of pre-service teachers present. In retrospect, perhaps we attributed how she engaged to simply having a bad day.

However, it became clear in Transcript 2 during our discussion on Thursday that how Monique engaged was perhaps more strategic than we had assumed. In line 29, when the group was questioned about why they did not seem to want to talk, Monique states: *We ain't want to offend nobody.* It is not clear who "we" is. Perhaps Monique is attempting to speak on behalf of some of her peers in the group. What is clear is that Monique was weighing potential responses and assessing risk. In line 31, she continues: *If I did I mean I would say sorry,* which continues to illustrate what we call identity consequences. Her statement suggests that she was concerned about how she would be perceived by the White people who were present during our CLIP session. Thus, in the initial exchange in Transcript 1, she does not fully engage. Monique's statement serves as an example of how these strategic moves are complex and fluid. What becomes equally interesting is that Monique was usually one of the most vocal students in the group, but when the context includes White people, she engages differently. Her statements in lines 29 and 31 suggest that when White people were present, she appeared to be negotiating not only how she engaged in the discussion, but also the possible identity consequences for her as a young Black woman.

Tension(s) and Race Conscious Reading

Based on the data, tension is a constant thread that runs throughout Double Reading. Just as Du Bois suggested in his understanding of double consciousness, tension is central to a theoretical construct of double consciousness, as evident in his reference to "two warring ideals." Similarly, we have outlined the importance of tension to Double Reading. One might argue that tension is present at multiple levels throughout both transcripts. Given our data, it became clear that tension is often in response to a race conscious read. We use the exchange between Dr. C and Erica during the book club discussion to illustrate tension and how tensions can surface after a race conscious read has been articulated. We suggest that Erica engaged in a race conscious read when she critiqued and articulated perceptions of Black manhood regardless of identity consequences. In line 36, Dr. C states: *Okay/So I mean—man/everybody has a concept or a notion about what it means to be a man/a Black man/ and I say Black man/is that what y'all were saying.* In line 37, Erica states: *Huh? . . . No!* and continues in line 39 with: *What is/ What is that! / How you gon say/ what the? . . . Ne'mind.* Erica openly challenges Dr. C's stance and makes tension more visible when she questions: *How you gon say/what the? . . . Ne'mind.* However, it is not until she is encouraged to continue in line 40 when Dr. C says: *No tell me Erica!* Erica's thus responds in line 41, stating: *You just don't say what's a Black man/ like/ you actin like you have to be like/ you have to act a certain a way to be a Black man or sumthin like that.* Erica critiques what she perceives to be a homogenized representation of Black men that depicts them as different from other men. Erica's response also hints at a larger tension that she might be responding to with regards to how Whiteness has informed perceptions about Black men, which can lead to a mainstream conscious read.

Other data suggest that Erica's family members who are Black males have highly influenced her thinking. In a separate interview during a follow-up focus group, Erica was asked to reflect on her thoughts about Black males. During the interview, she began to share a story about an incident with her brothers where she believed they were seen as criminals to a White passerby who came into contact with a group of young Black males on their way to a party. She observed: *Like when I'm around my brothers, we are not thinking about the person [White person] that is next to us, and people lock their doors when they see like a group of Black folk* (Focus Group Interview, 9/21/06). Erica's reflection on this event helps illustrate her level of awareness as to how Black people—Black males in particular—are perceived by dominant White society. Therefore, when Dr. C. raised the issue of Black males, it is likely that Erica drew on her prior knowledge and experiences of witnessing Black men like her brothers being depicted as threatening in a dominant White social context.

Bridging

Bridging, which is essential to Double Reading, is the last strategic move that we will discuss. Bridging is using the tensions that arise from differing reads to engage more deeply and to challenge others on issues of race and power. In Transcript 1, we begin to see bridging occur. Although we use this segment of the transcript to illustrate bridging, we want to acknowledge that multiple strategic moves could be occurring at once. As the exchange between Dr. C and Erica continued, Dr. C tried to clarify by summarizing what she believed to be Erica's stance. She states in line 47: *Okay so I guess I was just sayin/ Erica raises another point cause I said/ What does it mean to be a man and then I said Black man/ and she was like hold up, hold up you know/ you know/ you know like you tryna single Black men out like their different/ that's what I get.* In line 48, Erica states: *"Right, yeah,"* suggesting she agrees that she did perceive that Dr. C was constructing Black males as different, and Erica's perception was that "different" was being constructed in a negative way. However, in line 51, Anthony articulates a response that is counter to Erica's when he says: *But they are different! That's the thing.* Later in the same book club conversation, Anthony was asked to expound on his thoughts about Black males being different. He described Black males as having a certain "swagger" (Field Notes, 9/19/08). In this instance, Anthony associated difference with the possibilities of Black males having distinct, positive characteristics that set them apart from others (i.e., a swagger). Although Erica and Anthony articulated race conscious reads, both attached a distinct interpretation to the way Black male identity was being constructed in the conversation. However, Whiteness was an undercurrent that remained unarticulated in their reactions.

While the concept of difference was being negotiated back and forth in the participants' conversation, Whiteness never moved away from its position as the normative center of the conversation. The next few lines in the transcript excerpt begin to make visible how Whiteness was serving as a backdrop to the conversation about Black males. For instance, in line 61, AS states: *Some Black people act White/some people.* Suddenly, the conversation about Black males has shifted to Black males acting White. What becomes apparent is that as a result of CLIP scholars pushing back against the tensions and through the conversation about Black males, the undercurrent of Whiteness is made visible. In the following paragraph, we briefly discuss the implications of a Double Read model for the field of language and literacy.

CRITICAL PERSPECTIVE

Double Reading has the potential to help literacy scholars "re-search and re-see" how reading gets taken up by some youth of color in social contexts in which the "color line" (Du Bois, 1903) is ever-present yet constantly denied existence by many. We believe that the Double Reading model holds great promise for characterizing and understanding the educational experiences of youth of color by capturing strategic moves that inform how some Black youth engage in literacy learning. We suggest that to better understand and academically support Black youth, there must be epistemological conditions for multiple types of knowledge that affirm and help to better contextualize Black experiences. What the CLIP scholars have taught us is that Double Reading is made visible in an intellectual space where students can contest and grapple with contradictions in their lived experiences and the world around them. We liken the space of CLIP not just to a community, but also to the space of a family, a group of youth united by common experiences who can also engage in heated debates and still have a sense of mutual respect for each other.

Our collaboration with CLIP scholars also illuminates the importance of providing resources for practicing and pre-service teachers to scaffold students' racialized experiences as a means to help them articulate their overt and covert thought processes, particularly around culturally sensitive topics or areas of inquiry. It is through this sort of scaffolding that practicing and pre-service teachers can create familial spaces where young scholars can grapple with the competing and often contradictory messages they receive concerning what it means to be a person of color in various contexts, particularly in educational settings. We believe that if educators understand how double consciousness works in theory, then perhaps they can refine their pedagogical practices with youth of color in ways that prompt truer and deeper expression of ideals, particularly around issues of race (see, e.g., Fuligni, 2007). CLIP and the creation of the *Circle of Voices* book club are examples of how to support the literacy learning of young Black scholars where sensitive issues are seriously debated and critiqued. Central to the creation of literate spaces such as this is a belief in the literate strengths and possibilities of youth of color.

REFERENCES

Aldridge, D. (2008). *The educational thought of W.E.B. Du Bois: An intellectual history.* New York: Teachers College Press.

Bloome, D., Carter, S., Christian, B. M., Otto, S. O., & Shuart-Faris, N. (2004). *Discourse analysis & the study of classroom language & literacy events in a microethnographic perspective.* Mahwah, NJ: L. Erlbaum Associates.

Carter, S. (2007a). "Inside Thing": Negotiating race and gender in a high school British literature classroom. In C. Clarke & M. Blackburn (Eds.), *Research for Political Action and Social Change* (pp. 97–111). New York: Peter Lang.

Carter, S. (2007b). "Reading All that White Crazy Stuff": Black young women unpacking whiteness in a high school British literature classroom. *Journal of Classroom Interaction, 41,* 42–54.

Cross, W. E. (1991). *Shades of Black: Diversity in African-American identity*. Philadelphia: Temple University Press.

Du Bois, W.E.B. (1903). *Souls of Black folk: Essays and sketches*. Chicago: A. C. McClurg and Company.

Fanon, F. (1967). *Black skin, white masks*. New York: Grove Press.

Fordham, S., & Ogbu, J. (1986). Black students' success: Coping with the burden of acting white. *Urban Review, 18*(3), 176–206.

Fisher, M. T. (2007). *Writing in rhythm: Spoken word poetry in urban classrooms*. New York: Teachers College Press.

Fuligni, A. J. (2007). *Contesting stereotypes and creating identities: Social categories, social identities, and educational participation*. New York: Russell Sage Foundation.

Gadsden, V. (1995). *Literacy among African-American youth*. Cresskill: Hampton Press.

Gauker, C. (1994).*Thinking out loud: an essay on the relation between thought and language*. Princeton, NJ: Princeton University Press.

Goodings-Williams, R. (2009). *In the shadow of Du Bois: Afro-modern political thought in America*. Cambridge, MA.: Harvard University Press.

Greene, S., & Abt-Perkins, D. (2003). *Making race visible: Literacy research for cultural understanding*. New York: Teachers College Press.

Kinloch, V. (2010). *Harlem on our minds: Place, race, and the literacies of urban youth*. New York: Teachers College Press.

Kirkland, D. (2009). We real cool: Toward a theory of Black masculine literacies. *Reading Research Quarterly, 44*(3), 278–297.

Kumasi, K. (2008). *Seeing white in Black: Examining racial identity among African American adolescents in a culturally centered book club*. Ann Arbor, MI: UMI Dissertation Services.

Lee, C. (2001). Unpacking culture, teaching, and learning: A response to the pedagogy of power. In W. Watkins, J. Lewis, & V. Chou (Eds.), *Race and Education: The Roles of History and Society in Educating African-American students* (pp. 89–99). Boston: Allyn Bacon.

Mahiri, J., & Sablo, S. (1996). Writing for their lives: The non-school literacy of California's urban African American youth. *The Journal of Negro Education, 65*(2), 164–180.

McLaren, P. (1998). Whiteness is . . . The struggle for postcolonial hybridity. In J. Kincheloe, S. Steinberg, N. Rodriguez, & R. Chennault (Eds.), *White reign: Deploying whiteness in America* (pp. 63–76). New York: St. Martin's Press.

Morrell, E., & Duncan-Andrade, J. (2002). Promoting academic literacy with urban youth through engaging hip-hop culture. *English journal, 9*(6), 88–92.

Richardson, E. (2003). *African American literacie*s. New York: Routledge.

Spencer, M. B. (2005). Crafting identities and accessing opportunities post-Brown. *American Psychologist, 60*(8), 821–830.

Tatum, B. D. (1997). *"Why are all the Black kids sitting together in the cafeteria?" and other conversations about race*. New York: Basic Books.

Tatum, B. (1992). Talking about race, learning about racism: The application of racial identity development theory in the classroom. *Harvard Educational Review, 62*(1), 1–24.

Taylor, R. (1995). *African American youth: Their social and economic status in the United States.* Westport, CT: Praeger.

Voloshinov, V. N. (1973). *Marxism and the philosophy of language.* (L. Matejka & I. R. Titunik, Trans.). Cambridge, MA: Harvard University Press. (Original work published 1929)

Williams, C. (2007). The "Sound" of Blackness: African American language, social and cultural identities, and academic success in a middle school Language Arts classroom. Unpublished Dissertation. Vanderbilt University.

Willis, A. I. (1998). *Teaching and using multicultural literature in grades 9–12.* Norwood, NJ: Christopher Gordon Publishers.

Woodson, C. G. (1933). *The miseducation of the Negro.* Washington, DC: Associated Press.

PART II

The Buzz on Teaching and Community

Anne Haas Dyson and Celia Genishi

Mrs. Kay is teaching a science lesson. She explains to her 1st-graders that "we are animals. Human beings!"

"Human bees!" say the children, quite amused, and they buzz at each other. Jon then explains that the first human bees were made out of gorillas!

Mrs. Kay pauses . . . and then proceeds gamely, articulating with great care the distinction between "be-ings" and "bees." Meanwhile, the small "human bees" buzz under their breath for the rest of the lesson.

This vignette suggests: first, a central quality of "human bees"—our capacity for social attunement and connection; second, a critical if slippery cultural tool for human learning—that of speech; and, third, the challenges of formal teaching across experiential and sociocultural differences. These three themes are central to the following chapters on teaching and teacher education in urban settings and, more particularly, to the work of Souto-Manning, Haddix and Rojas, and Winn.

Mrs. Kay's children were not only responding to her but to each other; when one began buzzing, others followed, until a quiet chorus of amused "bees" accompanied the lesson. As human beings (or "bees"), we all have a biological capacity for identifying with and responding to others (Tomasello, 2009); this capacity is culturally organized and socially enacted. We are selective, though, in those with whom we identify and, thereby, those from whom we learn, and those whom we help.

All of our authors, as teachers, value humane, intellectually rich classroom communities in which students define and redefine their relationships to the broader society in part by defining their relationships to each other. Through illustrations of students' dialogue, and of their engagement with human experience as articulated through the literary and dramatic arts, the authors offer readers visions of communities in the process of "socio-ideological becoming" (Bakhtin, 1981, p. 295). At the same time, they collectively acknowledge the challenges inherent in teachers, and children, finding empathy for those defined as "others." They hope to support teachers and students in reimagining their relationships with diverse "others"—others embodied in peers and articulated in artful worlds. Those "others" have emotions, struggles, and pleasures that make possible a more nuanced, socially sophisticated, and intellectually open vision of self and of the common world (Greene, 1995).

Hence, Souto-Manning brings us into a Freirean cultural circle for teachers in a preschool serving a socioculturally diverse population. In those circles, teachers tell stories of their daily struggles and, through dialogue, imagine alternative possibilities for responding to their challenges. In the process, they forge connections among themselves as a group of educators with different perspectives but shared aims for engaging and supporting their students.

With Haddix and Rojas, we move back to an institutional setting within which we hope Winn's participants might thrive, a secondary English classroom. Haddix and Rojas examine the curricular materials—the literature textbooks, with their study guides—meant to inform the classroom teacher. In their focus on the texts' framing of literary works by Latino/a authors, they illustrate how language has the potential to limit dialogue, in part by categorizing others. Consider, for example, an assumption of a common "immigrant" experience among Puerto Rican American citizens and Mexican citizens. Individual history, taking shape in complex regional, societal, and legal circumstances, is lost . . . unless alert teachers raise critical questions and keep the dialogue, and visions of self and others, in motion.

Finally, with Winn we travel to a program for children who have moved unsuccessfully through many classrooms and, as young women, find themselves incarcerated and otherwise regulated by the juvenile adjudication system. The girls write, enact, and examine their experience in plays; in so doing, they articulate in fictional worlds the characters and situations of their experiential ones. Through these means, they experience some sense of themselves as agents with decision-making power in their lives. The girls do not simply adopt adults' hopes and dreams as their own but they do begin a dialogue of possibility, of imagining alternatives.

As all the chapters illustrate, we as teachers must have empathy for the categorized—the homeless, the refugee, "the silent or the fidgety or the hopeless child in the classroom" (Greene, 1995, p. 37). Mobilized by their own empathetic caring and human curiosity, teachers may reach out for intellectual and social connections with each other and with their students. In so doing, they contribute to classroom worlds where the buzz of human "bees" bespeaks a community of citizen learners, confidently reaching out to and transforming the world around them.

REFERENCES

Bakhtin, M. M. (1981). Discourse in the novel. In C. Emerson & M. Holquist (Eds.), *The dialogic imagination: Four essays by M. Bakhtin* (pp. 254-422). Austin: University of Texas Press.

Greene, M. (1995). *Releasing the imagination: Essays on education, the arts, and social change.* San Francisco: Jossey Bass.

Tomasello, M. (2009). *Why we cooperate.* Boston: M.I.T. Press.

CHAPTER 5

A Different Kind of Teaching

Culture Circles as Professional Development for Freedom

Mariana Souto-Manning

"Children learn what they live" (Nolte, 1998). So do adults. Thus, if we—teacher educators—want teachers to engage in critical, transformative education with their students, we must engage in this very same process in our classrooms. In this chapter, I describe the process whereby I involved teachers in transformative teacher education, doing what we propose they do in their own classrooms—embracing cultural conflicts as opportunities for learning.

As a teacher educator, I know that whether they are challenging curricula, administrative decisions, or assumptions about diverse learners, critical multicultural educators' work is never done (Cahnmann-Taylor & Souto-Manning, 2010). Affecting early educational settings to become more culturally relevant (Ladson-Billings, 1995) requires the ability to communicate through conflict, consider multiple perspectives, and break down barriers to social change. To foster multicultural curricula and teaching in early educational settings, we must acknowledge our cultural locations and privileges. To do so, we must communicate and learn through conflict while considering diverse perspectives in teacher education. It is not enough to talk the talk. If we teacher educators want to have an effect in classrooms and, by extension, with the educational experiences of children, we must be committed to walking the walk by doing what we propose in our own research.

Thus, this chapter documents the situated representation of transformative in-service teacher education (Dyson & Genishi, 2005)—a 2-year critical teacher study group. In it, I explore how eight early childhood teachers and I engaged in dialogue through differences of perspective. I share how I embraced the roles of ethnographer and action researcher to document the process of a problem posing approach to teacher education through culture circles (Freire, 1970).

In doing so, I hope that teacher educators will recognize the need to "examine the kinds of cultural conflicts . . . [in] diverse classrooms and to consider the best ways to help . . . teachers become multiculturally competent" (Weinstein, Tomlinson-Clarke, & Curran, 2004, p. 27). Here, I share my representation of the perspectives of eight early childhood teachers in a diverse urban community in the Southeast who experienced the importance of dialogue for sharing their most urgent, daily struggles as they created climates that affirmed diversity and enhanced students' agency in educational contexts.

CULTURE CIRCLES:
A PROBLEM POSING APPROACH TO TEACHER EDUCATION

"A culture circle is a group of individuals involved in learning . . . [and] in the political analysis of their immediate reality and national interests. In culture circles, reading demands more than decodification of linguistic symbols. It is viewed as political 'reading' of the world" (Giroux, 1985, p. viii). Over a period of 2 years and with eight early childhood teachers, I applied culture circles as a means of conducting in-service teacher education that was critical and transformative. I started from participants' individual and collective experiences—thematically investigating the realities and practices of their classrooms, and codifying those realities into artifacts or cases. I brought these themes back to the group for decodification (Souto-Manning, 2010). I chose a critical, transformative approach because, too often as a teacher, I sat through teacher development sessions that presumed to tell me what I should be doing in my classroom without knowledge of what I was in fact doing. I wanted to avoid the mantra: "Do what I say and not what I do." To accomplish this, I could not afford the excuses afforded by lack of time. I had to live the process with them.

Theoretically, culture circles are situated within a diversities framework (Goodwin, Cheruvu, & Genishi, 2008), valuing a variety of perspectives as opposed to conceptualizing differences as deficiencies. The process encompasses learning through conflict, considering multiple perspectives valid while moving toward critically transforming realities that are not a priori, predetermined realities. It proposes that authority can be dialectically negotiated (Freire, 1970).

SITUATED REPRESENTATION OF A CULTURE CIRCLE

In 2006, as an early childhood teacher educator, I decided to engage in generative, Freirean professional development. I believed that the critical cycle inherent to culture circles would allow teachers to collectively re-envision early education in their own settings, considering multiple perspectives and cultural practices. The university-affiliated preschool where this teacher culture circle took place consisted of seven classrooms, each with lead and assistant teachers. It served a population of approximately 120 children, of which one-third were at or below the federally established poverty line. The county in which this preschool was located had been identified by a federally funded study as one of the 10 poorest counties with populations of more than 100,000 inhabitants in the United States. Although the preschool served a diverse population, its student body did not mirror the county's socioeconomic landscape. The preschool functioned weekdays and year-round from 7:30 a.m. to 5:30 p.m. Lead teachers held bachelor's or advanced degrees related to early education, and assistant teachers held a child development associate credential. Teacher–student ratios recommended by the National Association for the Education of Young Children (NAEYC) were closely implemented and monitored. Creative Curriculum™ was adopted schoolwide.

The in-service teacher culture circle I discuss in this chapter met between August 2006 and July 2008. Every other week, eight teachers and I met to problematize everyday issues and engage in dialogic, collective, critical learning processes. During this time, as the culture circle facilitator, I engaged in ethnographic observations of participating teachers' classrooms and of our own culture circle to learn from the process through fieldnotes, video and audio recordings, interviews, and artifacts. I aimed to document the situated representation of transformative teacher education—a critical teacher study group.

Although I invited teachers to join the group, I followed their leads from the first meeting. What led the teachers and I to engage in this kind of exploration were themes emerging from their own practices and experiences, and furthermore, the many conflicts and tensions they were experiencing. I carefully documented their classroom practices and listened closely to what they said in the teacher study group. As I engaged in these actions systematically and recursively, I learned a lot from my observations. In striving to understand the complexities and nuances of what the teachers were saying and/or doing in the teacher culture circle, I probed further, not providing answers, but questioning. Questioning became a common component in our dialogues by which we developed trust. As I questioned the teachers myself, and the mandates that constrained our practices, they started questioning each other and their own practices as well as the larger discourses that were shaping (and often constraining) curricula and teaching in their classrooms.

Our learning community developed and teachers became comfortable exposing vulnerabilities and uncertainties.

In implementing Freirean culture circles in teacher education, I wanted to explore how early childhood teachers engaged in dialogue through differences of perspective. Therefore, I reframed my role as teacher educator, becoming both an ethnographer and an action researcher. I documented relevant themes generated from the teachers' classrooms and facilitated the teacher culture circle. Doing these things allowed the teachers and me an opportunity to embrace teacher education as a process of problem posing. In documenting the process, I wanted to learn about the power and possibilities of teacher culture circles, focusing on how the process occurred and its potential for transformative action. Specifically, I wanted to assess if and in what ways participation in a teacher culture circle propelled change and transformation in the lives of participants.

GETTING STARTED:
A GENERATIVE THEME AS AN INVITATION

We started purposefully focusing on issues of early literacy. As a former primary grades teacher, I had experienced a push-down model of traditional literacy practices. Genishi and Dyson (2009) documented that starting "in kindergarten, there is often a stark curricular shift" signaled by "prescribed literacy focused curricula" (p. 138). In the preschool I studied, the effects of such a shift were evident as parents questioned teachers as to why their children were not being taught to write letters conventionally and to develop graphophonemic awareness by age 3. Teachers were frustrated with having parents of children ages 2 and 3 pointedly ask them when their children were going to be writing letters and reciting the alphabet, and questioning why teachers were not employing products such as Baby Einstein™ flashcards to accelerate their children's literacy development. Addressing the tension I had observed in many classrooms—parents pushing for more structured literacy instruction and early childhood teachers feeling oppressed by such requests—I issued an invitation to teachers by email, as suggested by the preschool administrator. Because the tensions surrounding early literacy were real for the teachers, many of them came to the first meeting.

The First Meeting

In the first meeting, teachers came with notepads and pens, and slowly trickled into the room. I had reserved a space on the rug in the toddler classroom. This was an open space where we could sit in a circle on the floor to break some of the uneasiness often associated with power differentials and the traditional roles of teachers and learners. I told them that we were going to be talking about issues relevant to their classrooms. One of the teachers (who sat next to me) wrote "early literacy" on top of her notepad. Many were skeptical of this "professional development" experience because previous ones had involved detached, here-is-what-you-should-be-doing approaches. Reflecting on the experience, Lexy, one of the teachers, said:

> I was skeptical, but from the very beginning it was so educational and so interesting, and so just down-to-earth and personable. We . . . discuss[ed] everything, the issues we were struggling with in the classroom, our feelings, our thoughts, our teaching. . . . I just learned SO MUCH. . . . it was amazing to be part of a group learning together. No one knew all the answers, but just using some of the resources that they had, the ideas that they had, we just learned so much from each other.

In establishing a democratic culture circle, Shor (1990) asserted that the first task of the critical educator is to deconstruct authoritarian modes of discourse in conventional classrooms. In culture circles, students' experiences are invited, valued, and central to the construction of meaning. In a culture circle approach to professional development, teachers are recognized as agents and their voices are privileged. This is not a simple process, however. Freire (1987) wrote, "a progressive position requires democratic practice where authority never becomes authoritarianism, and where authority is never so reduced that it disappears in a climate of irresponsibility and license" (p. 212).

There is neither a simple definition of a culture circle nor a formula for implementing one, especially a culture circle in teacher education. Yet, an educator must dare to blur teacher and learner roles, positioning himself/herself vulnerably yet responsibly (Souto-Manning, 2010). Positioning myself vulnerably, I shared with participating teachers my experiences of constraints associated with literacy mandates and focused instruction. For example, I had experienced programs founded on "scientifically based reading research" according to No Child Left Behind mandates that censored books students could read and defined what counted as "good" reading (Souto-Manning, in press). I used my own teaching experience as a codification of what they were experiencing. James, one of the participating teachers, recounted that the first session "didn't start out as open." He continued:

> [Mariana] would come in and share some things we could relate to; like things that affected our classrooms, our teaching, but not talking about us directly. Then as we started feeling comfortable, she would share different things that she would see in the classrooms . . . she wouldn't say where, I think, but *what* she saw.

Soon, the notepads and pens were put aside and teachers began asking questions. They were still trying to determine particular pedagogical practices and approaches to use with their students. I informed the teachers that I did not have all the answers and that what works in one classroom may not work in another classroom. Instead, I posed questions and listened to their experiences. Freire (1970) proposed the use of problematization or the technique of problem posing to initiate dialogue. Taking learners' experiences as central to the literacy process respects their discourses and cultures while making learning relevant. The learner is therefore the protagonist in the culture circles. On this same point, James continued:

> Mariana was the facilitator . . . but she really would follow our leads, ask questions that helped us move ahead and look deeper at situations. So, I mean, originally, we're discussing literacy, issues that she had brought from our classrooms, and how we could change things, what pressures are keeping us from moving ahead, from progressing in our vision and practice.

James's comments demonstrate how engaging in "a peer problem-solving process" helped to ease the teachers' initial tensions and skepticism, which were transformed into a sense of curiosity. I told them that we could meet as often as they'd like, and that in between our scheduled meetings, I would document their classroom practices so the topics of our meetings would be relevant to their realities. Our teacher culture circles became spaces to seize conflicts as opportunities for learning.

Mollie, another participating teacher, explained the possibilities afforded by culture circles in teacher education. She indicated, "the teacher culture circle really encouraged the strengths-based perspective. . . . Focusing on the strengths, on what teachers are doing is so much more empowering and encouraging to them. I learned a lot from this and will continue to use that in my classroom." Mollie's sentiments show the power of engaging in professional development that values and extends teachers' pedagogical practices while using a pedagogical design that can be employed in teachers' classrooms. Her beliefs, which connected to James's ideas that the culture circles were powerful spaces for looking deeper at issues affecting their curriculum and teaching, proves that culture circles are a powerful format for transformative professional development.

Grounding Beliefs

Culture circles are grounded in the belief that "no educational experience takes place in a vacuum, only in a real context—historical, economic, political, and not necessarily identical to any other context" (Freire, 1985, p. 12).

Thus, in employing culture circles, teacher educators should investigate the context and practices generated by participating teachers themselves. Beyond being a generative process—a process that derives from the experiences and lives of its participants—culture circles are based on two foundational tenets: the political nature of education (Freire, 1985) and dialogue in the process of educating. Education is not neutral; rather, it is a means for change and transformation. It is not a one-person business, but a process whereby individuals come together and learn from each other and consider multiple perspectives. These tenets come to life within the context in which learners live; as they critically and politically analyze their problems, they use dialogue to progressively find solutions to those conflicts.

Overall, culture circles aim to foster *conscientização* (Freire, 1970), or critical meta-awareness. By engaging in the critical cycle inherent to culture circles (Souto-Manning, 2010), participants not only come to name issues, but learn to challenge the forces shaping them. Freire first proposed culture circles in the 1950s. According to Apple, Gandin, and Hypolito (2001), "in concrete terms, his methods of 'conscientization' with adults in literacy programmes was basically constituted by a process of coding/decoding linguistic and social meanings, organized through a number of steps" (p. 131). Although this curricular approach may initially appear as something from the past (Souto-Manning, 2010), it serves as an opportunity for freedom and possibility, for change in teaching and teacher education today (Ayers, 2010).

Steps in the Process of Culture Circles

The first step in culture circles, which encompasses the stance that knowledge is co-constructed, is to generate themes from the community/ies in which participants live. The generative themes are socially and culturally relevant to individuals and communities. In teacher education, these themes initially emerge from the professional lives of teachers within the context of their classrooms. A teacher educator repositions himself/herself as an ethnographer, seeking to document the cultures of classrooms and code data for relevant, recurring themes across time and space. This repositioning happens as the teacher educator takes the stance of a researcher engaging in comparative and thematic analyses—moving between transcripts, memos, notes, and relevant literature. Thus, the teacher educator commits time to study the classrooms of the teachers whom she/he is working with as he/she engages in simultaneous data collection and inductive thematic analysis of the collected data.

After being generated, themes are codified into cases, artifacts, drawings, and so forth, and are employed in dialogues within the circles. In the culture circles, these themes are deconstructed dialogically via a process of problem posing. Teachers can identify with the importance and urgency of an issue being discussed because of its situated occurrence in their classrooms; thus, they have an investment in resolving each issue and in finding possible solutions. Decoding relevant themes happens collectively through a process of dialogic problem posing. Specific "steps are taken to achieve the process of reading . . . [which] consist of a process of decoding written words . . . from a coded existential situation. This connection to the real existential situation is . . . crucial . . . enabling students . . . to use . . . knowledge to reconstruct their lives" (Apple, Gandin, & Hypolito, 2001, p. 132).

The culture circle curriculum is generated from the fabric of students' lives, and in the case of in-service teacher education, the curriculum is generated from the lives, practices, and beliefs of practicing teachers. Although a common theme may be initially identified (e.g., early literacy practices), the topics discussed and the group collectively negotiates the definitions of a given theme. Culture circles intend to eliminate the dichotomy between theory and practice that is often present in traditional schooling environments as practice depends on theory and theory depends on practice in the implementation, development, and maintenance of culture circles. Together, teachers theorize from their very practices.

The common aspects in culture circles are not prescriptive and need to be re-created as new instances occur and culture circles are implemented in different contexts across time and space (Souto-Manning, 2010). These common aspects are generative themes (including thematic investigation and codification), problem posing, dialogue, and problem-solving leading to action.

WHAT HAPPENED?: INSIGHTS FROM CO-REFLECTION AND ANALYSIS OF A TEACHER CULTURE CIRCLE

In this section, I recount how eight early childhood teachers and I dialogically co-reflected (Waff, 2009) and analyzed the process in which we engaged—the critical cycle in a teacher culture circle. We talked about the uniqueness of this process as participating teachers reflected on their previous professional development experiences, the process per se, and considered the effects this had on classroom practices. I use dialogue sessions to illustrate the process as a way to portray our collective analysis of our culture circle meetings. By doing so, I hope to shed light on the power afforded by a dialogic, problem posing approach to teacher education. In particular, as the teachers and I reflected on being part of culture circles, we illustrated how "A world may come into being in the course of a continuing dialogue" (Greene, 1995, p. 196). The dialogue below offers powerful insights on culture circles as places for learners to engage in problem-solving, the effects of culture circles on teachers' beliefs and practices, culture circles as polyphonic spaces, and culture circles as safe communities of learners. To demonstrate the power of culture circles, I provide key insights from participating teachers without interpreting the meanings of their insights.

Culture Circles as Places to Engage in Collective Problem-Solving

HILLARY: It provided a space, a way, an outlet for us to use, to talk about problems and issues in our classrooms. It was really good to hear all the ideas, what will be used, and good to hear that teachers actually have . . . similar issues in their classrooms. We came together, asked questions, tried to see what the problem was, and moved to problem-solving together.

MOLLIE: You know, recognizing that these were shared issues and that we could problem-solve together reinforced that it was a worthy amount of time. I think just talking about it and recognizing that we are not alone is therapeutic—not feeling isolated, alone. Issues that we all experienced were brought to the circle. Just the normal school day wasn't allowing us the opportunity to talk with your co-teachers about what's going on in and across the classrooms, and problem-solve. When you are not talking about it you feel like, am I the only one who sees this, am I the only one who feels this way? And the teacher group was really therapeutic in that way, just to be able to recognize how common and prevalent some of the issues were . . .

LEXY: And then we could talk and try to find answers together. We knew that many times there aren't the perfect answers or simple solutions for situations, and what works in one setting may not work in another. But recognizing that if this is going on in my classroom and in another, then teachers can collaborate and problem-solve together and feel like we can do it instead of feeling like there is no way, this is not for me, I am a horrible teacher.

SHANTE: Yeah, problem-solving through collaboration ((nodding)). It was really nice just 'cause it was very open, and you know if you had a problem, there was actually at least one other teacher who dealt with that, who can try to find solutions together, even if we knew that the same solution may not work as well in different classrooms.

CORRY: It wasn't just a place to take problems or talk about what's great in our classroom, but also a place where we can get to know one another. It was a place that allowed us to get to know each other as people, on a more personal level, and to get to know more about their needs and wants, issues, and goals. Because we cared about each other, we were invested in the process. To talk and try to find solutions, to ask hard questions, required trust and close relationships.

JAMES: One of the powerful things is that we did not oversimplify the process. After we talked and found some solutions, we would follow up and see what had worked, what had not, talk about the whys and if it had not worked. That became a theme to be addressed by the group . . . again.

MARILYN: But instead of getting upset about it, we knew that it was part of the process.

Effects of Culture Circles on Teachers' Beliefs and Practices

HILLARY: [Y]ou really had to be reflective in it. So the process, being reflective, then trying to really put into practice things that we were talking about in the study group, kept us honest.

LEXY: From the very beginning it was SO educational and so interesting, and so just down-to-earth and personable, you know. We were all just discussing and, I mean, I just learned SO MUCH. But when we left, we put those plans to action, and we supported each other, and we held each other accountable. We also started helping our kids learn from each other using that same circle idea. We also saw how very important it is to be part of a group, of a community for learning. Coming together and learning from each other was amazing . . .

JILL: I was able to take things that we talked about, strategies and solutions we talked about, and I feel like I was able to apply them in my classroom. So, it wasn't all about talk. It was talk and action.

LEXY: We listened and learned different ways to deal with particular situations. You get a totally different perspective from somebody else, and you can look at your problems or your stresses in a different way. So, if you're stressed out, you know, if you are part of a group, . . . then, at least you know that you are not, like, totally incompetent. ((Many teachers agreed))

MARILYN: Mariana had talked about, like, doing a gallery walk. She had seen something like that in a public school in New York City, to communicate what's going on in classrooms, and we all get to preview and talk about it. Then parents could come in and talk and see what's going on in the classrooms, 'cause . . . sometimes the parents really are unsure what's going on in the classrooms.

LEXY: We thought it was a good idea, but we decided to put together a brochure that talked about what were some of the core ideas that guided our teaching and decisions in the classroom. So, the teacher culture circles influenced our teaching and the way we communicated with parents.

JAMES: But I think one of the things we did not address well is the fact that everyone, the parents, they read it individually, they're not there experiencing it together. I think that, of course, what I learned from the teacher study group, is that we all experienced it together, and that, I think was what made the difference.

MARILYN: ((keeps nodding)) It was just that amazing!

JAMES: The . . . culture circles were grounded on a vision of change, which is an ongoing process. . . . If an issue is not addressed, it's gonna come back up again. . . . Besides dealing with everyday issues, this influenced my philosophy and approach to teaching.

MARILYN: Right, and just getting feedback on what you're doing in the classroom, which is huge. Thinking about what is and hoping for what is going to be, and taking this approach with our students, helping them think and question as they grow.

JAMES: Yes, yes, it is so important, it is so important!

CORRY: As a teacher, I can say that the effect of our teacher culture circles on me was to de-stress and think of ways to deal with issues on smaller and larger levels. . . . There was a community that allowed me to recognize the stresses of teaching as a process rather than personal punishment. Every time after we had a meeting, I felt I came away from there . . . feeling like validated or, helped in some way, or that I helped someone. So . . . that overall general feeling is what I think kept me wanting to be back, the empowering process that made me believe I can do this.

JAMES: I love teacher study group. It did kind of fire up my teaching. I started seeing how kids could ask questions and be critical too and how they had the power to change things. It inspired me to try new things because I knew I could try something and go to teacher culture circle and say, ooh, I tried this and this worked, and that didn't work and we could problem-solve together.

Culture Circles as Polyphonic Spaces Honoring Multiple Voices and Perspectives

MOLLIE: It was participant directed. A traditional seminar might be helpful if it's about topics that you're unfamiliar with, and somebody that's really knowledgeable in the area comes in and talks about their specialty. But all you do is listen and take it in. There is no connection between theory and practice. . . . In the teacher culture circle, we theorized from our practices, together. We really directed the conversation. . . . There was respect of difference and I think this is why it worked.

JILL: I found out, I found very quickly, all of us're very DIFFERENT too. I mean we're . . . all working toward the same goal, but we're doing it in different ways . . .

HILLARY: Yeah. There were some instances where we might disagree or we might talk about subjects that might be uncomfortable for a lot of people. It DIDN'T happen all the time, and when it did, it was dealt with respect.

SHANTE: In those times, Mariana was very good at keeping our focus, bringing it back to the issue. Sometimes, we realized that we tended to avoid conflict. But we learned that even though many of us had grown up thinking that conflict was bad, it was a place where we learned.

MARILYN: So, [the facilitator] asked us to keep bringing perspectives we were good at, listening, saying okay I hear what your concerns are, you know, but just bringing back the focus of what we were discussing. So, the facilitator . . . was important for all voices to be heard.

JILL: Yes, I definitely think so.

CORRY: But we had to keep reminding ourselves that many voices, opinions, experiences are part of what make a community so important, so we could learn from other teachers.

Culture Circles as Safe Communities of Learners

JAMES: One of the first things . . . [the facilitator] said was, this is not about teacher bashing, which I think, totally just like, made us go oh, okay. And it's like a whole wave of fear was removed.

CORRY: I definitely feel that our guard was let down and we could share anything that we wanted to, and we knew we wouldn't be looked down upon for thinking this, or we wouldn't be reprimanded. . . . It was a very safe place, and I think one of the biggest memories I have is of people getting emotional, even crying about something that was going on. . . . And just knowing that it stopped there, and people won't go like, oh, do you know that so and so was crying in the teacher culture circle last night, you know what I mean?

JAMES: Right, it wasn't that gossiping that usually happens.

MARILYN: It was a good time to meet other teachers, to see what they're about, 'nd all that. I felt isolated. Knowing who everyone was, what they cared about was important. We were not just teachers, but we were people with likes and dislikes. So, getting to know my coworkers as people, I really enjoyed that part of it too . . .

LEXY: It was okay to feel vulnerable, to not know, to be angry.

JAMES: Oh yeah, I totally agree with that. I think also the fact that, it was an open space, but we developed trust before we were asked to take personal risks.

LEXY: I think so. It was a safe haven. But it wasn't a place people crossed their arms. They put up their sleeves and got to work, talking and asking questions, and looking for solutions, and supporting each other. But the same people who comforted you, pushed you . . .

MARILYN: I feel closer to those teachers than I do to the teachers who were not in the culture circle, 'cause I feel like we shared that. . . .

JAMES: It was like the confessionary, a place where there were mysteries shared ((laughs)).

MARILYN: And they all got to be solved. Not by some other person or miracle, but by us.

JILL: It was like a support group, a place where the teachers go where it's kind o' like a safe area, where, um, we can just talk about different things going on as well as learn from each other and problem-solve together. I felt . . . that you can share ideas more openly, more freely.

HILLARY: It was a safe place, and I felt that it gave me a sense of community as we decided what we're working toward. I found it special, I got to know everybody and liked how we were working together to make things better.

JAMES: Mariana [the facilitator] really set it up from the get-go, she set this up as a safe place. . . . We all had great respect for that group of people and for the space it created.

SHANTE: . . . [P]robably one of the best things is that you felt comfortable enough to talk about anything in there. And you know, you didn't have to worry about, oh, if I say this somebody is going to go tell it to someone else. There was trust. . . . I remember there were a couple of things that I had brought in and was asking about. I walked away feeling that okay I can totally handle this now. . . . They gave me these possible solutions to try out, recognizing that they might work or might not. But these solutions were often better than anything any of us could come up with on our own because we thought of complicating factors as we talked about solutions.

CORRY: It was not like stuffy staff meetings, where you always sit there, sit on your hands, and bite your tongue. It was not a place

where you are being told what to do. . . . While there were tensions when questions were being asked, there was respect. I felt
that tension among our group was dealt with in helpful ways. I
honestly think that everyone felt that way. Sometimes, someone
would come in there not even knowing that they needed to talk
about something . . .

SHANTE: This was so helpful, being part of this community. I mean all
the other professional training that I've done has been so bor-
ing . . . somebody stands up there and just preaches at you. You
don't get to say anything, you don't get to do anything, you just
sit there . . . take it in and at the end of it, be like okay, none of
that is pertaining to me . . . . this was a group thing. We went
around and talked, and so EVERYTHING . . . pertained to you
because you had say so and you're not just sitting there, looking at your watch hoping it'll be time to go home. In the teacher
culture circle, we often were surprised by how late it was when
we finally . . . look[ed] at our watches.

CRITICAL PERSPECTIVE

The aforementioned exchanges showcase some transformative possibilities
afforded by culture circles in an urban context. As I think back on the study
and offer possibilities for the future, I reflect on a) foundational concepts
about culture circles that were outlined in this chapter, b) key insights from
this study, and c) what such insights might mean for teacher educators as
they re-envision support for teachers by addressing teaching and learning
tensions present in urban contexts.

First, culture circles are pedagogical spaces that significantly differ
from the norm for professional development. They do not have set curricula to be passed on to teachers. Teachers and teacher educators co-create
curriculum generatively. Second, in a culture circle, teacher educators consider what is taking place, carefully documenting the realities lived by its
participants as opposed to making assumptions regarding the experience
and brilliance of teachers. As action researchers, teacher educators systematically document the practices and actions of their students and seek
to create better educational environments and opportunities. While it is
easy for teacher educators to affirm that they do not have time to engage
in action research, it is important to not only talk the talk about the value
of rethinking teaching, but walk the walk by engaging in transformative
teaching themselves. Third, culture circles encourage teachers to engage in
action research by paying careful attention to what is happening in their

classrooms, finding points of tension to be addressed, and reworking their own practices.

Foundationally, culture circles start from the very lives and experiences of learners, problematizing the commonly known and seeking to collectively, dialogically foster better futures by challenging what *is* and envisioning what *could* be. Beyond fostering awareness of issues affecting the lives and communities of participants, culture circles seeks to foster meta-awareness by centering on questioning the reasons why a certain event is taking place or a certain issue is being mandated or perpetuated. Culture circles are conducive spaces for getting beyond simplistic explanations such as "I have to do this" or "This is just the way it is." Although there are many facets of culture circles through co-reflection, participating teachers and I realized that culture circles afforded ways to engage in professional development that mattered to them personally and professionally. Culture circles encouraged them to rethink their ways of teaching, consider many voices and perspectives, and build a community of learners in which participants could position themselves as vulnerable—where there was a great amount of trust and freedom to voice concerns and share victories.

Key insights from this study point toward the need to reconceptualize professional development in culturally relevant ways. Professional development should be fashioned as a place where colleagues engage in collective problem-solving and as a polyphonic space where multiple perspectives are not simply tolerated, but honored and respected. Clearly, this differs from the norm of in-service professional developments conducted on-site (in schools). Often, such professional development opportunities focus on passing information on to teachers and depositing knowledge in their brains (Freire, 1970). Typically organized around workshops or a single event with a preset agenda, they often do not allow for a community of learners to be developed. Professional development needs to recognize that teachers have agency. Teacher educators want teachers to honor children as creative human beings who enter classrooms with a wealth of knowledge. Thus, it is important that teacher educators re-envision professional development in a similar fashion.

Although this chapter offers a situated representation of teacher culture circles, I posit that it opens up possibilities in teacher education and professional development for freedom across contexts. I conclude with a call to action. I challenge educators at all levels to consider the structure and ideology implicit in culture circles. As we create, implement, and support spaces for ongoing professional development in schools and beyond, let's consider how we can serve as catapults for positive transformation, dialogically negotiating spaces of possibility!

REFERENCES

Apple, M., Gandin, L., & Hypolito, A. (2001). Paulo Freire, 1921–97. In J. Palmer (Ed.), *Fifty modern thinkers on education: From Piaget to the present day* (pp. 128–133). London: Routledge.

Ayers, W. (2010). Afterword. In M. Souto-Manning, *Freire, teaching, and learning: Culture circles across contexts.* New York: Peter Lang.

Cahnmann-Taylor, M., & Souto-Manning, M. (2010). *Teachers act up!: Creating multicultural learning communities through theatre.* New York: Teachers College Press.

Dyson, A., & Genishi, C. (2005). *On the case: Approaches to language and literacy research.* New York: Teachers College Press.

Freire, P. (1970). *Pedagogy of the oppressed.* New York: Continuum.

Freire, P. (1987). Letter to North American teachers (C. Hunter, Trans.). In I. Shor (Ed.), *Freire for the classroom: A source book for liberatory teaching.* Portsmouth, NH: Heinemann.

Freire, P. (1985). *The politics of education: Culture, power, and liberation.* Westport, CT: Bergin & Garvin.

Genishi, C., & Dyson, A. H. (2009). *Children, language, and literacy: Diverse learners in diverse times.* New York: Teachers College Press.

Giroux, H. (1985). Introduction. In P. Freire, *The politics of education: Culture, power, and liberation* (pp. xi–xxvi). Westport, CT: Bergin & Garvin.

Goodwin, A. L., Cheruvu, R., & Genishi, C. (2008). Responding to multiple diversities in early childhood education: How far have we come? In C. Genishi and A. L. Goodwin (Eds.), *Diversities in early childhood: Rethinking and doing* (pp. 3–10). New York: Routledge.

Greene, M. (1995). *Releasing the imagination: Essays on education, the arts, and social change.* San Francisco: Jossey-Bass.

Ladson-Billings, G. (1995). But that's just good teaching!: The case for culturally relevant pedagogy. Theory into Practice, *34*(3), 159–165.

Nolte, D. (1998). *Children learn what they live.* New York: Workman Publishing Company.

Shor, I. (1990). Liberation education: An interview with Ira Shor. *Language Arts,* 67 (4), 342–353.

Souto-Manning, M. (2010). *Freire, teaching, and learning: Culture circles across contexts.* New York: Peter Lang.

Souto-Manning, M. (in press). Accelerating reading inequities in the early years. *Language Arts.*

Waff, D. (2009). Coresearching and coreflecting: The power of teacher inquiry communities. In D. Goswami, C. Lewis, M. Rutherford, & D. Waff (Eds.), *Teacher inquiry: Approaches to language and literacy research* (pp. 69–89). New York: Teachers College Press.

Weinstein, C. S., Tomlinson-Clarke, S., & Curran, M. (2004). Toward a conception of culturally responsive classroom management. *Journal of Teacher Education,* *55*(1), 25–38.

CHAPTER 6

(Re)Framing Teaching in Urban Classrooms

A Poststructural (Re)Reading of Critical Literacy as Curricular and Pedagogical Practice

Marcelle M. Haddix and Mary Alexandra Rojas

Urban classrooms are overpopulated and underresourced, teachers have limited time to plan and collaborate for effective and efficient teaching, and teachers find themselves forced to rely more and more on prepackaged curricula and textbook anthologies. Given this picture of the current landscape of urban education, it is crucial that researchers investigate more powerful ways to assist teachers in reading and analyzing curricular materials, such as teacher edition (TE) textbooks, in order to enhance their own and their students' critical capacities and knowledges in relation to language, literacy, and culture.

In this chapter, we explore the importance of critical literacy in the curricular and pedagogical practices of educators who teach literature in urban school settings. We advocate moving beyond viewing literacy as an individual literary or technical skill and toward an understanding of literacy as situated social practices in communities and in the world. Specifically, we draw on the work of Luke (2000) to describe the practical aspects of critical literacy when teachers use TE textbooks. We consider, as an example, the situating of Latino/a literatures in TE textbooks. Then, we take up poststructuralist perspectives to further question the complex issues of power and authority as we seek to contest static constructions of knowledge. We conclude the chapter by highlighting specific kinds of classroom-based research, strategies, and pedagogical practices for using critical literacy frameworks in the teaching of literatures in urban settings.

TEXTBOOKS AND THE SITUATING
OF LATINO/A LITERATURES

In secondary English language arts classrooms, textbooks are a dominant source for teaching literature and for literary analysis. Although the practice of using textbooks for pedagogical purposes varies from teacher to teacher, studies show that a majority of public school teachers depend solely on textbooks (versus individual texts) as their main source for teaching literature, and many rate textbook anthologies as at least adequate in terms of their teaching suggestions and strategies (Applebee, 1993). In the context of urban education, this is particularly important to note, since in the current terrain of English education in secondary schools, the dependence on textbooks has not changed (Scherff & Piazza, 2008/2009). Determining what counts as literature in ways that include an explicit focus on the intersections of race, gender, and class is a challenging task, one that needs to be explored (Morrell, 2007).

The dependence on textbooks and the need to expand the scope of what counts as literature is significant when we consider the makeup of today's student population in urban school settings. The majority of students in today's urban schools are Black and Latino native-born and foreign-born youth. One of every five students in U.S. public schools is either an immigrant or the child of an immigrant, mainly from Latin America (Zentella, 2005). Because many U.S. Latinos/as trace their origin to Mexico, most statistics about Latinos/as reflect the experiences of Mexicans, negating the complexity of Latino/a heritages and identities (Zentella, 2005). Inter- and intra-group diversity in the Latino/a American experience is significant, yet monolithic treatment of this experience persists within our schools, and by extension, in our English language arts curriculum. The selection and representation of Latino/a literature in secondary English literature textbooks do not fully represent the complexity of Latino/a identities.

In her most current research, Rojas (2010) analyzed secondary English TE literature textbooks to understand how U.S. Latino/a identities are situated and framed via textbook editors' notes, suggested activities, and discussion questions. She found that although textbooks purport to present curricula that support critical readings of race, class, and gender and deal with issues of power, the selected literatures feature literary terms to teach certain skills that the textbooks, and those who design them, believe are valued by state/district-defined curricula. In addition, the literatures themselves are defined and "othered" as "multicultural" in contrast to or by what it is not considered—in this case, mainstream.

One example Rojas (2010) explored extensively is the inclusion of the work of Judith Ortiz-Cofer. Ortiz-Cofer is one of six U.S. Latino/a authors found in all TE texts who are identified as Puerto Rican, and she has the most selections of all Puerto Rican authors included. Her work is diverse in genre. Although her essays, poetry, and short stories are all represented, her short stories are most popular. Most of the pieces selected for inclusion in anthologies are taken from her book *The Latin Deli* (1993), published as a collection of prose and poetry. The work of Ortiz-Cofer appears in all grade levels—her short story "American History" was published in only 9th-grade textbooks; her short story "Catch the Moon" in only 10th-grade textbooks; and her poem "The Latin Deli: An Ars Poetica" in three different publishers' 11th-grade texts.

Ortiz-Cofer's works are mainly situated around the teaching of particular literary and technical skills—knowledge that is deemed important and appropriate for the grade level. Activities and suggested questions address specific skills or literary terms highlighted within the work in order for teachers and students to "see" how these works are manifested within each piece. Analysis and comprehension questions as well as project suggestions follow most works to extend the study idea. Primary focus, however, is on the terms and skills the textbook introduced. The following example demonstrates questions and activities for teaching her short story "American History," presented in a McDougal Littell TE textbook:

To provide students with help in perceiving cause-and-effect relationships, read aloud or write on the chalkboard the following question:

Which of the following was NOT one of the effects of the Kennedy assassination?

A. Eugene's mother tells Elena to go home.
B. School is dismissed early.
C. El Building is much quieter than usual.
D. Elena's mother asks her to go to church with her.

Guide students in selecting choice A. Help them recognize that Eugene's mother tells Elena to go home because she does not want Elena and her son to be friends.
(Applebee, Bermudez, Blau, Caplan, Elbow, Hynds et al., 2006, p. 300)

In less scripted activities, a section called Writing Options offers a few activities that extend terminology and skills aimed for the story:

1. Thoughtful Poem: Read the last paragraph of the story aloud, and ask students to list vivid details they might use in their poems. To make this assignment more challenging, have students base their poems on the symbol of the "green door of hope".
2. Different Ending: Encourage students to try to make the ending consistent in some way with events earlier in the story.
3. Speculative Essay: Before students begin writing, have them consider possible long-range consequences of the public event they choose.
(Applebee, Bermudez, Blau, Caplan, Elbow, Hynds et al., 2006, p. 303)

In these examples, the textbook editors encourage teachers to address the literary elements of plot and conflict, to emphasize the linearity of the story, and to guide students to select "correct" responses geared toward standardized test practices. These examples demonstrate ways in which the positioning of certain knowledges functions to fulfill particular objectives and privilege certain meanings while silencing many others.

WORKING WITH CRITICAL LITERACY

Critical literacy as a framework for reading and studying literature involves exploring complicated themes in the larger world. The tradition of critical literacy draws attention to what is included in and what is left out of a text and pushes us to identify the ideological underpinnings of texts. Underlying critical literacy frameworks is Freire's (1970/1982) notion that critical literacy is about "reading the world" and seeing the world from particular frames. Moving from theory to practice, however, many versions of critical literacy circulate. In a critique of the appropriations (or misappropriations) of critical literacy, Luke (2000) notes that for many educators and scholars in the North American context, critical literacy is often understood as including higher-order comprehension skills, such as the development of meta-cognitive reading strategies, reader response orientations, and analysis of authorial intent. Such an appropriation often sidesteps the systematic analysis of relationships of social, cultural, and economic power—concepts that ground a definition of critical literacy as situated within social practices in communities and in the world. Another dominant critical literacy agenda is that of Australian scholars (e.g., Comber, 2006; Gilbert, 1993; Janks, 2000) who began from the assumption that reading and writing are about power and that critical literacy goes beyond the individual toward an analysis and reconstruction of social fields. However, no one formula for "doing" critical literacy in classrooms exists, and many (e.g., Edelsky & Cherland, 2006; Vasquez, 2004) have challenged the promotion of critical literacy as a singular method or approach, as we do here. For example, while the four-tiered approach developed by Freebody and Luke (1990) presents necessary sets of social practices for literacy instruction—coding, text-meaning, pragmatic, and critical practices—this approach, Luke (2000) argues, is not sufficient in and of itself for literate participation in a complex and dynamic social world. Instead, a central aim of critical literacy is to foster, according to Luke (2000):

> A classroom environment where students and teachers together work to (a) see how the worlds of texts work to construct their worlds, their cultures, and their identities in powerful, often overtly ideological ways; and (b) use texts as social tools in ways that allow for a reconstruction of these same worlds. (p. 453)

Critical literacy is most often considered in terms of providing young people with tools to critique and question the world around them as they make sense of texts, including those mediated by the school environment and by popular and media texts. Many literacy researchers utilize a critical literacy framework in their work with urban youth populations (Bean & Moni, 2003; Morrell, 2002, 2007). Morrell (2007) writes, "no population requires critical literacy more than today's urban youth" (p. 6). He points out that because of the realities that many urban youth must confront on a regular basis, they will constantly have to interpret and critique texts, or linguistics and semiotic symbol systems, that position them as "Other." For example, with the dominant stereotyping of urban poor or people of color that persists within popular media and texts, young people are uniquely positioned to take on critical literacy as praxis, to take an activist stance toward challenging and changing such representations. Given that critical literacy incorporates and subsumes traditional literacies frequently taught in schools, urban literacy classrooms become ideal locations for critical literacy education that supports young people in their move toward engaged citizenship and personal emancipation (Morrell, 2007).

This latter point leads us to an examination of the role of teachers in urban school settings, and in particular, the use of TE textbooks to influence student learning in literature classrooms. Because so many teachers rely on textbook anthologies of literature, the TE textbook becomes significant for how teachers help students make sense of literary texts, and by extension, make sense of themselves and their worlds. Critical literacy holds great potential to challenge teachers to think about the ways they utilize TE textbooks in the English language arts classroom. Further, it provides necessary tools for teachers to critique and problematize the inclusion of particular literatures within the TE textbook while questioning how certain framings position teachers and their students. Critical literacy also encourages teachers to think beyond the development of individual skills and higher-order comprehension to take up how texts are produced by and reproduce larger social contexts. Beyond using a critical literacy framework to provide students with conceptual and technical skills and to foster attitudes toward language and texts, critical literacy proves useful for teachers to examine how literature and the teaching of literature are framed in TE textbooks and how such framings position them and their students.

What follows is an example of how we use critical literacy to examine ways U.S. Latino/a literatures are positioned within TE textbooks to tell and ignore particular stories about U.S. Latino/a identities. To illustrate this, we turn our attention to the publisher's suggestions included in various TE textbooks for teaching U.S. Latino/a literature, continuing with Judith Ortiz-Cofer's work as an example and highlighting discussion questions and suggested literary analyses that shape curricular and

pedagogical practices. We draw on Luke's (2000) "redefinition" of critical literacy as a starting point, where critical literacy is about "teaching
and learning how texts work, understanding and re-mediating what texts
attempt to do in the world and to people, and moving students toward
active position-takings with texts to critique and reconstruct social fields
in which they live and work" (p. 453). In analyzing how U.S. Latino/a
literatures are positioned within TE textbooks, we bring to the forefront
often tacit ideologies of power by examining textual devices—that is, how
reality is constructed textually and how the text positions readers. In essence, our use of critical literacy involves a close examination of text production and reception. In the analysis of how Judith Ortiz-Cofer's poem
"The Latin Deli: An Ars Poetica" is framed in TE textbooks and how such
framing positions U.S. Latino/a literatures (and identities), we began with
a two-tiered critical literacy questioning strategy:

- What are the practices and processes of exclusion and inclusion in
  social fields (an analysis of power); and
- What is the text trying to do to the reader (an analysis of positioning)?

These questions serve as starting points for considering the ways U.S.
Latino/a literatures and identities are framed in TE textbooks.

Positioning the Reader

There are major themes that emerge when looking closely at the TE textbooks' introductions and suggestions for how to teach Ortiz-Cofer's work.
These themes include her identity as woman, Latina, and writer in relation
to cultural differences around immigration, ethnicity, and economic class
and family situations. Through biographical and historical contextualiza-
tion, the TE textbooks' introductions of Judith Ortiz-Cofer situate her work
around her identity as writer and are centered around issues of immigration.
Although TE textbooks' emphasis in the framing of Ortiz-Cofer's work is
to teach technical terminology or particular skills, the contextualizing information that is offered seems to underscore her identity in particular ways.
The piece "The Latin Deli: An Ars Poetica," a poem that describes a corner/
family-owned store that promotes products of particular Latin American
countries and provides its customers with the chance to express their nostal-
gia and cultural affections, is introduced with an extended biography about
Ortiz-Cofer and her family. The biography describes her and her family's
moving to Paterson, New Jersey, from Puerto Rico to improve their economic situation. What follows are two excerpts from Holt Rinehart and
Winston's 11th-grade *Elements of Literature* TE textbook's introduction of
the poem:

The writing of Judith Ortiz-Cofer bridges two cultures; her feet are planted linguistically and culturally in the soul of both Puerto Rico and the United States. . . . Although Ortiz-Cofer details Latino experience, immigrants from a wide variety of cultures have felt the longings that she describes. Ask students to name places besides Puerto Rico, Cuba and Mexico from which people have emigrated to the United States. What cultural artifacts or traditions do these groups bring with them or seek? How did they adapt to the United States? (Beers & Odell, 2007, pp. 1174–5)

These excerpts instantly position Ortiz-Cofer as an immigrant who has a bicultural and bilingual identity. A critical literacy frame would push the teacher to question his or her own positionality in relation to the way the TE textbook tells Ortiz-Cofer's experience and to question the way the suggested introductions potentially position his or her students. A growing majority of urban youth in today's public schools are ethnic minorities who live in low economic conditions and are taught by White, English-monolingual, U.S. native-born, upper-middle-class females (Gomez, 1996; Zumwalt & Craig, 2005). Yet the majority of these students are Black and Latino native-born and foreign-born youth. The growing cultural and linguistic mismatch between teachers and students in urban school contexts is widely documented (e.g., Gomez, 1996; Kinloch, 2010; Ladson-Billings, 2005; Sleeter, 2001; Zumwalt & Craig, 2005). Therefore, when examining the audience assumed by TE textbooks, the reader is the White, English-monolingual, U.S. native-born, upper-middle-class female teacher. In this way, issues of race, class, gender, and linguistic identity are made neutral and assumed to be universal for all. In other words, publishers of TE textbooks make the assumption that their readers are the same. Further, these examples show how the teacher can potentially become more vulnerable not to question the text because she/he is already positioned in opposition to this immigrant identity. If she/he is to exercise teacher authority and demonstrate pedagogical content expertise in the English language arts classroom, the teacher may be more likely to rely on what the TE textbook suggests because she/he is distanced from this immigrant identity and may feel that she/he does not have the cultural and linguistic knowledge base. From a view that sees teachers as the knowledge producers and students as the receivers of that knowledge, this positioning of the teacher would appear disempowering and paralyzing. However, from a critical literacy stance, where teachers and students actively participate in a constant exchange of meaning-making and knowledge creation, the teacher's and the students' roles in urban classrooms are reimagined.

Also, these examples simplify the immigrant experience, implying that individuals who immigrate to the United States have similar "longings" as those described in the poem of Ortiz-Cofer. What the TE textbook's framing fails to do is to consider deep-seated historical and political undercurrents of the relationship of Puerto Rico to the United States. The unique political and historical connections of Puerto Rico to the United States make Ortiz-Cofer's articulated immigrant experience significantly different from those experiences of other Latin American immigrants, on the one hand, and immigrants from non–Latin American countries, on the other hand. In addition, since Puerto Ricans have been considered American citizens since 1917, access to Puerto Rico, both in geographical proximity to the mainland United States and in the ability to enter and exit at will, begs the question of their continued immigrant identity. This may, in fact, be an aspect that significantly contributes to the biculturalism and bilingualism in Ortiz-Cofer's literature. This aspect, then, serves as a form of resistance to the Anglo culture that has imposed its political power on the island. These are characteristics that cannot be quickly associated with the experiences of other U.S. Latino/a immigrants—or other immigrants generally, as the TE textbook offers—whose country of origin is a sovereign nation and whose culture and language may be associated strictly with it. In this sense, teachers can employ critical literacy as an analytic tool by interrogating various meanings of the immigrant experience. Some questions to ask include: What is meant by the "immigrant experience"? How are the experiences of immigration among U.S. Latino/a immigrants different? The same? What assumptions do these questions and exercises make?

Power: Who's Excluded? Who's Included?

In another TE textbook's introduction of "The Latin Deli: An Ars Poetica," editors from McGraw-Hill's Glencoe Literature series review the term *melting pot*, refuting it as a passé term and clarifying that "Today, there is a new cultural model that stresses the value of maintaining ethnic diversity in American society" (Wilhelm, Fisher, & Chin, 2007, p. 1140).

Additionally, the introduction provides general historical information about the influence that immigrants have had in American history and letters and presents students with new concepts that can be explored in the unit. Among others, these concepts relate to immigration and cultural diversity. Ortiz-Cofer's individual experiences are essentialized to fit into a generalized perception of the immigrant experience, an idea that is further universalized with/in the "new cultural model" that purports to value ethnic diversity as a contribution to American society and further assumes that ethnic diversity occurs as a choice. From a critical literacy stance, the teacher is called to question this "universal" immigrant experience and consider whose narratives and experiences are left out by assuming that ethnic diversity is a choice. Another framing considers that, for many people, ethnic diversity is a matter of making it, surviving, and understanding the power and positions of the dominant culture. The TE textbook introduction above suggests that achieving diversity comes without struggle or sacrifice, and that it can be plagued with issues of discrimination, bias, and identity crisis.

A critical literacy framing also asks the reader to consider whose world is represented in this text and whose world is left out. Ortiz-Cofer's work, like the work of other U.S. Latino/a authors such as Julia Alvarez and Sandra Cisneros, is anthologized as an example of multicultural literature. U.S. Latino literatures are often included with literatures that are part of newer or contemporary literary traditions such as those that grew out of the African American civil rights movement, women's movement, and related political movements among U.S. Latinos/as and other groups (Wilhelm, Fisher, & Chin, 2007). In the introduction above, the TE textbook editors emphasize a move toward inclusion of ethnic diversity. Yet, at the same time that this introduction encourages a "new cultural model" of diversity, it inadvertently separates out U.S. Latino/a literatures. When we rely on critical literacy for an analysis of power, we consider the ways a text that is labeled multicultural is produced in opposition to mainstream practices and representations. Mainstream literatures, then, remain untroubled and unchallenged as a hegemonic center. All other literatures and, by extension, identities, continue to exist as alternatives or as "Other." Dominant narratives remain in the center and alternative narratives remain an add-on to the dominant narrative—hence, the "new cultural model." Considering U.S. Latino/a literatures in this way excludes them from the American literature tradition.

ANALYSES WITH POSTSTRUCTURALIST PERSPECTIVES

Poststructuralist perspectives (e.g., Davies, 1994, 1997, 2000; Ellsworth, 1994; Miller, 2005) allow us to further question complex issues of power and authority that persist within the analyses of the TE textbooks' framing of U.S. Latino/a literatures and identities. Such perspectives provide a critique for contesting static constructions of knowledge. Developed in and from the work of various philosophers, including Derrida (1967/1998) and Foucault (1980), among others, poststructuralist theorists address issues of language, subjectivity, social processes, and institutions to understand existing power relations and to identify areas and strategies of change (Weedon, 1997). Within education, poststructuralist theories have been used to interrogate the very categories that situate what it means to be educated, what types of research are valid, and what kinds of questions can be asked about any given structure and process. By using a poststructuralist approach, we cannot claim to provide alternatives or models of particular methods or successful outcomes; instead, we offer "critiques and methods for examining the functions and effects of any structure or grid of regularity that we put into place, including those poststructuralism itself might create" (St. Pierre & Pillow, 2000, p. 6).

Primarily, we rely on Davies (1994, 1997, 2000), drawing from Foucault (1980), who defined discourse as a system of representation concerned with how the production of knowledge and meaning through discourse operated to regulate conduct. This considers the focus on the relationship between knowledge and power and how power operates within particular discourses (see also Hall, 1997). This view emphasizes that subjectivity is produced through discourse and rejects any essentialized form of subjectivity. Davies (1994) explains both the practical and theoretical notion of subjectivity this way:

> An individual's subjectivity is made possible through the discourses s/he has access to, through a life history of being in the world. It is possible for each of us as teachers and students to research the process of subjectification in order to see its effects on us and on the learning environments we collaboratively produce. (p. 3)

Specific to our task in this chapter, we draw on poststructuralist perspectives to extend our critical literacy analysis to contest the constructions of static knowledges by looking more at the context of teaching and learning. For example, while the critical literacy questions in the previous sections urge an analysis of power, answers to such questions risk becoming universalized and generalized when we fail to take into account how the knowledges are produced. In his criticism of the practical applications of critical literacy, Luke (2000) asked:

> What happens when a radical approach to literacy education moves in the tent of a secular state education system? Is it a matter of appropriation, repressive tolerance, and "selling out"? Is that really critical literacy or just a watered down version of educational progressivism? (p. 448)

This can happen when educators use critical literacy tools to render a "critical" reading of texts without elucidating the complex, dynamic ways the context in which the text is understood mediates such readings. From a poststructuralist perspective, teachers would complicate the critical literacy analysis and consider how it is mediated by the particular context, informed by specific subjectivities and discourses. This takes into account who is doing the critical analysis and within what discourses the analysis is framed. For instance, beyond asking what we mean by the "immigrant experience," we would ask instead what knowledges does this critical literacy analysis make possible and what does it leave out?

Also, a poststructuralist analysis disallows the treatment of U.S. Latino/a identity as a monolithic category, thus the move away from singular *identity* to pluralistic *identities*. Referring back to Davies's (1994) definition of subjectivity, an individual's sense of self through discourses is constantly reconstituted via their being in the world. Poststructuralist theories not only question what it may mean to be Latino/a or what it may mean to be an "immigrant," but they allow for an examination of the structure of TE textbooks as examples of classroom practices that function within specific discourses. This functioning allows particular ideologies, meanings, and subjectivities to be constructed about what it means to know, to teach, to learn, and about what is valued and by whom. The ways U.S. Latino/a literatures are positioned to be studied within what we would call a structural or even positivist/post-positivist or traditional perspective (Pinar, 2003)—where U.S. Latino/a literatures are used to emphasize terminologies and/or skills or perpetuate specific cultural views about what it means to be U.S. Latino—constitute subjectivities that privilege certain ways of seeing and reflect certain political interests.

Poststructuralist perspectives call upon us to problematize issues of teacher authority and the teacher's role in the critical literacy analysis. Similar to Ellsworth's (1994) critique of critical pedagogy as having the potential to empower groups of people, a critical literacy analysis risks the same if it fails to launch any meaningful analysis of or program for reformulating the institutionalized power imbalances between teachers and students, or of the essentially paternalistic project of education itself. In the absence of such an analysis and program, teachers' efforts are limited to transforming negative effects of power imbalances within the classroom into positive ones. Strategies such as student empowerment and dialogue give the illusion of equality while in fact leaving the authoritarian nature of the teacher/student relationship intact (p. 306).

Poststructuralist theories dismantle the idea of the teacher's critical literacy analysis as the new norm and aim to redistribute power in the analysis, positioning teachers and students as knowledge producers. Beyond that, poststructuralist theories urge us to continually "unsettle" every definition, category, or experience that we claim to know (Ellsworth, 1994), taking into account the particular discourses and subjectivities within which we operate.

Drawing on poststructuralist theories brings to the forefront the intended aims of a critical literacy perspective by making visible the ways in which certain knowledges function to produce particular meanings. Working from these perspectives, where discourses and subjectivities are taken into account, and recognizing our own situatedness (as teachers using critical literacy in the classroom), we can see how our critical literacy analyses construct meaning and how our interpretations affect and are affected by and through our processes and the discourses that we (un)consciously use.

CRITICAL PERSPECTIVE

In offering practical suggestions for how to use critical literacy when teaching literatures, we must first reiterate that there is no one way to do critical literacy and that we are not advocating for a singular approach or method. Instead, we adapt elements from Freebody and Luke's (1990) Four Resource model to highlight the kinds of questions that can serve as starting points for any critical literacy analysis:

- Who was the text written for?
- Whose perspectives and narratives are omitted or silenced by this text?
- What are the cultural meanings and possible readings that can be constructed from this text?
- What is the text trying to do to me? Or, how is the text positioning me as the reader?

It is important that students know that they are using a critical literacy approach when working with these texts. To further problematize the analysis and avoid constituting static constructions of knowledge, a poststructuralist critique can examine what critical literacy makes possible and what such analyses leave out. Questions that can be used to engage in a critical analysis may include:

- How is the literature and curriculum defined within this critical literacy approach?
- How is the analysis of these texts (literature and curriculum) defined by particular discourses?
- How can these discourses be altered, interrupted, resisted?
- What subjectivities constitute and are constituted through these discourses (and what "new" subjectivities might be constructed)?

This chapter presents a possibility for enacting curricular and pedagogical practices in urban classrooms. By restricting knowledge production and learning skills and themes that promote and maintain the status quo, other possibilities are negated, submerged, and dismissed, limiting those explorations that can lead to imagining new ways of seeing.

Understanding that the framing of literatures in TE textbooks can lead to particular conclusions provides an opportunity for alternate readings that expand and move the readings in ways that are not prescribed by the suggestions and recommendations outlined throughout the TE textbooks. Complicating the use of critical literacy as curricular and pedagogical practices by taking up a poststructuralist approach also requires that we take into consideration how our own situatedness and subjectivities as teachers, teacher educators, and researchers, and as Black and Latina women (among other categories), affected our interpretations of these selected TE textbook examples of the framing of U.S. Latino/a literatures. By doing so, new readings and ideas emerge that delimit the positioning of U.S. Latino/a literatures and identities in the secondary English classroom in urban contexts.

REFERENCES

Applebee, A. (1993). *Studies of curriculum and instruction in the United States.* Urbana: IL: NCTE.

Applebee, A., Bermudez, A., Blau, S., Caplan, R., Elbow, P., Hynds, S., et al. (2006). *The language of literature.* New York: McDougal Littell, Inc.

Bean, T. W., & Moni, K. (2003). Developing students' critical literacy: Exploring identity construction in young adult fiction. *Journal of Adolescent and Adult Literacy, 46*(8), 638–648.

Beers, K., & Odell, L. (2007). *Elements of literature: Essentials of American literature.* New York: Holt, Rinehart and Winston.

Comber, B. (2006). Critical literacy educators at work: Examining their dispositions, discursive resources and repertoires of practice. In R. White & K. Cooper (Eds.), *Practical critical educator: Integrating literacy, learning, and leadership* (pp. 51–65). Dordrecht, The Netherlands: Springer.

Davies, B. (1994). *Poststructuralist theory and classroom practice.* Victoria, Australia: Deakin University Press.

Davies, B. (1997). The subject of post-structuralism: a reply to Alison Jones. *Gender and Education, 9,* 271–283.

Davies, B. (2000). *A body of writing: 1990–1999.* New York: AltaMira Press.

Derrida, J. (1998). *Of grammatology.* (G. C. Spivak, Trans.). Baltimore: Johns Hopkins University Press. (Original work published 1967)

Edelsky, C., & Cherland, M. R. (2006). A critical issue in critical literacy: The "popularity effect." In K. Cooper & R. E. White (Eds.), *The Practical Critical Educator* (pp. 3–16). Dordrecht, The Netherlands: Springer.

Ellsworth, E. (1994). Why doesn't this feel empowering? Working through the repressive myths of critical pedagogy. In L. Stone (Ed.), *The education feminism reader* (pp. 300–327). New York: Routledge.

Foucault, M. (1980). *Power/Knowledge: Selected interviews and other writings 1972–1977.* Hassocks, UK: The Harvester Press.

Freebody, P., & Luke, A. (1990). Literacies programs: Debates and demands in cultural context. *Prospect: Australian Journal of TESOL, 5*(7), 7–16.

Freire, P. (1982). *Pedagogy of the oppressed.* New York: Continuum. (Original work published 1970)

Gilbert, P. (1993). (Sub)versions: Using sexist language practices to explore critical literacy. *Australian Journal of Language and Literacy, 16*(4), 323–332.

Gomez, M. L. (1996). Prospective teachers' perspectives on teaching "other people's children". In K. M. Zeichner, S. Melnick, & M. L. Gomez (Eds.), *Currents of reform in preservice teacher education* (pp. 109–132). New York: Teachers College Press.

Hall, S. (Ed.). (1997). *Representation: Cultural representations and signifying practices*. London: Sage Publications Ltd.

Janks, H. (2000). Domination, access, diversity, and design: A synthesis for critical literacy education. *Educational Review, 52*(2), 175–186.

Kinloch, V. (2010). "To not be a traitor of Black English": Youth perceptions of language rights in an urban context. *Teachers College Record, 112*(1).

Ladson-Billings, G. (2005). Is the team all right? Diversity and teacher education. *Journal of Teacher Education, 56*(3), 229–234.

Luke, A. (2000). Critical literacy in Australia: A matter of context and standpoint. *Journal of Adolescent and Adult Literacy, 43*(5), 448–461.

Miller, J. (2004). *Sounds of silence breaking: Women, autobiography, curriculum.* New York: Peter Lang.

Morrell, E. (2002). Toward a critical pedagogy of popular culture: Literacy development among urban youth. *Journal of Adolescent and Adult Literacy, 46*(1), 72–77.

Morrell, E. (2007). *Critical literacy and urban youth: Pedagogies of access, dissent, and liberation.* New York: Routledge.

Ortiz-Cofer, J. (1993). *The Latin deli. Telling the lives of barrio women.* New York: W.W. Norton.

Pinar, W. F. (2003). *What is Curriculum Theory?* Mahwah, NJ: Lawrence Erlbaum Associates.

Rojas, M. A. (2010). *Exploring US Latino/a identities with/in high school English textbooks.* Unpublished dissertation. Teachers College, Columbia University.

Scherff, L., & Piazza, C. (2009). Why now, more than ever, we need to talk about opportunity to learn. *Journal of Adolescent & Adult Literacy. 52*(4), 343–352. (Original work published 2008)

Sleeter, C. E. (2001). Preparing teachers for culturally diverse schools: Research and the overwhelming presence of whiteness. *Journal of Teacher Education, 52*(2), 94–106.

St. Pierre, E., & Pillow, W. (2000). *Working the ruins: Feminist poststructuralist theory and methods in education.* New York: Routledge.

Vasquez, V. (2004). *Negotiating critical literacies with young children.* Mahwah, NJ: Lawrence Erlbaum Associates.

Weedon, C. (1997). *Feminist practice and poststructuralist theory.* New York: Blackwell.

Wilhelm, J., Fisher, D., & Chin, B. A. (Consultant Eds.). (2007). *Glencoe literature: The reader's choice, American literature.* New York: McGraw-Hill.

Zentella, A. C. (2005). Perspectives on language and literacy in Latino families and communities. In A. C. Zentella (Ed.), *Building on strength: Language and literacy in Latino families and communities* (pp. 1–12). New York: Teachers College Press.

Zumwalt, K., & Craig, E. (2005). Teachers' characteristics: Research on the demographic profile. In M. Cochran-Smith & K. M. Zeichner (Eds.), *Studying teacher education: The report of the AERA panel on research and teacher education* (pp. 111–156). Mahwah, NJ: Lawrence Erlbaum Associates, Inc.

CHAPTER 7

Down for the Ride but Not for the Die

Theatre as Language for Incarcerated Girls

Maisha T. Winn

Every year from August through May, an ensemble of the not-so-usual suspects gathers in the waiting rooms of three southeastern regional youth detention centers (RYDCs) to prepare for playwriting and performance workshops with incarcerated girls. RYDCs are transitional centers for detained youth while they are waiting for their court dates to learn their fate. During these monthly 2-day workshops, the girls—hereby referred to as student artists—learn how to build ensemble through a variety of exercises and physical warm-ups in a program called Girl Time. Engaging the writing process through a series of brainstorming activities, student artists are put into pairs to write plays that revisit their life experiences. The girls work with teaching artists who are not only employed by a woman-centered theatre company, Our Place, but who also serve the community in various ways: as women's reproductive health advocates, an organizer of a youth radio program, and teachers in creative and drama programs throughout the city. Together, these teaching artists have committed themselves to working with incarcerated teen girls; thus, they position themselves as advocates for issues that impact the lives of girls and women.

Taking these things into consideration, this chapter examines how teaching artists in a women-centered theatre company help adjudicated teen girls use playwriting and performance to develop critical literacies. The term adjudicated refers to youth who have been tried or have had a decision made about their case. In essence, student artists "think and thus act for themselves"—by writing and performing in plays written by their peers (Fraden, 2001, p. 70). Student artists develop critical literacies in the Girl

Time program by re-reading, reinterpreting, and reimagining these scripts with the guidance of teaching artists and with the help of their peers. By re-reading scripts, both lived and imagined, these young playwrights and actors transform subaltern voices into voices of resistance while talking back and acquiescing to institutions of power. They also reinterpret scripts when they rehearse and perform their work. Student artists, teaching artists, and their audiences—junior correctional officers (JCOs), parents/guardians, and "outsiders"—who experience these plays are able to reimagine the lives of girls beyond the walls of detention centers. Therefore, theatre and the process of working in community to create and produce a play can help formerly incarcerated teen girls shift from the discourse of individualized failure to one that generates dialogue among the audience. For student artists, the process of writing a play is also about agency—having control over how their story is represented to others. Issues of representation guide the questions that the larger study poses, including:

- In what ways do playwriting and performance assist or enable incarcerated and formerly incarcerated teen girls in regional youth detention centers to revisit positions of power?
- When do they use playwriting and performance to talk back or acquiesce to institutions of power in their lives?

For the purpose of this chapter, I focus on a particular play, *Ride or Die*, written by Sanaa and Kaylen during one of the 2-day workshops at a regional youth detention center (RYDC) and interpreted by their peers in the extended summer program for girls who have been released. I examine the recurring theme "ride or die" because of its implications in the lives of girls who live in impoverished communities, attend underserved schools, and who are often "compelled to crime"—to borrow Richie's words—by participating in illegal activities with profound consequences (Richie, 1996). To define "ride or die" in the context of the student artists' lives, I defer to the girls themselves. "Ride or die" often refers to a relationship (typically between a man and a woman) that gives both parties a false sense of power. To "ride" is to be an active participant in often illegal activities or to be readily available for anything while serving as a partner and confidante as defined by the dominant member of the relationship. In some instances, participants in these relationships believe they have no other choice but to engage in the activities, an idea to which I return later in this chapter. Relationships with this dynamic are not limited to heterosexual relationships; queer youth, and lesbian girls in particular, have been forced into heterosexual relationships to protect themselves from the backlash they have received for their sexual identity by acquiescing to straight males for protection from homophobic predators (Richie, 2005). To "die" is to accept consequences that result from the ride. Although consequences do not always end in physical death, "die" can also refer to taking responsibility for an act and serving time in a jail or prison. Alternatively, one student artist asserted that "ride or die" could be affirming; a woman or girl could help her significant other begin a new life after incarceration. A "ride or die chick," then, is a woman or girl who is willing to "stick with" her significant other, which, as one student artist posits, may require one to "put [his/her] life in somebody." This construction of "ride or die," which did not originate in the urban, or inner-city, neighborhoods where many of the student artists emerged, has roots in a love story made widely known in American popular culture.

POPULAR CULTURE AND THE MAKING OF URBAN LEGENDS

Studies of popular culture and its role in education have examined ways to foster critical literacies among urban youth (Dolby, 2003; Jocson, 2005; Morrell, 2004, 2008). Dolby argues that popular culture "has the capacity to intervene in the most critical civic issues and to shape public opinion" (Dolby, 2003, p. 259). Scholarship on the use of popular culture in classrooms has looked beyond its mere relevance to students' lives (Fisher, 2007; Hill & Vasudevan, 2007; Kinloch, 2005). For example, Morrell (2004) posits that there are rigorous literacy tasks involved in employing popular culture, including helping students with "carefully discerning and interacting with the messages that bombard them on a daily basis" (pp. 44–45). Popular culture, then, can be viewed as a text that is "received by people and acted on, or as a 'lived experience' that is created by the people" (Dolby, 2003, p. 259). However, for youth and the adults who are their guardians and for teachers who are not engaged in practices that identify and critique messages in popular culture, there can be severe consequences. Meiners argues that "mainstream mass media" is also responsible for "the movement of youth of color into the prison industrial complex (PIC)" (2007, p. 82). In other words, people who have limited engagement with particular communities will rely on media images. Additionally, Black and Brown youth consistently see themselves portrayed as "superpredators" and "gangbangers" on television, in movies, and in the news.

Indeed, the "ride or die" trope is prevalent in urban America, where some young women have become "drug mules," have withheld evidence from law enforcement, and have been convinced that as a woman or a girl they will not get into as much trouble as their male counterparts. Stories like "Kemba's Nightmare," which was featured by *Emerge* magazine in 1996, depicted the reality that young women and girls were "casualties in the drug war" just as much as young men (Smith, 2005, p. 107). Kemba Smith, a college student, was romantically linked to a young man in the drug trade.

When her boyfriend was targeted, Smith was targeted as well and was eventually sentenced to 24.5 years with no prior convictions under the mandatory minimum sentencing laws. (Former president Bill Clinton, however, did grant clemency to Kemba Smith toward the end of his term.)

On the outset one could easily point a finger toward hip-hop music and culture, as people often do when there are problems concerning youth culture. Tupac's famed song "Me and My Girlfriend" certainly had its share of radio play, as did Jay-Z and Beyonce's retooling of the song. In these songs, women or girls follow the male's lead, for better or for worse. Women who are down to ride or die are upheld as devoted, dependable, and worthy of a man's attention and commitment. Consequently, those who are not down to ride or die are viewed as cowardly, untrustworthy, and replaceable, if not disposable. Both songs specifically cite the notorious Bonnie and Clyde crime couple. Bonnie Parker was only 19 when she met Clyde Campion Barrow in Texas in 1930. One of Parker's first known "ride or die" actions for Barrow was smuggling a gun to him in jail that he used to escape. By the time officers located Barrow, Parker, and other members of the Bonnie and Clyde gang on May 23, 1934, the gang had reportedly committed countless murders and robberies and had been involved with kidnapping. Bonnie and Clyde were eventually gunned down by officers in Sailes, Bienville Parish, Louisiana. The fact that this young White criminal couple in Texas in the 1930s has somehow influenced the lives of incarcerated teen girls and urban youth throughout the United States is not completely unexplainable, given that the ethos of Bonnie and Clyde hovers over American popular culture.

Although the most obvious artifact may be Warren Beatty and Faye Dunnaway's version of *Bonnie and Clyde*, released in 1967, American popular culture has always enjoyed its share of gangster movies and entertainment with a clear "rebel/criminal." In a study of incarcerated women who participate in The Medea Project: Theatre for Incarcerated Women, Fraden (2001) argues, "The rebel/criminal has always been an object of fascination in modern times . . . but alongside fascination, and even glorification, is a heightened fear of the criminal and political manipulation of that fear" (p. 128).

For teen girls who are facing abject poverty, the rebel/criminal fascination can have severe repercussions beyond movies, songs, and video games. Young people, and teen girls in particular, read and critique these images especially in a climate where they are becoming public enemies. However, it is not enough to consider the ways popular culture influences girls to participate in these relationships. Readings or misreadings of popular culture can also impact public policy and people's perceptions of who gets counted as a criminal and who is considered a citizen. Therefore, popular culture not only shapes the paths that youth select, but also influences how young people are situated in public policy (Fisher, 2006).

LANGUAGE, LITERACY, AND THE
SCHOOL-TO-PRISON PIPELINE

As "the world's most avid incarcerator" (Sudbury, 2004), the United States has earned its reputation as an incarceration nation by imprisoning more people than any other country. According to Fraden (2001), at the turn of the 21st century there were 1.8 million incarcerated people in the United States, 600,000 on parole, 3 million on probation, and 60,000 in the juvenile justice system. Currently, there are 2.3 million adults incarcerated in the United States out of an adult population totaling approximately 230 million (see Pew Center for the States Report, 2008). Scholars argue that the incarceration rate in the Unites States is both "gendered and raced" (Meiners, 2007). To be sure, the U.S. Department of Justice, Bureau of Justice Statistics report, authored by Snyder and Sickmund (2006), noted that 1 in 36 Latino men and 1 in 15 Black men age 18 or older are incarcerated. For Black men ages 20–34 the numbers are even more dismal; 1 in 9 in this age group is incarcerated.

The "gendering" of these rates suggests that there is 12 times the number of women incarcerated in the United States since 1970. Women and girls of color are being incarcerated throughout the world in disproportionate numbers. The recent report from the Pew Center on the States reveals that 1 in 355 White women is incarcerated as opposed to 1 in 100 Black women ages 35–39. The report insists that the female prison population "is burgeoning at a far brisker pace" than in previous years (Pew Center for the States, 2008, p. 3). Teen girls, and Black girls in particular, are "overrepresented" in the juvenile justice system (Fine & McClelland, 2006). Although there is a growing number of African American girls being incarcerated, "there is no new crime wave among Black girls" (Richie, 2005, pp. 75–76). In fact, Richie argues, "Despite the image that has been constructed of them, girls in jails, prisons, and detention centers and under state supervision are less dangerous to the world around them than the world is to them" (p. 76).

Fine and McClelland (2006) situate the growing numbers of incarcerated teen girls in a larger discourse of abstinence-only and heteronormativity in public school curriculum. Extending Fine's research on sexuality and education (Fine, 1988), Fine and McClelland assert that "abstinence only until marriage" (AOUM) curriculum further marginalizes teen girls who have been victims of sexual abuse and rape. Fine and McClelland's critique of this curriculum is intertwined with the large numbers of incarcerated girls and women who have reported that they were victims of sexual assault, abuse, and rape. Girls who have been abused are often silenced in the discourse of abstinence-only and not allowed to be considered innocent. Perhaps most disconcerting is that these girls need spaces to discuss, critique, and become knowledgeable about their bodies and their rights; however, they are seldom, if ever, afforded this opportunity.

Undoubtedly, literacy researchers and educators must join the dialogue that is taking place in urban education circles (Fisher, Purcell, & May, 2009; Fisher, 2005). The need for critical literacies in the lives of Black and Brown youth who have been routed through the school-to-prison pipeline is the difference between life and "civic death"—if not physical death. Gilmore (2007) uses the term *civic death* to refer to the denial of basic rights that are a result of carrying a jail or prison record. One of the most prevalent examples of "civic death" is the prohibition of voting for convicted felons. Physical death, according to Gilmore, refers to the unhealthy and unsafe conditions of jails and prisons. The sorting and surveillance of children in grades K–12 through procedures such as referrals and expulsions are "strong predictors" of incarceration. When schools are more concerned with students walking in a straight line and being quiet than engaging in discussions, higher-order thinking tasks, and inquiry-driven curriculum, particular students will only view school as punitive and puritanical. In the economic landscape of the United States, young people need multiple literacies to be considered for jobs with security and to have a variety of choices with regard to higher education. In a recent edited volume examining literacy as a "civil right," Lipman (2008) argues that the denial of "forms of literacy that are highly valued . . . is part of relegating whole communities to the low-wage, military, and prison-prep tracks in society" (p. 62). In resisting such relegation, especially of formerly incarcerated girls of color, I employ Boal's (1979, 1995/2006) idea that theatre is language. Boal posits that the language of theatre is especially helpful for prisoners (and guards) in repositioning them as active participants who re-create lives after imprisonment. To understand how the language and teaching of theatre can help incarcerated and formerly incarcerated teen girls develop critical literacies, I discuss my critical ethnography of the Girl Time playwriting and performance program. I focus on data collected during the 2006–2007 Girl Time sessions.

METHODS

This multi-sited ethnography follows participants across sites including three southeastern regional youth detention centers where the playwriting and performance workshops take place, a multi-service center where part of the summer program is held, and a playhouse that hosts the final part of the summer program, including a public performance. I have chosen a multi-sited critical ethnographic approach because of the shifting discourse in scholarship examining the lives of incarcerated and formerly incarcerated women. Sudbury (2004) asserts that most of this scholarship has focused on one-on-one interviews, which often lead to stories that personalize failure. Here, I hope to address larger systemic issues by moving across spaces with participants and focusing on student artists' cultural productions and interactions with written and performed texts. Girl Time allows me to move between the institutions that have detained the girls and those that seek their freedom through oral and written language. Also, a critical ethnography presupposes the researcher is "profoundly interested in the relationship of power (re)produced in spaces as marked by differently positioned subjectivities" (Gallagher, 2007, p. 56).

Participants

Participants include Girl Time teaching artists who volunteer to work at the 2-day RYDC workshops. Teaching artists are women involved in the arts in a variety of ways, including acting (in theatre, television, and films), costume design, and teaching. The summer program included four teachers, three of whom taught during the RYDC workshops, as well as the program director and founder. Student artists are girls who participate in the Girl Time summer program after being released from RYDCs or YDCs. Some are still on probation or under state-sponsored supervision. The summer 2007 cohort of student artists included 9 girls ranging in age from 14 to 16. Three girls had previously participated in the Girl Time summer program. Four girls learned about the summer program through their peer participation in a RYDC workshop while the remainder learned about the program through a probation officer or social worker. The youngest participant was the sister of a student artist. All of the girls in this cohort were African American and all but one were born in the same urban southeastern city at the same public hospital.

Data Collection and Analysis

As a participant observer, I kept fieldnotes at each site during teaching artist pre- and post-meetings and during the workshops. During the summer program I collected ethnographic video of sessions including warm-up activities, and sessions where student artists discussed and prepared for plays, the rehearsals, and the final performance. Also, I collected copies of all plays, which are a part of the Girl Time archive. I interviewed the core group of Girl Time teaching artists, including the founder and artistic director of the performance group that houses the program and the Girl Time program director. Interviews with teaching artists were conducted at my home at the convenience of each artist. Each interview was videotaped and accompanied by detailed notes. Student artists in the summer 2007 cohort, with the exception of one who declined, were interviewed at the multi-service center during the course of the program.

I used N6 qualitative research software to manage data. For this particular case, I worked with a transcription from the session for the *Ride or Die* pre-meeting with student artists who were cast in the play led by one of the teaching artists. Additionally, I worked with transcribed interviews of student artists who acted in the play and the student artist who wrote the play. Student plays were coded to find recurring themes such as "ride or die" and/or "Bonnie and Clyde." Coded fieldnotes from the workshop in which *Ride or Die* was produced, the summer program where it was performed, and interview transcripts with the playwright and actors were a part of this specific case. I used discourse analysis tools, and specifically Gee's (1999) questions for understanding situated meanings. Gee posits that a discourse analysis "by asking questions about how language, at a given time and place, is used to construe the aspects of the situation network as realized at that time and place and how the aspects of the situation network simultaneously give meaning to that language" (p. 92). Gee's framework was useful for learning about what was taking place in discussions around this theme and seeing how the plays became mediating tools among student artists, teaching artists, and audience members.

Researcher's Role

I was a participant observer, and my role changed depending on program needs. I have been trained as a teaching artist in Girl Time and have formally taught when there was a shortage of teaching artists for particular workshops. Prior to the study, I had very limited experience acting and ensemble-building in theatre. Spradley (1980) identifies five types of participant observers ranging from a "non-participant" to a "complete participant." Using Spradley's typology, I was an "active participant" in the summer program who learned in-depth about the "cultural rules" of a particular community (p. 60). Whether or not I participated as a formal "teacher," I engaged in all ensemble-building exercises and was given a role in leading or facilitating part of the workshops. I helped scribe for student artists as they brainstormed ideas and I worked side-by-side with new teaching artists.

RE-READING THE SCRIPT

The play *Ride or Die* is a story about a young woman, Starkima (also known as "Star"), who is involved with a married man named "Smoke." In the opening scene, Smoke and his wife, "Ashley," are just starting to wake up. As they both stretch and realize it is the morning, Smoke immediately barks at his wife, "Where my breakfast at?" When Ashley reasonably points out that she, too, just woke up, Smoke responds by slapping her and continues to threaten her until he is interrupted by the phone. As Ashley begrudgingly walks to the kitchen to make Smoke's breakfast, he proceeds to have a phone conversation with his girlfriend, or "ride or die chick," Star. As Smoke questions Star, "You sold all that work for me?" (Translation: Did you sell the drugs I gave you?) and "You turned up them tricks for me?" (Translation: Did you prostitute your body?), Star confirms, "Baby, I got all that money!" Star's reward is Smoke's affirmation, "That's why you my down chick." He instructs her to put on something "sexy" and leaves Ashley with the untouched breakfast, but not before he asserts that he wants *his* house clean by the time he returns.

When Star decides she does not want to "share" Smoke with his wife, she calls Ashley to torment her about the affair. However, when Star sees Smoke again, she lies and tells him that Ashley called her instead. In order to comfort Star and protect his income, Smoke makes it clear that he will put Ashley in her place once and for all. When Smoke confronts Ashley, he asserts: "[Star] is my money maker, my ride or die chick—she do thangs you won't! Things you don't do!" As Ashley tries to explain her side of the story, Smoke chokes her until her body becomes lifeless. When Smoke calls Star to tell her of his murderous deed, Star is overwhelmed rather than overjoyed. By the time Smoke gets to Star's hotel room, the police are hiding behind the door, anxiously waiting to arrest him for his wife's murder. As the police officer handcuffs Smoke, he looks at Star incredulously and shouts, "I thought you were my ride or die chick." Star proclaims, "I was down for the ride, but I ain't down for the DIE!"

When student artists first performed this play, they were met with thunderous applause and shouting by their peers. In each subsequent performance, girls in the audience jumped out of their seats and gave each other multiple high-fives. One of the teaching artists marveled, "This is one of the first times the woman was not the sacrificial lamb for the man." Given the success of the performance and the powerful representation of female identity, I believe it is important to revisit the pre-meeting that led to the performance. During the pre-meeting, Kaya, the Girl Time program director and director for this play, asked the student artists to explain what they liked about the play:

> KAYA: We're going to do this talk that we usually do like we did the last time but we're going to abbreviate it a little bit but it's really important. I want you to think about your characters—first of all tell me what you like. Tell me what you like about the play. One specific thing.
>
> DENISE: I have something! I have something to say y'all. I like that I get to be the cop because I get to put the handcuffs on somebody.

KAYA: Good. Good—Good. What part rings true for you? Or maybe
    it didn't happen in your life but to somebody you know or some-
    thing you saw on TV. What part rings true for you?

NIA (RAISING HER HAND): See he—wait hold on. In this (pointing to
    the script)

KAYA: Unh huh

NIA: He-he-he kind of the boss in this.

KAYA (INTERRUPTING NIA): I—I'm kind of

NIA: Oh. I'm (pointing to herself) kind of the boss so I like being in
    control. But in the end cause—personally I wouldn't kill nobody
    but uh . . . I thought—I picked the one who is actually going to
    snitch on me in the end even though I know it was wrong, you
    know what I'm saying? She go'n snitch on me in the end so either
    way it goes I was either going to get locked up for that or some-
    thing else—

Denise, the student artist with the most Girl Time experience, delighted
in the opportunity to be the authority figure in this particular context. Not
only was she playing a police officer, but she was able to handcuff Smoke.
Denise's appropriation of incarceration discourse was not just a way to embrace her character, but also an opportunity to be on the side of the "law,"
given that she is not the pursuant but the pursuer. After Denise responded,
Kaya changed the question to elicit more detailed responses. In the new
question, "What part rings true for you?", Kaya left space for students to
opt out of disclosing personal experiences by reminding them the stories
could come from other sources like television. Nia, who played Smoke,
wanted to discuss her character, but Kaya had to remind her to use the first
person. It was important to Nia that she underscored to the group that she
would never kill anyone. After establishing distance from Smoke and his
actions, Nia shifted to first-person voice. In fact when I interviewed Nia,
a self-described "female stud lady," she indicated that playing a man was
"easy." However, playing an abusive man was an entirely different matter:

> I'm not an abusive person and I don't sell drugs . . . so it was hard for
> me to get in someone else's place as far as beating your female and
> killing someone. I'd never do that so it was hard putting myself in that
> position.

Student artists relished the opportunity to play the male characters. In
most of the original plays written by student playwrights in the detention
center workshops, men appear as emotionally and physically abusive. The
girls play male roles with great pride as they try to impress peers with authentic linguistic practices. When a student portrayed a male character to

the satisfaction of her peers, the audience members rose to their feet, raised their fists in the air and called out to the performer. During the "talk-backs" after performances and read-throughs, most girls favor male characters and praise student artists who demonstrate the most authenticity. Nia and her peers were teaching and learning a new language—the language of theatre. Boal (1979) asserts that theatre is both a "weapon for liberation" (p. ix) as well as a distinct language: "By learning a new language, a person acquires a new way of knowing reality and passing that knowledge to others . . ." (1979, p. 121). In the discussion, Nia noted that it was particularly troubling that Smoke chose Star over Ashley since ultimately Star snitched on him. Lisa, who played the "ride or die chick" had an opportunity to share her thoughts about her character:

> KAYA (TURNING TO LISA): What do you like? Any certain part of it you like or anything that rings true for you?
> LISA: I like the end when she says she was down for the ride instead of the die
> KAYA: What do you like about it?
> LISA: I mean . . . I was like his girl or trick or whatever you call it and she was I think his wife. And I mean, I know I shouldn't have called her and it was wrong but I don't know (Lisa starts to shrug).
> KAYA: What are you saying, "I was down for the ride but I ain't down for the die?"
> LISA: I mean was down for the ride for him. You know I was going through everything for him—
> KAYA: You're getting money too!
> LISA: Yeah, yeah.
> KAYA: You're getting something out of it too don't you think?
> NIA: I know man.
> KAYA: I think you're a business woman . . . so you're down for that but you're not down for what?
> LISA: To die. I mean I'm not down with like—
> NIA: Killin' folk.
> SHOSHANA: You like that she stands up for herself.
> LISA: Yeah!
> [Nia starts hitting her chest with her fist.]

Star's declaration was powerful because it conveyed the idea that for many of the girls, there are levels of wrong. Therefore, crime and criminals were not fixed in the minds of student artists, but rather permeable based on what kind of crime was committed. Because many student artists have been detained for running away or survival crimes such as prostitution, they do not consider such acts as severe as the one Smoke committed by abusing and murdering his wife.

Kaya and Lisa's understanding of Star differed greatly. Lisa viewed Star as a victim who was passive and a bit reluctant to stand up to Smoke. Kaya disrupted this idea with her observation about Star, "You're getting money too!" Here, Kaya repositions Star as an active participant, or as a "business woman," in Smoke's activities. Kaya was not only pushing Lisa to think about her character, but also shift the discourse from women or girls having to go along with a man's program to women or girls with the ability to make their own choices. Kaya also wanted to provoke Lisa in order for her to consider Star's complexities. She asks, "So you were down for that but you're not down for what?" As this discussion unfolds, Nia began to instigate as she embraced Smoke's character. Shoshana, the intern, took a more sympathetic stance toward Star's decision and thus Lisa's portrayal of Star. Shoshana saw Lisa as being proud that her character stood up for herself at the end. Although Lisa was seemingly protective of Star during the pre-meeting, she was more critical of her character during her interview. Lisa maintained that Star's declaration, "I was down for the ride but not for the die" was still her favorite line: "[Star] just lets go . . . that was strong words . . . it was wrong how she did him because you supposed to be there 'til the end. She lied. Star was wrong." Here, Lisa is torn between Star's powerful words and actions and what Lisa considers contradictory actions. Lisa appreciated how Star "just let go" and believed Star's words were strong. However, Lisa also thought that Star was "supposed to be there 'til the end." Lisa's response begs the question: When is it acceptable to change directions or choose another path? Ride or die, in the context of Lisa's response, was a contract—either you were in or out, but there were shades of gray. This was a real scenario for student artists; they did not need to be convinced that this story was possible if not true:

> DENISE: I like the part of the play when Ashley and Smoke—I mean stuff happens like that for real. Folks just wake up and get pimp slapped by they nigga' 'cause—oh—they man because they ain't fixed dinner or something to eat and I know people like that in real life. Like I know some folks that some stuff happened like that not the part where he kills her but stuff happens like this in real life.
>
> KAYA: Where the man turns on you.
>
> DENISE: Yeah. Yeah.
>
> KAYA (TO GABRIELLE): What do you like about the play?
>
> GABRIELLE: The part when he get locked up in the end because he was a bad person.
>
> [Laughter]

Denise was so convinced that the story represented reality that she became very comfortable in her explanation. In her effort to demonstrate the realness, Denise recounted women who "wake up and get pimp slapped." Denise corrected herself when she used the n-word and replaced it with "they man." While there were no written rules in Girl Time about censorship, the n-word and other vulgar language were not allowed in the RYDCs. Gabrielle, who participated in previous summer programs, took on Ashley's role so well that she was rather passive during the discussion. However, Gabrielle was clear that she liked the fact that Smoke got "locked up." This was not the only instance of Gabrielle viewing the world through an either/or lens. When she described her own life, she explained that when she was in elementary school she was "smart," "happy," and "good." However, according to Gabrielle, once she went to junior high school, she "turned bad." In Gabrielle's eyes, Smoke was a "bad person" and that was the main fact to take from the play. Katie moved the discussion from likes and dislikes to a more focused character study:

KAYA: Now close your eyes for a second. Think of one thing that your character really wants. What does your character want? What does your character really want? What are you trying to get?

DENISE: Lock up Smoke.

KAYA: Yeah, not just Smoke but—

NIA: I'm trying to get to the money really and truly and I ain't need nobody is stopping me—

KAYA: Excellent. You want money.

NIA: Yeah.

KAYA: That's a good thing. You can go through that all the while. You get pretty crazy over money, don't ya'?

NIA NODS IN AFFIRMATION.

KAYA (TO GABRIELLE AND LISA): What do you guys want?

GABRIELLE: I think I wanted love and attention 'cause he wasn't showin' me enough love. He'll leave me and I'll still be there with him.

KAYA: Do y'all have a baby or not? You can decide.

NIA (GRINNING AT GABRIELLE): Yeah girl.

KAYA (TO LISA): What do you want?

KAYA (TO NIA AND GABRIELLE): How long you been together?

NIA: Five years.

GABRIELLE: Five and a half years.

KAYA: That's a long time to turn around and kill her.

NIA: Oh I killed you (pointing to Lisa) or I killed her (pointing to Gabrielle)?

EVERYONE AT ONCE: You killed her (pointing to Gabrielle).

NIA: Oh, we only been together for a year. No, we been together
    (voice trails off)
. . .
KAYA: Y'all talk about it. Y'all can decide. This is something that the
    audience doesn't have to know.
NIA: 'Cause I wouldn't want my kids to see nothing like that. So I'd
    say we been together for about five and a half years. No kids.
KAYA: Do you think Smoke cares what his kids see?
NIA: I don't know.

Student artists learned the skill of making inferences by creating the backstory for their characters. As Nia and Gabrielle tried to imagine the history of Smoke and Ashley's relationship, time became a central issue. Kaya noted that 5 and a half years might be a long time for a couple to be together only to have the husband murder the wife. Nia was not convinced of this perception; however, she was adamant that Smoke and Ashley did not have children. Nia's context clue was that her character committed murder and that fact in itself was enough for her to conclude that no children were involved. Nia, now voluntarily using the first person, explained, "'Cause I wouldn't want my kids to see nothing like that . . .", referring to Smoke choking Ashley. Kaya questioned whether or not a man who murders his wife would even care about what his children witnessed:

KAYA: I'm just putting it out there. You decide. What do you want?
    (Turning to Lisa)
NIA: What you want baby?
NIA: Get that money.
LISA: Star wants—
KAYA: I want.
LISA: I want money. I want Smoke thrown in jail, I guess.
SHOSHANA: What's the bigger thing about it?
NIA: 'Cause if I had never kilt Ashley?
GABRIELLE: You want to make him happy.
LISA: Yeah.
NIA: Yeah. So::: What you—I mean—
LISA: I'll do whatever—
KAYA: You::: want to be happy.
LISA (ADDRESSING NIA): Yeah, I'll do whatever to make you feel right.
NIA: Because if I had never kilt Ashley . . . so would you?
LISA: I want to be happy—

By this time Nia has morphed into Smoke; she flirts with the other girls who smile at her and shake their heads. Lisa was still having a difficult time with her character, Star, but tried to reconcile what her character wanted out of this situation. Initially, Lisa follows Denise and Gabrielle's one-dimensional view of Smoke that positioned him as the sole villain. However, the intern, Shoshanna, and Nia pushed Lisa to take it one step further. Nia suggests that if Smoke had not murdered Ashley, then Star may have continued the relationship. Gabrielle, who had been relatively quiet throughout the discussion, forges a potential link between Ashley and Star; these two women were focused on pleasing Smoke even to their own detriment. Nia asserted her point again but framed it as a question in the hopes of learning if Lisa believed Star would have given Smoke another chance had he not committed murder. Lisa left Nia's question unanswered, but remained determined to portray Star as full of yearning and desire. Shoshanna, not completely satisfied but building empathy for Star, made a final attempt to have the group consider Star's perspective:

> SHOSHANNA: 'Cause now Smoke lo:::ves money, right? But he's a little crazy about it. Everybody needs money right? To pay the bills and things like that. That might be how Star is—she might need money to pay the bills but she's not okay with it if it means bad things are happening—
>
> NIA: Goin' killin' people.
>
> KAYA: And figure out do you really like him or are you just working with him?
>
> LISA: I like him. I like him.
>
> KAYA: You just workin' for me.
>
> KAYA: Okay. But you say here, "I got this. She won't be his wife for long."
>
> NIA: Told you.
>
> KAYA: You say some things and you turn him in but you don't have to decide that right now.

Shoshanna's final push helped Nia make her case. Nia, who started out trying to distinguish herself from Smoke, did not want her character to be the only one who was wrong or "bad." Nia challenged Lisa's depiction of Star as only wanting to make Smoke happy and going along with his plans. Continuing to instigate, Nia asserted, "You (Star) just workin' for me," as if to say that Star really did not care about Smoke but wanted money.

CRITICAL PERSPECTIVE

One of the most important lessons teachers and teacher educators can learn from Girl Time, and the *Ride or Die* play and performance in particular, is the importance of youth advocacy through curricular choices. Playwriting and performance are essential tools for urban youth who have important stories to tell but who are seldom asked to tell them. The power of theatre, in the words of Boal (2006), is that it "helps make dialogue possible" (p. 116). Given the "circuits of dispossession" (Fine & Ruglis, 2009), and the consistent diploma denial for urban youth, the need for dialogue between and among students, teachers, and policymakers could not be more timely and important.

The work presented in this chapter demonstrates the ways teaching and teacher education extend beyond the walls of traditional school spaces in effecting positive change in the lives of urban youth. It is essential for teachers, teacher educators, and others invested in the lives and literacies of young people to understand how Girl Time, in addition to other programs across the country, can serve as sites of resistance and places to understand how and why youth, particularly girls of color, feel vulnerable. Teachers can take up aspects of this work in their classrooms through innovative writing activities that are based in collaboration, performance, dialogue, empathy, and reflection. The opportunity to create plays and perform in them gives youth, in this case incarcerated and formerly incarcerated girls, a window to view alternatives as real or possible. Learning how to become another character invites students to question and critique these scenarios without focusing on themselves.

REFERENCES

Boal, A. (2006). *The aesthetics of the oppressed*. London and New York: Routledge.

Boal, A. (2006). *The rainbow of desire: The Boal method of theatre and therapy*. London and New York: Routledge. (Original work published 1995)

Boal, A. (1979). *Theatre of the oppressed*. New York: Theatre Communications Group.

Dolby, N. (2003). Popular culture and democratic practice. *Harvard Educational Review, 73*(3), 258–284.

Fine, M. (1988). Sexuality, schooling, and adolescent females: The missing discourse of desire. *Harvard Educational Review, 58*(1), 29–53.

Fine, M., & Ruglis, J. (2009). Circuits and conquences of dispossession: The racialized realignment of the public sphere for U.S. youth. *Transforming Anthropology, 17*(1), 20–33.

Fine, M., & McClelland, S. I. (2006). Sexuality and Desire: Still Missing after All These Years. *Harvard Educational Review, 76*(3), 297–338.

Fisher, M. T., Purcell, S. S., & May, R. (2009). Process, product, and playmaking. *English Education, 4*(4), 337–355.

Fisher, M. T. (2005). Literocracy: Liberating language and creating possibilities. *English Education, 37*(2), 92–95.

Fisher, M. T. (2006). Earning "dual degrees": Black bookstores as alternative knowledge spaces. *Anthropology and Education Quarterly, 37*(1), 83–99.

Fisher, M. T. (2007). *Writing in rhythm: Creating literate traditions for urban youth.* New York: Teachers College Press.

Fraden, R. (2001). *Imagining Medea: Rhodessa Jones and Theater for Incarcerated Women.* Chapel Hill: University of North Carolina Press.

Gallagher, K. (2007). *The theater of urban: Youth and schooling in dangerous times.* Toronto: University of Toronto Press.

Gee, J. P. (1999). *An introduction to discourse analysis: Theory and method.* New York: Routledge.

Gilmore, R. (2007). *Golden gulag: Prisons, surplus, crisis, and opposition in globalizing California.* Berkeley: University of California Press.

Hill, M. L., & Vasudevan, L. (Eds.). (2007). *Media, learning, and sites of possibility.* New York: Peter Lang.

Jocson, K. (2005). "Taking it to the mic": Pedagogy of June Jordan's *Poetry for the people* and partnership with an urban high school. *English Education, 37*(2), 132–148.

Kinloch, V. F. (2005). Poetry, literacy and creativity: Fostering effective learning strategies in an urban classroom. *English Education, 37*(2), 96–114.

Lipman, P. (2008). Education policy, the politics of race, and the neoliberal agenda: The urgency to reclaim social justice in literacy teaching. In S. Greene (Ed.), *Literacy as a civil right: Reclaiming social justice in literacy teaching and learning.* New York: Peter Lang.

Meiners, E. R. (2007). *Right to be hostile: Schools, prisons, and the making of public enemies.* New York: Routledge.

Morrell, E. (2008). *Critical literacy and urban youth: Pedagogies of access, dissent, and liberation.* New York: Routledge.

Morrell, E. (2004). *Linking literacy and popular culture: Finding connections for lifelong learning.* Norwood, MA: Christopher-Gordon.

Pew Center on the States. (2008). *One in 100 behind bars in America 2008.* Washington, DC: The Pew Charitable Trusts.

Richie, B. (2005). Queering antiprison work: African American lesbians in the juvenile justice system. In J. Sudbury (Ed.), *Global lockdown: Race, gender, and the prison-industrial complex.* New York: Routledge.

Richie, B. (1996). *Compelled to crime: The gender entrapment of battered black women.* New York: Routledge.

Smith, K. (2004). Modern day slavery: Inside the prison-industrial complex. In J. Sudbury (Ed.), *Global lockdown: Race, gender, and the prison-industrial complex.* New York: Routledge.

Spradley, J. P. (1980). *Participant observation.* Australia, Canada, Mexico, Singapore, Spain, United Kingdom, United States: Wadsworth.

Synder, H. N., & Sickmund, M. (2006). Juvenile offenders and victims: 2006 national report. Washington, DC: U.S. Department of Justice, Office of Justice Programs, Office of Juvenile Justice and Delinquency Prevention.

Sudbury, J. (Ed.). (2004). *Global lockdown: Race, gender, and the prison-industrial complex.* New York: Routledge.

PART III

Studies on Popular Culture and Forms of Multimodality

Colleen Fairbanks and Detra Price-Dennis

Considering adolescents' uses of what they call "unsanctioned" literacy in classrooms, Heron-Hruby, Hagood, and Alvermann (2008) write:

> What is interesting about this situation is not that adolescents are slipping a meaningful part of their lives into schools and past classroom doors, but rather that young people have much to teach us, as adults, about the ways in which their uses of popular culture texts work to reference, discredit, or complement other standardizing practices, such as school literacies. (p. 314)

The chapters in this section, authored by Jocson and Cooks, Kim, and Paris and Kirkland, take seriously the potential of such agency and the possibilities of youth literacies to speak back/to school practices. In another sense, they also extend beyond speaking back/to. They provide a means of understanding the "verbal artistry," as Paris and Kirkland call it, that characterizes such literacies and reminds us of the serious playfulness and agency that, as English teachers, we value in such artistry.

The students, teachers, researchers, and activists in these chapters engage in literacy practices rooted in the exploration of "textual relationships of power" (Luke, 2000) whereby popular culture and critical pedagogy function as catalysts for resistance, critique, and hope. In this way, the students' textual performances become a means to push against the forces that would otherwise marginalize them and to put voice to other, more hopeful, possibilities. Conversely, these chapters also illustrate the importance of teachers who welcome students' "unsanctioned" literacy practices, help them read critically their own and others' texts, and create access for multiple literacies and languages. In this way, such teachers support students' efforts to compose textual performances that demonstrate students' capabilities in academic spaces. Jocson and Cooks, Kim, and Paris and Kirkland all foreground the sophisticated nature of the multiple literacy practices that urban youth engage as a result and in spite of the exclusion and marginalization they typically manage in school. When tools of popular culture such as hip-hop lyrics, MySpace, poetry, and texting converge with critical literacy, collective resistance against institutional inequities is set in motion. In each example, we gain a deeper understanding of how students draw on real life experiences to name; how their literacy practices revise standardized school practices; and how they disrupt barriers that interfere with their ability to compose, write, perform, and embody their own stories. In many ways, popular culture and literacy create a fracture in the classroom that gives space for students to assert their agency and their humanity.

REFERENCES

Heron-Hruby, A., Hagood, M. A., & Alvermann, D. E. (2008). Switching places and looking to adolescents for the practices that shape school literacies. *Reading & Writing Quarterly, 24*, 311–314.

Luke, A. (2000). Critical literacy in Australia: A matter of context and standpoint. *Journal of Adolescent and Adult Literacy, 43*(4), 448–461.

CHAPTER 8

Writing as a Site of Struggle

Popular Culture, Empowerment, and Politics of (In)Visibility

Korina Jocson and Jamal Cooks

In an era following George W. Bush administration's response to educational reform, factors such as ability tracking, de facto segregation, low expectations, and the use of non-innovative curricula, to name a few, still characterize the undemocratic or subtractive elements of schooling (Darling-Hammond, 1997; Noguera, 2003; Valenzuela, 1999). Many children attend schools that lack the capacity to build on or add to their strengths, culturally and linguistically. In particular, many children of historically marginalized groups in the United States have been relegated to positions of academic underperformance and blamed for their "own" failure. These conditions continue to mask a failed sociopolitical infrastructure and what has been termed an apartheid educational system (Kozol, 2006). Specifically, a major concern for educators is that many middle and high school students, especially low-income and students of color, lack grade-level writing skills. Based on national language arts frameworks/standards, African American students, for example, are scoring 30 points lower on reading assessments than their White counterparts (National Assessment of Educational Progress, 2008).

Adolescent literacy development is complex, requires an expanded notion of text (e.g., Internet, music, film, television, and so on), and draws on immediate feedback from adults and peers (Alvermann, Hinchman, Moore, Phelps, & Waff, 1998). Given that many students from nondominant backgrounds continue to perform below grade-level proficiency, teaching and research on adolescents must not only examine schooling contexts but also how adolescents and their teachers use literacy to teach and learn (Moje, Young, Readence, & Moore, 2000). In this chapter, part of our charge is to reconceptualize literacy and reexamine the incorporation of popular culture in the classroom. Many theoretical models have emerged that attempt to subvert the mainstream cultural expectations that exist in education and replace them with ways of learning that more fairly reflect the diversity of backgrounds in our schools. They go by a multiplicity of names such as culturally relevant pedagogy, cultural inclusion, and critical pedagogy, among others (Ladson-Billings, 1994; McLaren, 1994; Meier, 1996; Oakes & Lipton, 1999/2003). Bartolome (1994) succinctly describes the goals of these practices when she asserts the need for a humanizing pedagogy that respects and uses the realities, histories, and perspectives of students as an integral part of educational practice. An appropriate means to incorporate the real-life experiences of students is to incorporate popular culture into the teaching and learning process. By popular culture, we mean the various sites of ideological struggle between dominant and subordinate cultures. Specifically, we mean the terrains of exchange that can be expressed through music, art, film, television, magazines, newspapers, and other mass media forms. These terrains of exchange are permeable and provide ways for the meanings and positionalities of dominant and subordinate participants to shift in context. Popular culture is rife with power-laden values and customs that through relevant pedagogies and approaches can promote literacy development (Morrell, 2004).

Popular culture is gaining ground in many classrooms. Due in part to the changing nature of 21st-century literacies, more and more teachers employ a response-based cultural studies approach to engage students (Carey-Webb, 2001). Although this is so, there are still those who oppose using popular culture in the classroom as a teaching tool. Important to note are the few reasons why. First, some teachers may be unfamiliar with the prevalent popular culture of today's youth. Teachers need to learn and understand youth popular culture, including poetry and spoken word, in order to make connections with students and to help build critical consciousness. Second, some teachers may feel that forms of popular culture to enhance classroom instruction are inherently amoral, inappropriate, or a waste of time, and they are not willing to sacrifice classroom norms to use them. Certainly, aspects of popular culture have had a history, even if unfairly maligned, of violence and overrepresentation of sex and criminal behavior. However, this history entrenched in the commodification of particular cultural forms does not preclude the value of other existing forms. Teachers need to assess their feelings, their comfort levels, and their boundaries before using popular culture in the classroom. Finally, some teachers may have attempted to integrate popular culture into their curricula; however, the material may not have been as relevant to students, leading to mixed or poor results. Eliciting students' knowledge and experience is key in the process (Cooks, 2004; Kirkland, 2004). For us, the incorporation of popular culture into classroom curriculum should be purposeful and meaningful.

YOUTH POETRY

Scholars have examined the relevance of poetry in the lives of urban youth, particularly among youth of color, in ways where youth poetry is situated within and responds to aspects of popular culture (Fisher, 2007; Jocson, 2008; Kinloch, 2005; Mahiri, 2004; Meacham, 2003; Morrell & Duncan-Andrade, 2002). Their work has provided alternative views to traditional top-down approaches common in schools and classrooms. Situated amid a growing hip-hop culture, its focus has been to tap into students' experiences and funds of knowledge in ways that would allow for culturally relevant exchanges with texts and interactions between teachers and students. Such perspectives on student-centered approaches emphasize the power of youth voice and the importance of creating a learning environment that strengthens and nurtures it (Weis & Fine, 1993). In line with such perspectives, this chapter draws on theories of empowerment and critical pedagogy to examine the experiences of students and teachers engaging poetry through a university-urban school partnership in northern California. What follows provides a lens into a unique educational project that brings outside collaborators into high school English classrooms. Central to the discussion are students writing about relations of power and the politics of (in)visibility, and teachers changing pedagogies while affirming the value of collaboration with community partners in urban education. Insights from students and teachers have implications for teaching and learning in multicultural settings. We depart from previous theoretical discussions of empowerment by providing practical examples of both students *and* teachers exploring what it means to engage poetry in personally and socially empowering ways.

EDUCATIONAL ISSUES IN CONTEXT

Today, it is not news that the poor and minority youth populations who need the most resources still receive the least. In a time when waging a war abroad is given more attention than "wars" at home, the crisis in many urban schools only worsens as community organizations and other locally based agencies are, at best, reduced or eliminated. Given these conditions, we turn to youth poetry in the context of a university–school partnership at Bellevue High to understand various manifestations and possibilities of empowerment. Bellevue High is a racially diverse school that houses more than 3,100 students, approximately 33% Black, 37% White, 11% Chicano/

Latino, 11% Biracial, and 8% Asian/Pacific Islander and/or Other. The university–school partnership stems from a university-based undergraduate program called June Jordan's Poetry for the People (P4P) at the University of California at Berkeley. The program provides a place for students from various backgrounds to develop writing skills and shine in a form of literacy practice that turns silence into language and action (Muller & the Poetry for the People Blueprint Collective, 1995). One of P4P's educational objectives has been to reach out into the community and take poetry beyond the university walls, leading its proponents to create partnerships with local organizations and institutions.

As high-stakes testing and privatization of schools have become ultimate choices for improving the educational experiences of young people, it is all the more important to tap into the power of collaboration and innovative teaching and to pay attention to some successful ways schools have gained ground to better serve students (Borthwick, Stirling, Nauman, & Cook, 2003; Jocson, 2005; Kirschenbaum & Reagan, 2001). We are not suggesting that creating partnerships or using poetry as a pedagogical tool would solve every educational crisis present in urban learning environments. Rather, we are suggesting that an examination of students' and teachers' work related to poetry can serve as one means of moving educators and other youth advocates a step closer to improving current educational practices. Before we turn to poetry, it is important to review empowerment in education.

EMPOWERMENT IN EDUCATION

Empowerment has its foundation in the sociohistorical meaning of "power"— a socially constructed concept that is neither bounded nor unidirectional. Though commonly defined as a person's strength or controlling influence, power manifests as a result of asymmetrical relations based on race, class, gender, ability, and age groupings as well as distribution of cultural goods (Apple, 1995). This latter definition advocates a view of power in terms of inequality and the hierarchical positions and processes that form it. Contemporary popular mantra such as *power is knowledge/knowledge is power* derive from what Foucault (1976/1980) calls the release or re-emergence of subjugated knowledges, or "blocs of historical knowledge which were present . . . that have been disqualified as inadequate . . . located low down on the hierarchy" (p. 82). It is through the reappearance of local popular knowledges, typically confined to the margins, that criticism performs its work. But what is power in relation to empowerment?

Ashcroft (1987) defines power as the capability to produce or manifest in action, one's cap/ability to act. Power is a construct that takes into account "self-power" or individuals' belief in their cap/abilities to act in such a way that "to empower" means to bring to a state of cap/ability to act ("to enable"). It is a process that involves bringing oneself or an outside person forward to power ("to be enabled"). Thus, to empower is to facilitate the process of acting and constructing reality and knowledge that is recognized by others. In this sense, empowerment becomes *the act and the process of en-abling*, that which is the primary objective of education. To further illustrate the relationship of empowerment to education are perspectives in the area of critical pedagogy.

Developed in the late 1970s, the area of critical pedagogy examines the orientation for teaching and learning both on the micro and macro level. Though it is not a unitary strategy or approach to education, critical pedagogy responds to competing notions of the schooling process and its objectives (McLaren, 1994). Its principles take into account history, cultural politics, and economics, as well as tease apart socially constructed concepts such as power, ideology, and hegemony. On the one hand, theorists of critical pedagogy reject the simple notion that schools as democratic institutions provide equal access and opportunities to or serve the interests of minority groups. Viewing schools as sites of reproduction, they make a clear distinction between *schooling* as the mere transfer of existing knowledge and a mode of social control, and *education* as a more dynamic process involving active subjects who are committed to transforming society (Apple, 1995; McLaren, 1994). On the other hand, theorists of critical pedagogy also note the centrality of subjectivity in the construction of knowledge, identity, and history in classrooms and other sites of practice. They emphasize the possibilities for contradictions and discontinuities that may arise as teachers and students take on their roles, while putting forth the importance of self-reflexivity in the process (Ellsworth, 1989; Gore, 1992; Luke, 1992). A key concept among the different strands of critical pedagogy is *agency*, not only in the areas of teaching and learning, but also and more significantly in the process of both self and social transformation.

Freire (1970) makes explicit the relationship between the oppressed and the oppressor. The notion of *conscientizacaó* (loosely translated as "intersubjective consciousness") is central to raising the level of one's awareness about liberatory possibilities and actions against forms of oppression, both educationally and socially. It is part of critical pedagogy rooted in liberatory possibilities that continues to examine the potential power (read: ability) of local actors to transform existing inequalities through contradictory dimensions or acts of resistance (Apple, 1995; Darder, 1995; Giroux, 2001; hooks, 1994; Luke, 1992; Shor 1992, 1996). This view reasserts the political nature of schooling and the roles of students and teachers participating in productively disruptive work. As we will point out, counterhegemonic practices through a particular engagement with poetry both in and out of the classroom shape the possibilities for empowerment.

MINIMUM WORDS, MAXIMUM IMPACT

The partnership between Poetry for the People (P4P) and Bellevue High was established in 1996. P4P's pedagogy centered on redefining poetry based on three guiding principles, such as 1) honoring students, 2) using words to change the world, and 3) treating poetry as serious, imaginative work. In P4P's university course, readers, and other compilations, it was not uncommon to find contemporary multicultural works, including those by E. Ethelbert Miller, James Weldon Johnson, Nikki Giovanni, Audre Lorde, Cornelius Eddy, Haas Mroue, Naomi Shihab Nye, Nicolás Guillen, Lorna Dee Cervántes, Martín Espada, Janice Mirikitani, and Jessica Hagedorn. These works offered an array of perspectives, genres, traditions, topics, and styles from which to draw; also, they served as points of departure for group discussions and writing assignments. Topics such as survival and racial and sexual oppression, as well as notions of home/land, language, and self as a subaltern were an integral part.

Additionally, P4P asserted the following objectives *with* and *for* its students: 1) to create a safe medium for artistic and political empowerment, and 2) to democratize the medium of poetry to include "the people," or populations that have been historically denied equal access and representation (Muller and the Poetry for the People Blueprint Collective, 1995). In a joint effort to sustain artistic and political empowerment, Jordan along with student-teacher-poets (STPs) in the program explored various means to "democratize" poetry beyond the confines of the university campus. They drew upon Dewey's (1916) notion of democracy through education to challenge and shape the role of schools in developing a just society.

Specifically, P4P's flagship partnership with Bellevue High provided 9th- to 12th-grade students the kind of personal attention typical of any writing workshop. It involved 8–12 college student-teacher-poets (STPs) entering high school English classrooms and facilitating writing workshops 3 days a week and lasting approximately 4 to 6 weeks. STPs adhered to P4P's mantra of "minimum words, maximum impact." For students, this mantra served as a writing guideline across different topics by paying attention to word choice, specificity, clarity, and purpose in their writing process. For teachers, this mantra, along with P4P's democratic stance on poetry, was central to the expansion of their pedagogies.

From Skits to Student Writing

In one 11th-grade American literature classroom, a skit was performed by two STPs as an introduction to the writing topic of profiling. The skit demonstrated two strands of thought and experience, one from a Chicano in his early 20s and the other by a Filipina American in her late 20s. Derogatory remarks were exchanged between them, making explicit constructions of race, class, and gender. Just as explicit were related issues such as poverty, il/legal immigration, language, violence, crime, and drugs. Overt racist and sexist statements became the focus of what seemed like a theatrical performance, a teaching strategy that both STPs decided would safely convey different types of profiling in the crudest and most exaggerated way. There was certainly a shocking effect, as the room grew silent. In the ensuing class discussion, students used different narratives to describe instances of profiling that occurred on and off the school campus. Several shared their frustrations, for example, with the police and the intrusive interactions they faced on a daily basis. One student noted, "These pigs, man, they're on you and you feel like you're being watched all the time. They need to chill." Another added, "You could be walking getting lunch or something and then all of a sudden there they go rounding you up." Similarly, other students were explicit about acknowledging that being Black or female, wearing baggy jeans or just being young, automatically placed them in the limelight. In the midst of this fruitful dialogue, topics such as youth violence, police harassment, racism, sexism, and classism served as generative themes (Freire, 1970)—relevant points that connected students' individual experiences to larger social phenomena. Both STPs noted that students began to see the value of dialogue in combating social inequities as well as the significance of voice through speaking up and, subsequently, through writing to augment the potential for change. At the end of class that day, students commented positively on the unique approach for raising critical subjects such as race and racism in the classroom. One student said, "You guys are crazy, but it worked," a remark that the STPs happily received. June Jordan, seated discreetly among students in the classroom, overheard the comment. Later, during a group debriefing, she challenged the STPs to further contemplate race, identity politics, and effective instruction in urban schools. Specifically, Jordan noted that there are myriad ways to confront human experience and that no matter the circumstances, the power for potential change lies in the naming of the experience. Naming through poetry was one of them.

In addition to the skit and interactive lecture, poems in the printed reader were also used for instructional purposes. The poems were carefully selected to represent certain conditions that related to students' experiences through the use of language and inclusion of specific details. Sometimes, poems struck students' attention simply by face value. For example, one particular poem on race and gender that students found magnetic was "Poem for Anyone Who Thinks I'm Not African Enough" by Uchechi Kalu:

Sorry
I forgot
My spear
At home
(quoted in Jocson, 2008, p. 115)

During a large-group discussion, STPs asked students to identify possible meanings in this four-line poem and, technically, how it manifested P4P's mantra—"minimum words, maximum impact." Several students pointed out the resemblance of the poem's limited syllable count to the haiku form. Others noticed the difference between the title and the actual verse, the former having 9 words and 15 syllables compared to the latter with only 7 words and 9 syllables. This observation about impact and intensity of language, for many, became an invitation to probe the depth of the poem's message as it related to the larger discussion on profiling.

African American student Carolyn particularly liked the poem's brevity. However, rather than focus on concise structure, Carolyn chose to compose a page-length poem as a response to the assignment on racial profiling. Her purpose was to openly share multiple accounts of stereotyping without being verbose. Carolyn revealed that what began as a three-page poem was later condensed into one page, a writing process that included several in-class workshops and revisions on her own. She noted the application of P4P's guidelines to her work to make the poem much more "clean and sharp" than the original version. According to her, "That's what I do most of the time after I finish. Take out [what's] irrelevant and cut it down to size." Below illustrates Carolyn's completed assignment and reflects a rhetorical choice conveying invisibility and racism.

Can You See Me?

1   When you think Black
      You think guns going glack glack
      Sending shots through your neighborhood
      Stores
5   There's no turning back
      You wack, you scared
      Can you compare
      To all the lashes I got across
      My back
10   Seek
      The curse in my eyes
      The flare of my nose
      The adrenaline in my chest
      The grinch in my teeth

15   The bitch in my breath
     Why the hell
     You gotta be so
     Difficult
     Listen to me when I tell you
20   What's on my mind
     The truth
     Twisted up but I spit it out
     So let it be known
     What the guns in their hands is all about
25   You
     Don't see me
     You see right through me
     You want me locked up as much as the next man
     Do I look like a hoodlum to you?
30   I'm not the Black you know
     I'm the Black you will know
     So I ask
     Once more
     Can you see me?

Along with alliteration and consonance to create poetic rhythm, Carolyn used the phrasal unit "can you see me" (in the title and line 34) to invite others into a dialogue, what she deemed to be often missing in classrooms, school grounds, and other youth-filled environments. Carolyn recalled taking the time to "brainstorm and free write for a while to get the poem right" and to bring forth issues she "really wanted to discuss." For her, writing topics such as profiling served as a conduit for representing experiences that have gone unsaid for far too long:

> Like for racial profiling, there's not too many people that talk about how a lot of African Americans are treated and put down in some situations. So *somebody* had to say something about it.

Carolyn also pointed out how writing enabled her to reach out and communicate with others. Her poem, "Can You See Me?", from the lens of empowerment, is constitutive of the language of critique and the language of possibility occurring within a site of practice. It denotes power at play in the writing process (Gore, 1992).

> Seeing myself. Being able to express yourself in another way. Like the way I took on the whole poetry thing was that being youth as it is, you know, it's already hard for us to speak out or what not. And that

was just another way of me speaking out and letting people hear what I have to say.

Indeed, completing a poetry assignment on profiling does not equate to empowerment. Suggestive here is the *en-abling* that happens through careful engagement with poetic texts in ways that open up doors for young people to take an active part in shaping and representing their social worlds. Carolyn's poem is illustrative of one possibility toward self and social empowerment.

Teaching and Changing Pedagogies

P4P's presence at Bellevue High also shaped teachers' experiences. Historically, a total of 8 English teachers and 12 different classes had been involved in the partnership (see Appendix B). Ms. Tanner, the third English teacher to host P4P, indicated that social networking between teachers was key to the partnership's early beginnings. Recommendations for P4P as "a really good group of people to work with" occurred mostly by word of mouth, and eventually spread across different classes and grade levels. Published anthologies provided concrete evidence of student work in individual classrooms and later, along with other relevant materials, served as poetry samples to urge other teachers. Sets of curricular materials, in particular the lessons on the "haiku" form and "rhythm and rhyme," added to teachers' repertoire in teaching poetry.

Noteworthy was teachers' openness to innovate classroom practice through collaboration. Among the six teachers interviewed in the study (4 White females, 1 White male, 1 South Asian female), two expressed that they felt fearful in the beginning, while others admitted the complexities and nuances of "teaching poetry with an edge." One teacher specifically noted the importance of embracing the power of hip-hop music and culture to connect with students, but revealed that she did not know how. Turning to P4P as a teaching partner allowed these teachers to address multiculturalism in new ways and further develop relevant teaching ideas in the classroom. Teacher testimonials describing their individual experiences in the partnership are too long to outline here. Instead, the examples that follow paint a representative picture of what it was like to step back and share their classroom with collaborators, participate in the writing process, and take hold of changing pedagogies. An important point to make in relation to empowerment is that teachers enabled themselves to confront hegemonic, often authoritarian, practices in the micro-context of poetry (Sleeter & McLaren, 1995).

According to Ms. Best, who taught 11th-grade American literature, the idea of having a 6-week-long collaboration with P4P began as a conversation with different people in her department. She asked a number of colleagues how she might be able to "invigorate things in my classroom" by tapping into what she had been observing at that time as youth's growing interest in spoken-word poetry. It was then when she discovered the different organizations already present in her school and within the larger San Francisco Bay Area community. Subsequently, Ms. Best invited both P4P and a literary arts organization called Youth Speaks (www.youthspeaks.org) into her classroom, identifying them as important resources in "making teaching and learning a bit more meaningful." She realized what each program had to offer students and over time used this knowledge to shape her teaching practice within Bellevue's small learning community.

> To be honest, the reason why I would want to have Poetry for the People is that there is a different feeling about the student teacher poets . . . there is *more* of an interaction between the poets and the students . . . .when Youth Speaks comes to my class, they come for a one-time or a two-time thing. . . . They sort of fit into a different niche in my classroom.

That initial collaboration in Ms. Best's classroom culminated in a final reading held at the university campus. Students' poems were published in an anthology, which piqued the interests of several other teachers.

Later, Ms. Moore, a 10th-grade world literature teacher, became convinced of P4P's student-centered approach to complement the goals in her small learning community. Similar to Ms. Best, she was interested in innovative practices through the facilitation of in-class writing group workshops by college STPs, with an emphasis on revision and the writing process. What she discovered was the salience of her own participation in workshops that afforded her a different role in the classroom. It was a conduit for understanding teacher-student dynamics.

> It was, I think, *this* contact [during writing workshop] . . . I felt comfortable turning over my class . . . I really felt like I got to sort of participate in my classroom more . . . and this interaction allowed me to see students differently, and students saw *me* differently.

For Ms. Moore, writing group workshops provided new learning moments to relate and strengthen her relationship with students. It gave her a chance to take on a student-centered approach, to not act as the sole facilitator or, in her words, "the one always in charge in class." Active participation in small groups during writing workshop broke grounds for a more democratic classroom.

In another instance, Ms. Tanner invited P4P into her mainstream senior poetry class for a 4-week collaboration. She wanted to draw upon the expertise of racially diverse college STPs to connect with her savvy college-bound students because, in her own words, she "just had no knowledge of hip-hop" and wanted to "kick it up a notch" by learning about it as well. The incorporation of "rhythm and rhyme" into the teaching of poetry was helpful to connect students' existing literacy practices to the craft of writing. What she did not realize was that the writing process would require her, similar to Ms. Moore's experience, to be just as active as her students during writing workshop.

At the final reading event held on the university campus, the embodiment of students' and Ms. Tanner's experiences in the form of poems became the basis for human connection. That night, Ms. Tanner also "gave it a go" and shared a satirical poem as an example of what transpired in her teaching and learning experience with P4P. She surprised many students with her use of candid language as well as her animated performance on the microphone. It was something that students had never witnessed.

> I decided to read my poem about Martha Stewart. It was critical of her crimes, of corporatism, of how some people get away with stuff and how others don't. It felt good to write about what's been on my mind, you know, and to share the process *and* the podium with students. *That* was awesome. I think I'll do that more in class.

Breaking codes of silence during a night of reading alongside students, teachers, parents, STPs, and community members, the poetry *of the people* bounced off the university's ivied walls and filled the not-so-ivied air. It was a night made possible by local actors enjoined by the power of words.

CRITICAL PERSPECTIVE

The experiences of students and teachers in P4P offer some insights into the complexities of teaching and learning in multicultural settings. First, the use of skits and provocative writing topics explicitly linked literacy and power in ways that recognize poetry as a medium of expression for both artistic and political empowerment. Second, for students like Carolyn and teachers like Ms. Best, Ms. Moore, and Ms. Tanner, poetry served as a means to communicate matters of importance, including the politics of (in)visibility, racism, and differential treatment, among others. Writing became a site of struggle where meanings were created and positionalities named. Third, the presence of teaching partners such as P4P's student-teacher-poets extends classroom pedagogies by tapping into community resources, co-constructing knowledge through poetry, and actively participating in the writing process. For teachers, the presence of collaborators became a type of professional development that strengthened their relationships with students and further developed their existing approaches to writing instruction. The collaboration was by no means a flawless relationship. Although there were advantages in allowing teaching partners and other collaborators to take part in the classroom, there were also challenges in hosting them (both administratively and pedagogically) and negotiating a power-laden space. Deciding when and how to step back or confronting contradictions to teaching norms were constant among teachers' experience.

Students and teachers represented in this chapter remind us that there is no one-solution formula. What we have highlighted here is one instantiation of popular culture and empowerment that tap into poetry writing as a site of struggle. That is, inscribing words about relations of power and entering power-laden terrains in discursive form. Poetry writing provided generative instances for further negotiating the social construct of power. Additionally, it afforded a unique entry into reimagining writing as a site of negotiated power. Through naming, reflection, and action, critical pedagogy in the context of a university–school partnership manifested with local actors actively participating in productively disruptive work. As illustrated by student and teacher experiences in P4P, en-abling self included a critical reading *and* writing of existing conditions in schools, communities, and society at large. This en-abling remains key in education.

REFERENCES

Alvermann, D. E., Hinchman, K. A., Moore, D. W., Phelps, S. F., & Waff, D. R. (Eds.). (1998). *Reconceptualizing the literacies in adolescents' lives.* Mahwah, NJ: Erlbaum.

Apple, M. (1995). *Education and power.* New York: Routledge.

Ashcroft, L. (1987). Defusing "Empowering": The what and the why. *Language Arts, 64,* 143–156.

Bartolome, L. (1994). Beyond methods fetish: Toward a humanizing pedagogy. *Harvard Educational Review, 64*(2), 173–195.

Borthwick, A., Stirling, T., Nauman, A., & Cook, D. (2003). Achieving successful school-university collaboration. *Urban Education, 38*(3), 330–371.

Carey-Webb, A. (2001). *Literature & lives: A response-based, cultural studies approach to teaching English.* Urbana, IL: National Council of Teachers of English.

Cooks, J. (2004). Writing for something: Essays, raps, and writing preferences. *English Journal, 94*(1), 72–76.

Darder, A. (1995). Buscando America: The contribution of critical Latino educators to the academic development and empowerment of Latino students in the U.S. In C. Sleeter & P. McLaren (Eds.), *Multicultural Education, Critical Pedagogy, and the Politics of Difference* (pp. 319–347). New York: State of University of New York Press.

Darling-Hammond, L. (1997). *The right to learn: A blueprint for creating schools that work.* San Francisco: Jossey-Bass.

Dewey, J. (1916). *Democracy and education: An introduction to the philosophy of education.* New York: Routledge.

Ellsworth, E. (1989). Why doesn't this feel empowering?: Working through the repressive myths of critical pedagogy. *Harvard Educational Review, 59*(3), 297–324.

Fisher, M. (2007). *Writing in rhythm: Spoken word poetry in urban classrooms.* New York: Teachers College Press.

Foucault (1980). *Power/Knowledge: Selected interviews and other writings 1972–1977.* New York: Pantheon. (Original work published 1976)

Freire, P. (1970). *Pedagogy of the oppressed.* New York: Continuum.

Gore, J. (1992). What we can do for you! What *can* "we" do for "you"?: Struggling over empowerment in critical and feminist pedagogy. In C. Luke & J. Gore (Eds.), *Feminisms and Critical Pedagogy* (pp. 54–73). New York: Routledge.

Giroux, H. (2001). *Theory and resistance in education: Towards a pedagogy for the opposition.* Westport, CT: Bergin & Garvey.

hooks, b. (1994). *Teaching to transgress: Education as the practice of freedom.* New York: Routledge.

Jocson, K. M. (2005). "Taking it to the mic": Pedagogy of June Jordan's Poetry for the People and partnership with an urban high school. *English Education, 37*(2), 44–60.

Jocson, K. M. (2008). *Youth poets: Empowering literacies in and out of schools.* New York: Peter Lang.

Kinloch, V. (2005). Poetry, literacy, and creativity: Fostering effect learning strategies in an urban classroom. *English Education, 37*(2): 96–114.

Kirkland, D. (2004). Rewriting school: Critical writing pedagogies for the secondary English classroom. *Journal of Teaching of Writing, 21*(1&2), 83–96.

Kirschenbaum, H., & Reagan, C. (2001). University and urban school partnerships: An analysis of 57 collaborations between a university and a city school district. *Urban Education, 36*(4), 479–504.

Kozol, J. (2006). *Shame of the nation: The restoration of apartheid schooling in America.* New York: Three Rivers Press.

Ladson-Billings, G. (1994). *The dreamkeepers: Successful teachers of African American children.* San Francisco: Jossey-Bass.

Luke, C. (1992). *Feminist politics in radical pedagogy.* In C. Luke & J. Gore (Eds.), *Feminisms and Critical Pedagogy* (pp. 25–53). New York: Routledge.

Mahiri, J. (2004). Street scripts: African American youth writing about crime and violence. In J. Mahiri (Ed.), *What they don't learn in school: Literacy in the lives of urban youth* (pp. 19–42). New York: Peter Lang.

McLaren, P. (1994). *Life in schools: An introduction to critical pedagogy in the foundations of education* (2nd ed.). New York: Longman.

Meacham, S. (2003, April). "Reader writer freedom fighter: Tupac Shakur and the struggle between liberatory and 'thug life' in Hip Hop music." Paper presented at the annual meeting of the American Educational Research Association, Chicago, IL.

Meier, D. (1996). *The power of their ideas: Lessons for American from a small school in Harlem.* Boston: Beacon.

Moje, E., Young, J., Readence, J., & Moore, D. (2000). Reinventing adolescent literacy for New Times: Perennial and millennial issues. *Journal of Adolescent and Adult Literacy, 43*(5), 400–410.

Morrell, E. (2004). *Linking literacy and popular culture: Finding connections for lifelong learning.* Norwood, MA: Christopher-Gordon.

Morrell, E., & Duncan-Andrade, J. (2002). Promoting academic literacy with urban youth through engaging Hip-Hop culture. *English Journal, 91*(6), 88–92.

Muller, L., & The Poetry for the People Blueprint Collective (Eds.). (1995). *June Jordan's Poetry for the People: A revolutionary blueprint.* New York: Routledge.

National Assessment of Educational Progress. (2008). *The nation's report card: Reading 2008.* Washington, DC: U.S. Department of Education/National Center for Educational Statistics. Retrieved March 21, 2010, from http://nces.ed.gov/nationsreportcard/

Noguera, P. (2003). *City schools and the American dream: Reclaiming the promise of public education.* New York: Teachers College Press.

Oakes, J., & Lipton, M. (2003). *Teaching to change the world.* Boston: McGraw-Hill. (Original work published 1999)

Shor, I. (1992). *Empowering education: Critical teaching for social change.* Chicago: University of Chicago Press.

Shor, I. (1996). *When students have power: Negotiating authority in a critical pedagogy.* Chicago: University of Chicago Press.

Sleeter, C. E., & McLaren, P. (1995). Introduction: Exploring connections to build a critical multiculturalism. In C. E. Sleeter & P. McLaren (Eds.), *Multicultural Education, Critical Pedagogy, and the Politics of Difference* (pp. 5–32). New York: State of University of New York Press.

Valenzuela, A. (1999). *Subtractive schooling: U.S.-Mexican youth and politics of caring.* Albany: State University of New York Press.

Weis, L., & Fine, M. (Eds.). (1993). *Beyond silenced voices: Class, race, and gender in United States schools.* Albany: State University of New York Press.

CHAPTER 9

Is It Bigger Than Hip-Hop?

Examining the Problems and Potential of Hip-Hop in the Curriculum

Jung Kim

The generation of adolescents coming up in school today has never known a world without hip-hop. Hip-hop has sold more albums than any other music genre in history and its influences can be seen in everything from art to fashion, language, and even advertising. With its urban and political roots, hip-hop has given voice to groups that have been historically marginalized and disenfranchised in our country—the poor, urban, Black and Brown, and young. In addition, it has quickly expanded to similar populations abroad (e.g., New Zealand's Maori). Contextualizing hip-hop in this manner, in conjunction with the rapidly diversifying face of today's school population (National Collaborative on Diversity in the Teaching Force, 2004), it is hardly surprising that some educational researchers and teachers have begun to investigate how hip-hop can be used in classrooms. Though there have been attempts to describe how students use hip-hop in out-of-school contexts, there has been relatively little work done on how hip-hop is and can be used within schools by practicing teachers. Of additional concern is how hip-hop can be structured as a site of resistance and empowerment for students.

Undoubtedly, the roots of hip-hop point to its existence as a site of empowerment and resistance for countless people. Stemming from the experiences of urban minorities, hip-hop, "a transnational, global art form capable of mobilizing diverse disenfranchised groups" (Potter, 1995, p. 10) is deeply rooted in African traditions and in the discourse practices of African American language such as call-and-response, signifying, and improvisation (Campbell, 2005; Perry, 2004; Richardson, 2003). For this reason, scholars have argued that hip-hop's growing popularity is due to its reflection of urban ghetto life and the artistic, public voicing of a set of experiences that were ignored (acts of disempowering) for centuries in this country (Clay, 2003; Stapleton, 1998). Clearly, hip-hop holds great pedagogical promise and potential for educators, given the ways young people have taken it up in their out-of-school literacy practices.

As more educators are becoming aware of the value of tapping into students' out-of-school literacy practices, they are beginning to bring hip-hop into the classroom. They recognize that hip-hop is not only an important part of students' lives and identities, but a resource that affords multiple avenues of learning and access to empowerment and resistance. Educator-researchers (Duncan-Andrade & Morrell, 2008; Fisher, 2004; Hill, 2009; Mahiri, 2004) have examined how students use literacy in their out-of-school lives and how they "read" the texts of popular culture in complex ways. Such educator-researchers have sought to uncover ways to bring hip-hop texts and practices into the classroom to support students' critical literacies in ways that provide them with world skills they will need to be successful. This chapter, part of a larger study, builds upon and expands arguments articulated by various scholars and educator-researchers by investigating how one teacher engages with students in bridging their out-of-school literacy practices, particularly around hip-hop, into school-sponsored work. The teacher highlighted here seeks both to encourage and sustain spaces for critical and academic learning.

The work discussed here is particularly timely, given the increasing gap between the cultural and linguistic diversities of today's students and the decreasing racial, ethnic, cultural, and linguistic diversities of the teaching force. This reality poses a number of troubling issues with literacy learning and teaching, including: how literacy, as a social practice (Barton, 2001), becomes mainstreamed along race and class lines, and how deficit-oriented labels such as "at risk" and "underperforming" are often and unfairly associated with urban students of color in deprecating ways (Noll, 1998; Moje, 2000; O'Brien, 2003). Insofar as hip-hop is concerned, it becomes rather interesting how it is overly criticized for being harmful when primarily White-audience music genres such as heavy metal, which contain similar themes, are less publicly trounced (Ross & Rose, 1994). There is clearly a need to question why hip-hop and its consumers/participants get demonized in light of its contribution to students' literacy practices and to current literacy research.

Studies have documented the obstacles, lowered expectations, and failures experienced by working-class students in classrooms (Anyon, 1980; Nagle, 1999) and the lack of/misrepresentation of students of color in the stated and hidden curriculum of school (Corley, 2004; Willis, 2002). Not only do youth understand these disempowering messages, but they may also internalize them (e.g., Bowman & Howard, 1985; Keating & Sasse, 1996). However, they often choose not to be passive recipients of oppressive practices, but rather, work to actively engage in resistance (De-Blase, 2003)—working to sabotage school literacy (Howard, 2003; Steele & Aronson, 1995; Stevenson, 1997) or creating separate niches and identities for themselves in nontraditional literacy spaces (Moje, 2000).

To critique these disempowering messages, this chapter examines the possibilities of critical pedagogy rooted in hip-hop as a way to trouble the waters of the current state of education and its ongoing failure to adequately prepare many youth for life beyond school walls. In order to take up this framework, this chapter first examines how hip-hop and its five elements—breakdancing, MC'ing, DJ'ing, graffiti, and knowledge—allow for multiple modes of access and expertise. In particular, I argue that hip-hop, rising out of the Bronx in the 1970s, is reflective of the kinds of critical literacies (e.g., Freire, 1997; Hagood, 2002) and multiliteracies (Cope & Kalantzis, 2000; New London Group, 1996) that comprise today's cutting-edge literacy work. As such, I describe hip-hop as *improvisational and experimental, critical, dialogic, collaborative and democratic,* and *evolving* (Chang, 2005; Rose, 1994; Smitherman, 1997). These aspects of hip-hop are foundational to how teachers can begin to unlearn previous ways of thinking and be open to new understandings of learning and of classrooms.

Recontextualizing the framework of the five elements for a classroom assumes differential expertise and talents. Individuals, in the contexts of both hip-hop and education, have a variety of experiences to draw from and share. In this manner, classrooms should allow for multiple modes of expression and participation in order for students to demonstrate their various capacities. This chapter, then, documents the pedagogies and practices of a high school English teacher, Florence Ballard, who incorporates hip-hop into her classroom. It draws upon an understanding of hip-hop as a metaphor for designing (New London Group, 1996) new ways of teaching and learning and begins to unpack the purposes and possibilities of a hip-hop-infused curriculum as part of literacy education. By using hip-hop as a lens through which to examine Florence's classroom, we are better able to observe and understand how this one teacher creates, incorporates, and builds upon her students', as well as her own, understanding of hip-hop to work toward critical and academic success.

TEACHING WHAT'S IMPORTANT TO THEM: FLORENCE BALLARD AND HIP-HOP

Florence Ballard is an African American woman who is deeply committed to issues of equity and social justice, and is engaged with hip-hop in the classroom. She has been teaching for over 10 years, both in a small central city in Illinois and in public schools in Chicago. I met Florence at a state university when we were both enrolled in the English secondary teacher certification program. At the time, Florence was a doctoral student who was also pursuing certification. Upon completion of the certification program (she is no longer working on her doctorate, but plans to finish it one day), Florence and her daughter moved to the city to care for her ailing mother. During Florence's time in the city, she has taught at two schools (and her daughter has been a student at both schools) where the student demographics are completely African American. At the time of the study, Florence and her daughter are both at Lake Academy, the same high school from which Florence had graduated years ago. It is Florence's 2nd year teaching there, yet she seems like a veteran of the school. She is highly connected to her students, lives in the community, and is in constant contact with her students' parents and guardians. In terms of hip-hop, Florence does not participate in its actual production, but she does use a variety of contemporary hip-hop artifacts in the classroom to engage students and make her teaching relevant to their lives.

The context for this research, Lake Academy, is a South Side community area high school, which means the school is open to students living in a district-defined attendance area. However, special programs, such as the school's International Baccalaureate (IB) program, are widely popular among students inside and outside of the attendance area. The IB program, for instance, requires a minimum of a Stanine 6 in math and reading on the 7th-grade standardized exams. (Stanines are scores that range from a low of 1 to a high of 9, with 5 designating average performance. National stanines, like national percentile ranks, indicate a student's relative standing in the national norm group.) Students who qualify and apply for the IB program are then accepted through a random lottery. The school's Web site boasts of two students receiving the full IB diploma and 84 individual subject certifications. Because of the IB program, Lake Academy is considered one of the district's "better than average" schools.

It was at Lake Academy where I observed the classroom practices of Florence and her students over the course of a semester. I audio recorded sessions and, on occasion, videotaped them. Detailed fieldnotes, along with interviews and collected artifacts (e.g., writing samples, lesson plans, handouts, photographs of student work), served as additional data. Through systematic processes of data coding and analysis, a primary intention of this work was to examine teacher rationale for action and to understand how students make sense of the curriculum and respond to hip-hop as a pedagogical practice.

DEFINING HIP-HOP

Florence incorporates hip-hop into her classroom to create a more student-centered curriculum. According to Florence, she employs hip-hop in the

classroom because of her desire to tap into materials that students find relevant and meaningful to their lives. In her words, hip-hop "makes teaching
relevant because you're teaching what's important to them." For Florence,
hip-hop is deeply tied to the artistic and creative endeavors of the African
American experience—not just historically, as seen in its roots in Black oral
traditions (Richardson, 2003), but in its present-day ability to speak to, for,
and about the experiences of Black youth (Clay, 2003). It is this connectivity
to her students that drives her understanding of hip-hop and its uses in the
classroom, and that guides how she creates innovative teaching and learning
opportunities.

Because Florence's understandings of hip-hop shape the way she conceptualizes a hip-hop pedagogy, it is necessary to unpack her meanings of
hip-hop. This is particularly significant in examining how her understandings correspond or conflict with students' understandings. At the most basic
level, Florence defines hip-hop as: "A synonym for the new generation, or
today's generation, their cultures, their values. Uh, what's significant in their
life . . . artistically, lyrically. Linguistically is what I should have said." She
continues: "And musically. Just dealing with culture, with art, and how they
use the art, this art in their lives."

Although Florence does describe hip-hop as tied to African American
arts—the history, culture, and arts tied to the Black experience in America—
she neither specifically cites hip-hop's five elements nor does she really discuss hip-hop beyond music. Instead, she connects hip-hop with African
American culture as she emphasizes the relevance and usability of hip-hop
in and for students' lives. Another way I frame this perspective is by describing how hip-hop can serve as both a mirror and a window for students—
how youth are attracted to hip-hop because of its ability to speak to their
lived experiences, on the one hand, as well as their hopes and dreams, on
the other hand.

As a mirror, hip-hop helps students to see "what's significant in their
lives . . . their cultures, their values," as these things are reflected in the stories, words, and culture of hip-hop. One of the major reasons Florence uses
hip-hop in her classroom is because she wants to acknowledge and validate
what students deem important to them as she helps them engage in critical
literacy practices: "I have to validate them and what—where they're at, and
then bring them up to the next level." She understands that hip-hop acts as
a mirror that reflects back what students see or want to see in their everyday
lives.

Additionally, hip-hop can act as a window by relating to the opportunities potentially afforded to its participants and consumers. In Florence's
words, hip-hop is also about "how they use . . . this art in their lives." This
can range from participants using hip-hop to gain status and recognition or
employing it for personal and creative expression, to participants making

choices about their identities based on the ways hip-hop is consumed. In this manner, the very focused connections to hip-hop that Florence makes with and for students' lives serve as the centerpiece of her teaching and her interactions with students.

TEACHING AS IMPROVISATIONAL AND EXPERIMENTAL

From breakdance battles to rap ciphers, hip-hop has a deep tradition of improvisation and experimentation. Hip-hoppers must be flexible and react quickly to the various challenges of their craft. Whether reacting to an opponent in a battle or to the changing moods of an audience, the most successful hip-hoppers are the ones who can quickly modify what they are doing and build upon what is available to them—such as the weak rhymes of their opponent, the crowd's enthusiasm for power moves over footwork, or the accelerating or slowing beat of the DJ. However, hip-hoppers must also be experimental and innovative in ways that do not simply imitate or mimic the success and talent of others. Thus, they are constantly trying out new techniques and skills in an attempt to push themselves to the next level of performance and accomplishment.

Similar to effective hip-hoppers, educators must be able to react to the needs, challenges, and abilities of their students, as well as improvise and try new, innovative teaching techniques. Nieto (2006), citing Jenoure (2000), discusses improvisation as one of the qualities of effective teachers. She explains improvisation as "a metaphor for creativity within structure. Improvisation means being prepared for uncertainty, both the joy and the frustration of it. This requires a great deal of elasticity" (p. 468). This kind of responsiveness and willingness to work with the unpredictable flow of a classroom of learners welcomes student interaction and participation. Just as hip-hoppers are often aware of their audience, Florence, a trained teacher, takes into consideration materials, resources, and artifacts that are engaging, relevant, and important to her students. Doing so helps her to facilitate provocative classroom discussions and create rigorous curriculum. She creates space in her classrooms for students to have a voice.

Such improvisation supports a class that "collaboratively creates its own knowledge, sometimes in a way that no teacher could have managed or planned" (Sawyer, 2004, p. 199). This kind of work cannot be fully anticipated in the pre-packaged scripted curricula that many schools are implementing today, especially as some schools mandate that every subject-matter grade-level specific teacher be on the same page as their colleagues on a daily basis. As Sawyer argues, improvisation is a central component to effective teaching, a key difference between novice and experienced teachers, and a characteristic evident in Florence's classrooms.

Both improvisation and experimentation manifest in Florence's classroom in two broad ways. One way is through the creation and/or implementation of a curriculum that is innovative. Such a curriculum incorporates nontraditional texts and films, and creates activities that push beyond the teaching of basic educational skills. Often, Florence eschews more canonical texts and traditional literary assignments in favor of ones that are more culturally and personally relevant to students. In doing so, she more creatively addresses the requisite English language arts skills that students need. Florence's understanding of hip-hop as explicitly tied to African American experiences manifests in this kind of Afrocentric curriculum, which explores texts and artists grounded in the Black experience and creates more opportunities for students to make personal connections to the literature, lessons, and discussions.

On a broad level, Florence constructs units and draws on curricular resources that many may consider integral to a standard curriculum for English language arts. She does teach traditional ELA skills such as characterization through a critical, social justice–oriented framework; however, she also includes texts and assignments that are often not a part of ELA curricula. For instance, Florence draws upon her connections to the community—because she lives in the neighborhood, she sees her students outside of school and shares some of their experiences, such as avoiding certain blocks because of shooting—and her observations of students' interests and experiences, which pave the way for learning experiences that are stimulating and a curriculum that addresses the sociocultural contexts of the classrooms.

The second semester of Florence's class begins with the Harlem Renaissance and includes Lorraine Hansberry's *A Raisin in the Sun* and Nella Larson's *Passing*. It quickly extends to a study of more contemporary African American artists such as Gregory Hines and Judith Jamison. As the culminating project for this unit, students are required to write a detailed research paper on a contemporary African American artist. Following this unit is one that invites students to study the life, poetry, film roles, and written appreciations of Tupac Shakur. The final projects for this unit are two poetry analysis papers and a memorized oral performance of Tupac's poems. Interwoven throughout these units are more novel activities such as studying vocabulary unit words through contemporary music to better understand their definitions and use. These two units address standard American literature topics and themes and teach requisite academic skills, as well as bridge more contemporary texts and experiences that are more relevant to today's students.

Although Florence's curricular innovations could be considered experimental or nontraditional, this kind of openness is seen even more in the discourse of her classroom. The traditional Initiate, Respond, Evaluate (Lapp, Fisher, & Wolsey, 2009) pattern of discourse, as well as its lack of effectiveness in encouraging engagement or deep discussion, has been well documented in countless classrooms. However, the discourse in Florence's classroom is much less structured and more free-flowing. Extensive, unplanned discussions are integral to the classroom culture. Furthermore, she not only "allows" these kinds of conversations to occur—in fact, she often takes a peripheral role during these conversations—but also builds on what her students bring up both in future discussions and curriculum. In other words, instead of just acknowledging what students share in class and then moving on with the lesson plan, students' ideas actually get taken up and built on in the class period. Furthermore, the conversations that occur in the classroom are *collaborative and democratic*, as student-initiated ideas are not only welcomed and validated by Florence, but are a part of the official discourse of the class.

This kind of classroom culture brings forth some very intense and thought-provoking discussions that otherwise might not occur. For example, during a discussion of Benitha's romantic relationships in *A Raisin in the Sun*, the class has an extensive discussion on the nature of relationships between African American men and women—specifically, the treatment (whether or not exaggerated or stereotyped) of some African American women by some African American men. During this discussion, students divulge horrific stories of abuse and domestic violence within their families, frank commentary on their parents' relationships, and their own ongoing attempts to make sense of it all. This sharing of students' personal, familial experiences relays the *dialogic* nature of the kind of teaching that Florence engages, as there is a very concrete sense of the context of students' lives in and out of the classroom. Florence also pushes students to practice self-reflexivity as they seek to make sense of their lives, the lives of the literary characters, and of the world (real or imagined).

The innovation in such work is not just in creating room in the curriculum for student voice and participation, but in skillfully interweaving multiple strands of the African American experience into teaching. Florence's classroom exists as an intersection of past, present, and future, where students learn from and draw on historical understandings and traditional texts and skills, as well as their own experiences, to create new learning/meaning. Florence is able to create room for these things to exist in the space of her classroom. I have been in many classrooms in this district, and this is the first classroom where I have seen such an intense level of dialogue and interaction between and among students. The fluidity of texts, perspectives, experiences, and relationships makes this space unique.

TEACHING AS CRITICAL AND DIALOGIC

Hip-hop is ever-aware of its past, present, and future. Its community-centered, politically charged roots can still be seen in its various iterations today, as artists draw upon and branch out from these roots. Hip-hop artists are continuously situated in a sociohistorical space, as well as in dialogue with each other. Although some artists are notorious for "beefs" with their contemporaries, invoking discussions about the future of hip-hop, others work collaboratively with each other while building on what has come before—across elements, time, and with their audiences—to achieve their best performances. All in all, hip-hop does not exist in isolation, but is deeply connected with its producers, consumers, and critics.

By drawing upon understandings of hip-hop as dialogic and critical, I seek out the application of these understandings in practice by exploring how Florence situates and contextualizes herself, her students, and her classroom within the community and world, as well as in relation to each other. Cultivating these experiences through the curriculum, personal relationships, and values upheld in the classroom, Florence works toward creating dialogic classrooms. This, in turn, helps her and her students to consider their own perspectives when taking a critical stance, whether toward texts or situations. They ponder their own beliefs and their enactment of those beliefs to determine where they stand within situations—how they are empowered or disempowered to act on behalf of themselves or others. Ultimately, the goals of this type of classroom extend beyond the four physical walls toward the ongoing development of individuals beyond content learning.

The dialogic nature of this classroom creates groundedness and positionality for Florence and her students. Because it helps situate them as individuals, they are better able to consider who they are in relation to others, particularly within situations of power. They consider who they are as individuals, as well as members of various groups (most often within a racial group), and how this impacts them and their place in society. This kind of deliberation affords a variety of opportunities to be critical.

There has been a great deal of writing around being "critical" in education today, from critical literacy (e.g., Hagood, 2002; Van Sluys, 2004) to critical pedagogy (e.g., Kincheloe, 2004; McLaren, 2006). Critical theories are most often about empowering disenfranchised or marginalized groups to learn about power structures and to question the status quo. However, there is still a need for additional work that moves these same groups toward active engagement with *how* to change the systems that they critique (Brookfield, 2003). There can also often be an assumed understanding that the bearer of this critical thinking is still somehow "right" or that he/she is less open to the same critiques he/she is advocating for other domains (Jay

& Graff, 1995). Teachers are still in positions of authority and power after all, and there remains the danger of becoming part of the same system or pattern of behaviors one critiques.

In many ways, this parallels the ongoing evolution of hip-hop. As previously stated, hip-hop (the music and its artists), emerging from the politically charged neighborhoods of New York City in the 1970s, demanded to be seen and heard. From public transportation to the radio waves, hip-hop sought to critique a flawed system and give voice to those previously ignored (the music of Public Enemy serves as one example). However, as some of the music became increasingly violent, misogynistic, and homophobic, and as "gangster rap" gained in popularity, hip-hop's critical edge was questioned. Although some of today's current artists are still considered "conscious" or politically aware, there is much writing and discussion about the soul of hip-hop and where its future lies. Educators are aware of both hip-hop's potential and its flaws, yet they still embrace its possibility as part of a pedagogy that invokes the critical within their students. They understand that, like hip-hop, there is the potential for multiple levels of consciousness and understanding within individuals, perhaps even conflicting ones, and that hip-hop can provide a way to begin to unpack and explore these understandings.

One of the first fathers of critical pedagogy, Paulo Freire, describes this theory as being concerned with raising individual's critical consciousness, their *conscientizacao* (Freire, 1997). Instead of domination or oppression, it is concerned with freedom. It seeks to humanize all, both oppressor and oppressed. Freire argues that no one can be fully human while preventing others from being so: "To be literate is *not* to be free, it is to be present and active in the struggle for reclaiming one's voice, history, and future" (Freire & Macedo, 1987, p. 11). Critical pedagogy is explicitly tied to a transformative element.

To this end, a critical pedagogy framework is essential in the kinds of teaching described in this study. It requires one to learn how to question not just existing power structures, but also one's own role within those power structures and ways to advocate for positive change. Florence's classroom, for example, demonstrates how the dialogic nature of that learning space encourages students to question power dynamics as they explore their positionings within a local context and their situatedness within the larger sectors of the world.

This point can be seen in the ways Florence challenges her students to examine their power as consumers in the music they purchase. Although much of hip-hop's initial and continuing allure has been its depictions of urban life and its voicing of previously silenced groups, people have come to critique some of it as glorifying and advocating violence. Rather than uncovering the experiences of a people, it serves to perpetuate the inequity and injustice that already exist rather than ameliorate them. She challenges her students in asking them to ponder, "Why are you buying that?" and whether they truly believe in the message or values a product (e.g., rap song, television show, and so on) is promoting. This idea even extends into the homes of her students with her discussion of the cable television program *Flavor Flav's Flavor of Love*, a reality dating show. Realizing the immense popularity of the program with her students, she assigned them to watch it, which involved some curious parents contacting her. Florence taught both parents and students about the background of Flavor Flav, his past drug addiction and inability to support his family, and that this was a grandfather they were "trying to get with." According to Florence:

> Well, I had a mother tell me that she couldn't enjoy the *Flavor of Love* anymore once I started. . . . Oh that, that made some parents upset because that—that made—that, that touched their soul. That they had to look at him as the grandfather pimpin' these women who were the same ages as your daughter. Daughters, your oldest daughters. Uh, it reminded them of men that they'd dealt with. It reminded them of situations that they're going through.

By connecting the details of a popular television program to the realities of their own lives, individuals were able to critique the messages being promoted and reframe the meanings of such productions within their own lives.

Florence encourages students to question the status quo along with their everyday beliefs. As students form their own opinions, Florence expects them to have well-thought-out ideas that they can effectively defend to various audiences. Not unlike the battles between various hip-hoppers where challengers and defenders must be prepared to assert their skills over one another, Florence's students must be ready to assert themselves when challenged. Being critical is not only about questioning the status quo but also each other and being able to respond accordingly. Whether commenting on the nature of relationships between African American men and women or discussing abuse, students are expected to clearly articulate their reasoning on the issues and engage with one another. Florence places a particular emphasis on examining issues within the community, paired with the expectation that her students will not only engage in those issues but commit to addressing them. Ultimately, her understanding of being a critical educator is preparing students to be fully empowered to show up and participate in their own lives and in larger society.

Finally, although Florence could have been more explicit in addressing specific actions students could or should be taking as part of a critical pedagogy, she does cite many examples of famous individuals who work to "give something back to the community." She talks about KRS-One's recent antiviolence rally at a local school that had a student fatally shot right outside, T.I.'s charity work, and Young Joc's discussions about faith. They recognize, on varying levels, the social and economic injustices in society and work toward providing greater opportunities for the disenfranchised. Florence holds these people up as individuals to emulate and encourages her students to look toward learning from their example.

TEACHING AS COLLABORATIVE, DEMOCRATIC, AND EVOLVING

According to Lincoln (1995), "the avowed purpose of education in the United States has been to educate citizens for participation in democratic processes . . . [although] we have often done otherwise" (p. 89). Educators, then, have a responsibility to help students gain the skills and experiences necessary to fully participate as active, critical citizenry: "As gatekeepers of culture, they are also uniquely positioned to become revolutionary usurpers of culture in the interests of enhancing critical possibilities for social change" (O'Loughlin, 1995, p. 114). Educators can participate in the creation of democratic classrooms by considering these conditions and helping students develop voices of their own. This not only entails helping students realize how they author their own voices, but allowing the rehearsal of these voices within the safety of the classroom or school in an effort to encourage students to apply this learning beyond the confines of the classroom. Through the sharing of students' stories, interests, and experiences—which encourages them to question their beliefs and those of others—youth and educators can collaboratively propose new meanings of literacy learning (Camangian, 2008; Fisher, 2009; Kinloch, 2010; Kirkland, 2010).

This kind of polyvocalism or multi-voicedness is part of a critical pedagogy. It welcomes the emergence of a wide range of roles, voices, and issues, even if they are in conflict or contradiction with each other. Similarly, hip-hop straddles and encompasses many partialities—such as the blatant misogyny of Nelly's "Tip Drill" music video to the pro-girl, feminist slant of various b-girl organizations. The same art form that gave birth to hyper-capitalist gangster rap also gave birth to socially progressive "backpack rap." Thus, Flavor Flav can be both part of a socially and politically conscious hip-hop group (Public Enemy) *and* have his own reality dating television show featuring scantily clad women.

Within the classroom, Florence must not only confront these truths and contradictions within hip-hop, but within the students, and in society. She teaches her students about who Flavor Flav is beyond the image presented on the television show, the complexities of T.I.'s community service and felony weapons charges, and their own complicity or resistance to a variety of messages. Teaching about the misogyny in some rap songs is not just about abstract notions of feminism but about how someone is talking about their mothers or sisters. Discussing the nature of romantic relationships in popular culture, in literature, or in their own lives, students interrogate their beliefs and own inherent contradictions. In seeking to examine these kinds of multiple truths more closely, Florence prepares students to be aware of not only their own views and to be able to expand upon and act upon these views, but to learn how to listen to and engage with others as well. Thus, the kind of teaching and learning that occurs within her classroom is more fluid and multidirectional, as knowledge is collaboratively constructed and critiqued.

As Florence strives to enact these principles in her classroom, she acknowledges that one of her biggest concerns is in creating a sense of community and collaboration with her students. Therefore, she is purposeful in how she acknowledges her students' stories and experiences in ways that attempt to ensure that students are recognized and validated as individuals. Encompassed within this is an understanding that sometimes these stories or experiences will come into conflict with one another. Florence embraces the conflict and potential cacophony that can emerge as she recognizes that so many voices cannot always merge into a single, unified harmony— sometimes not even within the same individual. This mirrors the contradictions within hip-hop itself and its own evolution as an art. Tupac Shakur, known for his mantra of a "Thug Life" and depictions of violence in his raps, also studied ballet in high school; a student who discusses his disappointment with his father's treatment of his mother also has a reputation as a "player" in his high school. There is room, though, both in hip-hop and in Florence's classroom, for these kinds of complexities, and it is the community fostered in her classroom that allows these kinds of truths to be shared.

One particularly poignant example of how this sense of community manifests in her classroom involves a student cutting class. Humphrey is a special education student who is almost always in class but rarely participates. In most classrooms, he would have slid by unnoticed by the teacher and/or his peers. However, one day when Florence is taking attendance, she notes that he is absent and wonders aloud whether anyone has seen him. She is promptly informed by several students that he is cutting class and sleeping in the library. Immediately, several students volunteer to go get him; however, Florence takes it upon herself to leave, with another student in tow, to retrieve Humphrey. When they bring him back, he grins sheepishly and the class cheers, punctuated with shouts of, "You've got to learn, too!"

In a classroom where the students refer to each other as "Sister" or "Brother" and by name, where each student is recognized and validated, and where there is a deep sense of community and collaboration, risks can be taken and leaps made in teaching and learning. Florence's classroom is a special space, but it does not necessarily have to be the only one of its kind.

By examining what it is that hip-hop offers in terms of possibilities in education and what we can learn from it and from teachers who effectively utilize it in their classrooms, we can begin to more fully explore the potential it offers.

CRITICAL PERSPECTIVE

Much of what is commercially available today that touts a hip-hop curriculum or that offers to show teachers how to use hip-hop in their teaching is problematic. Whether it offers pre-created handouts pairing rap lyrics with canonical texts, increased SAT vocabulary, or improved student engagement, most of these programs package hip-hop in overly simplified ways. It reduces hip-hop only to rap music (versus a culture or movement with a history and a context) and as a gimmick to achieve a more traditional kind of education—what I refer to as the "condiment effect." Without actually changing how education works, these programs seek to shake on a little hip-hop or pop culture to make traditional teaching and learning more palatable to increasingly disenchanted students.

In this chapter, I have argued for a more complicated understanding of hip-hop and of teaching and learning using hip-hop as critical pedagogy. This is not to say that such a pedagogy is not without its faults, potential problems, or hiccups. In fact, even on the most basic level, I find that Florence and her students do not agree. In small-group interviews, almost all of Florence's students say point-blank that they do not think she uses hip-hop in her teaching. However, what is revealed is that Florence has a richer and more complex understanding of hip-hop than her students think. In fact, when I query her about the perplexing nature of her students' responses, Florence replies that her definition of hip-hop is much broader than her students' definitions. For Florence, hip-hop is representative of a culture and a way of thinking and being in the world that includes, but is not just limited to, music (the latter of which is how her students *see* hip-hop). Teaching with hip-hop is not so much about using the artifacts of hip-hop as it is about drawing upon the pedagogical promise, or essence, of hip-hop as *improvisational and experimental, critical, dialogic, collaborative and democratic,* and *evolving* (Chang, 2005; Rose, 1994; Smitherman, 1997). With this understanding, Florence's classroom embodies a deeper sense of hip-hop.

This raises a larger question of why use hip-hop—or popular culture—in classrooms. What is hoped to be accomplished, and for what end? Invoking the points made at the beginning of this chapter, the increasing disparities in outcomes for students from nondominant groups indicate that something is not working in today's educational system—or, for the more cynical readers, that something is working exactly the way it is meant to (i.e., that those in power remain in power and those who are marginalized stay on the margins). If we are serious about changing education and changing these outcomes, shaking on a little popular culture will not be enough. An understanding of hip-hop as improvisational and experimental, critical, dialogic, collaborative and democratic, and evolving can be extended beyond hip-hop into a greater understanding of teaching and learning. Ultimately, as a teacher in my larger research project, from which findings in this chapter are derived, puts it, "It's not really about hip-hop." It is more about teaching something that you are passionate about, that resonates with your students, and about being conscious and reflective about teaching and learning.

In recent years, Chicago has received national media attention for the large number of public school students who have been victims of violence, most of these purportedly gang-related. There have been scores of articles on what to do, press conferences, and rallies, all attempting to address and remediate the realities of being a young person living in certain pockets of the city. Florence's school lost a senior to the violence of the streets that year. He was shot outside a school at which he was taking classes on the weekend. Florence is very aware of the realities of her students' lives and she seeks to arm her students with the self-awareness and critical eye to engage in the injustices of the world. She is doing everything she can to "reach and teach" every student, to offer alternatives to the violence they see around them, and the opportunity to make choices to be fully engaged both in their classrooms and in larger society. This *is* bigger than hip-hop.

REFERENCES

Anyon, J. (1980). Social class and the hidden curriculum of work. *Journal of Education, 162*(1), 67–92.

Barton, D. (2001). Directions for literacy research: Analysing language and social practices in a textually mediated world. *Language and Education, 15*(2), 92–104.

Bowman, P. J., & Howard, C. (1985). Race related socialization, motivation, and academic achievement: A study of black youths in three-generation families. *Journal of the American Academy of Child Psychiatry, 24,* 134–141.

Brookfield, S. (2003). Critical thinking in adulthood. In D. Fasko (Ed.), *Critical thinking and reasoning: Current research, theory, and practice.* Cresskill, NJ: Hampton Press.

Camangian, P. (2008). Untempered tongues: Teaching performance poetry for social justice. *English teaching: Practice and critique, 7*(2), 35–55.

Campbell, K. E. (2005). *"Gettin' our groove on": Rhetoric, language, and literacy for the hip hop generation.* Detroit: Wayne State University Press.

Chang, J. (2005). *Can't stop, won't stop: A history of the hip-hop generation.* New York: Picador.

Clay, A. (2003). Keepin' it real: Black youth, hip-hop culture, and black identity. *American Behavioral Scientist, 46*(10), 1346–1358.

Cope, B., & Kalantzis, M. (Eds.). (2000). *Multiliteracies: Literacy learning and the design of social futures.* London: Routledge.

Corley, M. (2003). *Poverty, racism and literacy.* Columbus, OH: ERIC Clearinghouse on Adult, Career, and Vocational Education, Center on Education and Training for Employment, College of Education, the Ohio State University. (ERIC Document Reproduction Service No.ED475392)

DeBlase, G. (2003). Missing stories, missing lives: Urban girls (re)constructing race and gender in the literacy classroom. *Urban Education, 38*(3), 279–329.

Duncan-Andrade, J. M. R., and Morrell, E (2008). *The art of critical pedagogy: Possibilities for moving from theory to practice in urban schools.* New York: Peter Lang.

Fisher, M. T. (2004). "The song is unfinished": The new literate and literary and their institutions. *Written Communication, 21*(3), 290–312.

Fisher, M. T. (2009). *Black Literate Lives.* New York: Routledge.

Freire, P. (1997). *Pedagogy of the oppressed.* New York: Continuum.

Freire, P., & Macedo, D. (1987). *Literacy: Reading the word the world.* New York: Routledge.

Hagood, M. C. (2002). Critical literacy for whom? *Reading Research and Instruction, 41*(3), 247–265.

Hill, M. L. (2009). *Beats, rhymes, and classroom life.* New York: Teachers College Press.

Howard, T. C. (2003). Culturally relevant pedagogy: Ingredients for critical teacher reflection. *Theory into Practice, 42*(3), 195–202.

Jay, G., & Graff, G. (1995). A critique of critical pedagogy. In M. Berube, & C. Nelson (Eds.), *Higher education under fire: Politics, economics, and the crisis of the humanities* (pp. 201–258). New York: Routledge.

Jenoure, T. (2000). *Navigators: African American musicians, dancers, and visual artists in academe.* Albany: State University of New York Press.

Keating, D., & Sasse, D. (1996). Cognitive socialization in adolescence: Critical period for a critical habit of mind. In G. R. Adams, R. Montemayor & T. Gullota (Eds.), *Psychosocial development during adolescence: Progress in developmental contextualism.* (pp. 232–258). New York: Sage.

Kincheloe, J. L. (2004). *Critical pedagogy primer.* New York: Peter Lang.

Kinloch, V. (2010). *Harlem on our minds: Place, race, and the literacies of urban youth.* New York: Teachers College Press.

Kirkland, D. (2010). English(es) in urban contexts: Politics, pluralism, and possibilities. *English Education, 42*(3), 293–306.

Lapp, D., Fisher, D., & Wolsey, T. D. (2009). *Literacy growth for every child: Differentiated small-group instruction, K–6.* New York: Guilford Press.

Lincoln, Y. S. (1995). In search of students' voices. *Theory into Practice, 34*(2), 88–93.

McLaren, P. (2006). *Life in schools: An introduction to critical pedagogy in the foundations of education.* Boston: Pearson/Allyn and Bacon.

Mahiri, J. (Ed.). (2004). *What they don't learn in school: Literacy in the lives of urban youth.* New York: Peter Lang.

Moje, E. B. (2000). "To be part of the story": The literacy practices of gangsta adolescents. *Teachers College Record, 102*(3), 651–690.

Nagle, J. P. (1999). Histories of success and failure: Working class students' literacy experiences. *Journal of Adolescent and Adult Literacy, 43*(2), 172–185.

National Collaborative on Diversity in the Teaching Force. (2004). *Assessment of diversity in America's teaching force: A call to action.*

New London Group. (1996). A pedagogy of multiliteracies: Designing social futures. *Harvard Educational Review, 66*(1), 60–92.

Nieto, S. (2006). Solidarity, courage and heart: What teacher educators can learn from a new generation of teachers. *Intercultural Education, 17*(5), 457–473.

Noll, E. (1998). Experiencing literacy in and out of school: Case studies of two American Indian youths. *Journal of Literacy Research, 30*(2), 205–232.

O'Brien, D. (2003). Juxtaposing traditional and intermedial literacies to redefine the competence of struggling adolescents. *Reading Online, 6*(7).

O'Loughlin, M. (1995). Daring the imagination: Unlocking voices of dissent and possibility in teaching. *Theory into Practice, 34*(2), 107–116.

Perry, I. (2004). *Prophets of the hood.* Durham, NC: Duke University Press.

Potter, R. (1995). *Spectacular vernaculars: Hip-hop and the politics of postmodernism.* Albany: State University of New York Press.

Richardson, E. (2003). *African American literacies.* London: Routledge.

Rose, T. (1994). *Black noise: Rap music and black culture in contemporary America.* Hanover, CT: Wesleyan University Press.

Ross, T., & Rose, A. (Eds.). (1994). *Microphone Fiends: Youth Music and Culture.* New York: Routledge.

Sawyer, R. K. (2004). Improvised lessons: Collaborative discussion in the constructivist classroom. *Teaching Education, 15*(2), 189–201.

Smitherman, G. (1997). "The chain remain the same": Communicative practices in the hip hop nation. *Journal of Black Studies, 28*(1), 3–25.

Stapleton, K. R. (1998). From the margins to mainstream: The political power of hip-hop. *Media, Culture, & Society, 20,* 219-234.

Steele, C. M., & Aronson, J. (1995). Stereotype threat and the intellectual test performance of African Americans. *Journal of Personality and Social Psychology, 69*(5), 797–812.

Stevenson, H. C. (1997). Managing anger: Protective, proactive, or adaptive racial socialization identity profiles and manhood development. *Journal of Prevention and Intervention in the Community, 16,* 35–61.

Van Sluys, K. (2004). Engaging in critical literacy practices in a multiliteracies classroom. *53rd Yearbook of the National Reading Conference,* Scottsdale, AZ. (53RD) 400–416.

Willis, A. I. (2002). Dissin' and disremembering: Motivation and culturally and linguistically diverse students' literacy learning. *Reading & Writing Quarterly, 18,* 293–319.

CHAPTER 10

"The Consciousness of the Verbal Artist"

Understanding Vernacular Literacies in Digital and Embodied Spaces

Django Paris and David E. Kirkland

We must deal with the life and the behavior of discourse in a contradictory and multi-languaged world . . . Langauge—like the living
concrete environment in which the consciousness of the verbal artist
lives—is never unitary.
—Bakhtin, *The Dialogic Imagination*

I live in this liminal state between worlds, in between realities, in
between systems of knowledge, in between symbology systems.
—Anzaldúa, *Crossing Borderlands*

These words from Bakhtin (1981) and Anzaldúa (quoted in Lunsford,
2004) speak to one another across decades and vast cultural distances in
ways crucial for understanding the present moment of literacy in the lives of
urban youth. For Bakhtin, it is essential that language and literacy scholars
and educators understand oral and written communication as it reflects and
challenges a multilingual, multi-voiced landscape of difference and power,
at once contradicting and embracing official notions of official languages.
For Anzaldúa, to live through writing and speaking in such a world is to
straddle multiple spaces in the *borderlands* (Anzaldúa, 1987/1999) between
systems of meaning-making that are variously positioned as prestigious and
deficient by the dominant world.

In this chapter, we look to explore the "life and behavior of discourse" in the present moment of urban youth culture in order to illuminate the realities that urban youth occupy and challenge through the "symbology systems" of the written word. We seek to understand the *heteroglossic* reality Bakhtin (1981) called "the consciousness of the verbal artist" (p. 288) by listening to and learning from the many verbal artists we have worked with in urban youth communities. We conceptualize *youth communities* as groups of young people engaged in shared activities with shared valued meanings about those activities. The *youth spaces* and *canvases* of these communities are defined by communication and interaction primarily between youth through these shared activities and valued meanings. The verbal artists—African American, Latino/a, and Pacific Islander adolescents from our studies of language and literacy—inscribe and ascribe stories and selves across digital and embodied spaces using *vernacular literacies* that challenge existing theories of learning spaces and the purposes of literacy. We use the term *vernacular literacies* to describe the close relationship between the oral and written word in youth literacy practices that voice ethnic, linguistic, and countercultural identities upon everyday youth canvases (e.g., computer screens, phones, skin, clothing, paper). Vernacular literacies, we suggest, "represent that mode in which the political and the popular conjoin indentifactory pleasure with ideological resistance" (Farred, 2003, p. 10). These young people enact vernacular literacies across multiple borderlands at once—the borderlands at the edge of the oral and the written as well as those at the boundary of the digital and embodied. Through challenges to the nature of space and literacy, the vernacular literacies of youth push language and literacy scholars and educators to consider how our pedagogy and research must account for expanding visions of where, how, and why youth practice literacy (Kirkland, 2009).

WINDOWS INTO THE ORAL/WRITTEN AND DIGITAL/EMBODIED DICHOTOMIES

We begin by meditating on two literacy events produced by young people in our research. The first is a brief text message exchange from Paris's (2009, 2010) research in the urban West and the second is a social networking exchange from Kirkland's (2009) research in the urban Northeast. We view these youth inscriptions through discourse analytic lenses to illuminate the ways such literacy practices of the present resist two core dichotomies that continue to limit our field's understanding of contemporary youth space literacies: the oral/written dichotomy and the digital/embodied dichotomy.

"Chiln wit ma friends": Text Messaging and the Oral/Written Dichotomy

The first example in our discussion is a text message exchange Paris had with Rochelle, a 15-year-old African American young woman he worked with during a yearlong study of language, literacy, and difference among Latino/a, African American, and Pacific Islander youth in the urban West. This text exchange will serve as an initial window into the ways youth's texting across digital and embodied spaces challenges the oral/written dichotomy. During this study, Paris exchanged hundreds of text messages with youth, all adolescents who attended the same urban high school. On this day, he was driving back from another section of the metro area when Rochelle began a literacy exchange via their cellular phones. A brief excerpt follows. (We reproduced youth literacy acts as they were authored, maintaining youth spelling, capitalization, and punctuation in all data examples.)

ROCHELLE: Wat u doin
PARIS: Wuz drvin back from Hayward now just chillin n you?
ROCHELLE: Chiln wit ma friends

This text, like the hundreds of electronic media exchanges Paris had with youth across ethnic groups, showed Rochelle employing linguistic features of African American Language (AAL) in her writing as well other acts of resistance to Dominant American English (DAE) writing conventions. AAL is a systematic variety of English spoken as at least one of the varieties of English by many African Americans (see Green [2002] and Rickford & Rickford [2000] for a full account of all the AAL features described in this chapter). AAL has a rich historical and continuing tradition in the literature, spiritual practices, music, and everyday lives of African Americans. Far beyond the mere efficiency of print often linked to text messaging (as in Rochelle's omission of the "h" in "what" as well as the lack of a question mark), Rochelle participated here in writing the sound system of AAL into her phone. Her choices of "doin" for the DAE "doing" and "wit" for the DAE "with" are examples of two common consonant replacements in the sound system of spoken AAL and other nondominant Englishes. Similarly, Rochelle's texting "Ma" instead of "My" is an example of monopthongization—the transformation of the two vowel sound sequence in "My" (m-ah-ee) to a long one vowel sequence in "Ma" (m-ah)—a phonological feature common in AAL and some southern varieties of American English. It is important to note that "Ma" does little for efficiency. Undoubtedly, Rochelle knew how to spell "doing," "with" and "my" conventionally, but chose in this and all her texting to resist such conventions. Paris, too, participated in resistant spellings here with "Wuz" and

AAL phonology and lexicon in "chillin." This authentically reflected his text messaging practices outside the research, as well.

Beyond the sound of spoken AAL, Rochelle's texting of "u" for "you" and omission of the "h" in "Wat" not only aid in the efficiency of the text, they are also examples of what sociolinguists term *eye dialect*—alternative spelling that does not change the sound, but indexes vernacular language. That is, "u" and "Wat" sound the same as "you" and "What," but mark the discourse as both resistant to dominant norms and representative of youth vernacular languages. We see such choices as resistance because youth made conscious counterchoices to DAE spellings and constructions as a means of communicating what they perceived as their authentic voices. In Paris's conversations with Rochelle and her peers about such textual choices as AAL and eye dialect, youth discussed the attempt to have text messages "sound" like the author of the text.

In addition to AAL phonology, AAL grammar was also essential to many of the text messages Paris exchanged with youth. Miles, an African American young man Paris worked with, texted to Paris, "We so raw" (5/11/07) in response to an exceptional play in a professional basketball game he and Paris were watching in different locations. In his brief, one line text, Miles used one of the major features of AAL grammar by omitting the copula in "We ø so raw" (for the DAE "We *are* so raw"). Basically, AAL speakers (and here, writers) have the option of omitting the "is" or "are." "Raw" (here meaning "extremely good") is also an example of how Miles employed the *semantic inversion* (Smitherman, 1977) common in the AAL lexicon, where the dominant meanings of words are repurposed and often reversed. Throughout the year, Paris documented numerous examples of AAL lexicon, phonology, and grammar in the text messages of Black and Brown students (see Paris, 2009, for a full account of AAL sharing across ethnicity in this study). Figure 10.1 provides examples of AAL features common in the text messages.

This use of AAL grammar, phonology, and lexicon in the text messages of urban youth shows a close relationship between vernacular talk and text messaging that goes beyond a mere efficiency of print and even beyond the resistant orthography evident in alternative spellings. Rochelle, Miles, and the other youth of color in Paris's work were being particular users of written language by indexing ethnic, linguistic, and youth identity through uses of AAL. All of these youth were to some extent bidialectal AAL speakers, but representing the vernacular in writing is a more conscious act than the often unconscious act of using vernacular in speech, particularly when authors are writing words and grammatical constructions they use and know well in DAE. These features also made their way onto more traditional canvases in Paris's study through youth written rap lyrics and the writing youth did on clothing and backpacks (see Paris, 2010).

Figure 10.1. AAL Features in Text Messages

Feature Example

Phonology

Monopthongization: ma {my}
Consonant Replacements: ing to in (ŋ to n): goin, doin
th to d (ð to d): da {the}, diz {this}
Th to t (θ to t): tanx {thanks}
R and L Vocalization: fo sho {for sure}, skoo {school}

Lexicon

Ducez {a salutation meaning "peace"}
Hela {local adjective for "extremely"}
Hatr {a person lacking respect}

Grammar

Zero Copula: we ø da champz
Regularized Agreement: the tickets is 10
Immediate Future Tense Markers: We Fnah {getting ready to} graduate; Ima
leave {I'm going to leave}

These text messages, a vital artery of written communication in youth space and beyond, were vernacular literacies which pushed against the separation between oral and written language as youth attempted to actively inscribe their everyday voices and experiences as Black and Brown youth into the keypads of their phones. They were attempts at capturing embodied orality in printed form. The oral/written dichotomy has been at the heart of decades of arguments about the superiority and civilizing capacity of the written word over the spoken one (Collins & Blot, 2003). Critical theorists and researchers of language and literacy have pushed hard against this separation for many decades, in effect debunking the overarching written/oral split in favor of contextualized understandings of the uses of language (Dyson, 2005). The foundation of this thinking has been built on investigating the intersections of language, literacy, power, and identity in particular social and cultural moments and communities as the field of language and literacy has moved from monolithic/decontextualized understandings of language and literacy to situated/contextualized understandings of languages and literacies (Bakhtin, 1981; Heath, 1983; de Certeau, 1984; Street, 1984).

Contemporary research has taken the lead of these sociocultural literacy scholars as the first decade of this century has seen an explosion of new digital avenues for inscription and a continual evolution of more familiar literacy canvases. Text messaging, of course, is only one of these new and evolving avenues. Other current work on the ways urban youth literacies marry the oral and written in acts of identity includes scholarship on spoken word (Dyson, 2005; Fisher, 2005), hip-hop lyrics (Alim, 2006; Hill, 2009; Kirkland, 2007, 2008; Mahiri, 1998), and online communication (Alvermann, 2008; Kirkland, in press; Knobel & Lankshear, 2008; West, 2008). These vernacular literacies engage in a multimodal performativity that spans various media between the oral and written, the textual and otherwise symbolic, the static word and the moving word, the dominant voice and the marginalized one (Lunsford, 2007). (It is important to note that current multimodal forms of writing are challenging the primacy of dominant print literacy, though they are in no way new. Anzaldúa [1987/1999] and Baca [2008] have shown such writing, using the visual and performative at the heart of Mesoamerican written communication systems that were systematically destroyed by conquistadors in favor of alphabetized print dominance.) Our chapter seeks to extend this long and continuing work that has pushed against the oral/written dichotomy by foregrounding the ways vernacular literacies index ethnic, linguistic, and countercultural identities through infusing the written word with the oral one.

In addition to the ways Rochelle and her peers' text messages used AAL features against the backdrop of DAE conventions, these messages were also written and delivered over cellular phones, often accompanied by visual artifacts such as photographs. These messages, then, brought the spoken together with the written on an everyday youth canvas. To fully grasp the educational value of vernacular literacies, language and literacy scholars and educators must not only look at *how* the writing happens, but also *where* it happens. In the following section, we analyze a literacy act from Kirkland's research to push a dichotomy that is less theorized but nonetheless crucial to our research and teaching with the verbal artists of urban youth communities: the digital/embodied dichotomy. Although there is increasing energy on this subject in genre theory (Duke & Purcell-Gates, 2003; Gee, 1996; Perry, 2009), Kirkland fuses Smitherman's (1977) and Bakhtin's (1981) notions of discourse to illustrate the digital/embodied dichotomy and the ways that it breaks down in a Twitter conversation.

"You Are a Beautiful Reality": A Twitter Conversation and the Digital/Embodied Dichotomy

The second example is of a social networking exchange Kirkland archived from the Twitter page of one of his research participants, Maya. The exchange depicts a conversation between Maya, an adolescent Black female, and her friend Kisha, also an adolescent Black female. Fusing multiple languages and digital dialects (e.g., textspeak, AAL, and modified dominant English) and the politics of converging words/worlds, the conversation between

Maya and her friend Kisha serves as a window into what we are calling the digital/embodied dichotomy that so many schools impose. Schools operate as if digital spaces were indeed separate from physical ones, where in fact the fluidity of space in this postmodern era makes "distributed cognition" a more plausible reality (Wertsch, 1991) and, therefore, spatial rigidity problematic (Kirkland, 2009).

By "digital" we are referring to the new electronic landscapes/templates where new literacy practices are happening (cf. Alvermann, 2008). By "embodied" we are referring to the more concrete forms in which and spaces where literacy has traditionally taken place. We offer the exchange below, one from among hundreds of digital artifacts that Kirkland collected from October 2006 to August 2009, to comment on the digital/embodied dichotomy. The exchange is reprinted here with the permission of both Maya and Kisha.

KISHA: hiya lady. ur performance last night was soooo demanding and felt!! seemed like 2 mins not 4 :) love yooou!!!!!

MAYA: I been on vacation in my own city for the past 4 days . . . Thank u

KISHA: Where you been?

MAYA: At the Women's Voices showcase here to see R.A.C.

KISHA: I think I do too much. "Sometimes I wish that I was less of a woman."

MAYA: "if u r a Jack of all trades, you're a master of nothing"

KISHA: Sometimes I amaze myself. I'm not quite sure how I do it all the time but it's painful to be the better person.

MAYA: when you can accept a situation for what it is, you will learn peace.

KISHA: Remember whut I said last night. You're on another level awesome, woman. And I wasn't playing. (thank you)

MAYA: Ginger tea.

KISHA: "Maya was my sister in another life"

MAYA: (Yes. We were amazing in our beauty, pain, healing, goddess stance. Pouring your soul out #truth) thank you.

KISHA: thank you darling. I try.

MAYA: Let go and breathe. Heal.

KISHA: i will. love ya.

MAYA: we have to talk more. but thank you so much for tonight. im gr8ful to know you. Getting ready for the photo shoot with maceo!

KISHA: always, dear Maya. You are a beautiful reality. I hope to see you sooner than later.

MAYA: i love you. Heal.

Similar to the text message exchanges in the examples above, the young women's discourse in this exchange is highlighted by the possibilities and limits of digitized vernacular languages and literacies: abbreviated (as opposed to elaborated discourse); symbolic intermingling among alphanumeric characters to abbreviate phonemes; creative usages of punctuation and spellings to suggest feeling, thought, and emotion; context-specific meanings, and plays on case usage (i.e., capitalization/lowercase) to intimate importance, degree, and familiarity. These digital distinctions presuppose a kind of digital dialect where language is performed and played with to the degree that it communicates a wealth of meaning among individuals who share and can understand its more nuanced cadences.

This dialect is often distinguished by spaces (digital/embodied) that both Maya and Kisha navigate and the beautiful brush of Black undertones beneath the audacious sounds of their voices and the standardizing force of language to which each of these voices submits (Bakhtin, 1981). Yet, beyond too easily distinguished spatial differences is the rude and eloquent remembrances of a mother tongue translated into digital verse—for example, a common grammatical feature of AAL that finds a presence early in the exchange. Its familiar face is revealed in both Maya's and Kisha's usages of the perfect progressive form of the verb *to be*, as in: "I been on vacation in my own city for the past 4 days" and "Where you been?" However, for much of the exchange, the two young women rehearse their thoughts in what we term here Modified Dominant American English (MDAE), a form of English that erases culturally specific syntax features while particular elements of an individual's linguistics identity survive. Further, in their appropriation and reaccentuation (or discursive modification) of DAE, these young women demonstrated their agency over form and space, sanctioning a language between the borders of a digital/real dimension that curved to their very intentions and purposes. Hence, the tenuous elements of social and cultural struggle that played out in Maya and Kisha's physical world lived in their speech. It was transferred from its embodied form and resolved in this digital exchange, where the irony of Black Talk set in the Whiteface of DAE has survived.

In these survivals are various elements of linguistic identity that surface throughout the exchange. They reveal Black essences or forms of discourse (see Figure 10.2), which are modes of cultural expression that carry particular meanings/messages (Smitherman, 1977). Such forms of discourse are embodied in Black cultural spaces. Not to be outdone, Black forms of discourse—linguistic constructions of Blackness—are prevalent in Maya's and Kisha's digital exchange. For example, Kisha signifies in the cultural linguistic sense (Smitherman, 1977) when she writes: "I think I do too much. 'Sometimes I wish that I was less of a woman' . . . it's painful to be the better person." There is also the Black discursive form of braggadocio present

Figure 10.2. Examples of AAL Discourse Forms in the Twitter Conversation

Form	Definition	Example
Signification	A form of verbal irony and play that exploits the gaps between expected discourse and what is actually revealed.	"I think I do too much. 'Sometimes I wish that I was less of a woman' . . . it's painful to be the better person."
Braggadocio	A verbal strategy characterized by cleaver boasts and skillful language techniques for bragging.	"Sometimes I amaze myself. I'm not quite sure how I do it all the time. . . ."
Call and Response	A type of verbal and nonverbal interaction between speaker and listener characterized by a statement follower by a spontaneous (and usually affirming) rejoinder.	The call: "Remember whut you said last night . . ." The response: "Ginger tea."
Metaphysical Transcendence	A leitmotif in African American women's discourse that operates as strategy for and indication of internal and collective strength. It also expresses the spiritual overcoming of the Black female metaphysical dilemma (see Shange, 1977).	(a) "Maya was my sister in another life." (b) "let go and breathe [and] Heal."

in the exchange, revealed in one of the young women's turns: "Sometimes I amaze myself. I'm not quite sure how I do it all the time. . . ." Such modes of discourse transcend the digital page, playing out patterns of embodied expression that predate the technology.

Perhaps another, more deeply entrenched and persistent discourse hovers over the text of the young females' conversation; that is, the (discourse of) metaphysical dilemma (Shange, 1977). Kirkland has written about this discourse in another work (Kirkland, in press). In it, he argues that a latent theme of dilemma is present in the digital and embodied spaces in which Black females inhabit and ascribe meaning through their interpretations of life—even when those interpretations happen in seemingly standardized ways or in virtual spaces. The borders of this discourse (and the dilemma/transcendence it reveals) are not confined to recognizable locations or even to this life, for Kisha makes this point well when she explains: "Maya was my sister in another life." Still, this discourse fashions itself between the invisible borders of the young women's digital/embodied realities. In this space, the digital/embodied dichotomy becomes a mirage, and distinctions that have made digital and physical spaces separate disappear. Therefore, insisting upon a digital/embodied split seems unhelpful in helping researchers and educators make sense of literacy exchanges. A new language takes shape between the arbitrary distinctions of space highlighted by the fascination of the media through which individuals write. This new language offers a new space (Kirkland, 2009) that unites the common language of African American culture, a known genuflection to a historical social context where two young women, as Maya said, "let go and breathe [and] Heal."

Notwithstanding, the abbreviated sentences and paced aspectual elements of writing online have done much to change where and how people write (Hull, 2003; Miller, 2001). And although digital multimedia and multimodal elements of literacy are quite literally changing the literacy game (Gee, 1996), they have not seemed to change why people write. Albeit a snapshot of a larger conversation, the exchange between Kisha and Maya hints at the consistent themes of writing, themes as ancient as Adam that are today being performed on the digital page. There, we see an unlikely show of enduring gendered/raced themes, performed in the subtle discourse forms that trap cultural ideas shaped in words and particular ways of using them. We see these ideas in Maya's and Kisha's discourse of dilemma which, in a fine African American traditional sense, trades on the calls and responses of preachers and their congregations (Moss, 2003): (call) "Remember whut you said last night . . ." (response) "Ginger tea" (used here like the term *Amen*). In this case, the call bears witness to the young women's acts of rejoinder to one another, to their shared sociocultural history (Bakhtin, 1981). Their exchange is testimony to a linguistic complexity that is in every linguistic event, digital or embodied. This complexity is culturally communicated and performed through the completion of an ascribed thought, which itself summons a context unknown to an outsider, a meaning that is deeply intrinsic, powerfully personal, but also profoundly cultural.

Between Maya and Kisha, the dichotomy between digital and embodied spaces breaks down. Whether in the context of a computer screen or in another community setting, words become forms of testifyin in the way that Smitherman (1977, 1999) uses the term to describe how AAL users employ the transcendent discourse of survival past struggle to shape a larger, collective narrative self (cf. Morgan, 2000), or as Maya puts it: "We were amazing in our beauty, pain, healing, goddess stance." The tribute to history, to a past rooted in something, which is alive in Maya's and Kisha's words, is also spiritual and at once didactical and communal. These metaphysical, or what Richardson (2003) calls meta-linguistic elements of Black discourse, transcend space and even time. And through their written representations, a historical voice capable of penetrating the spatial schism between the digital and physical universe is present. Between Maya and Kisha, the discourses of being Black and female online are barely different from those of just being Black and female.

Further, in the digital space, which suddenly mirrored the young women's embodied spaces, Maya and Kisha uttered timeless thoughts—encouraging and inspiring—needing no affixation to the properties of place. Instead, they ascend upward from the digital pulpit of a converted computer screen, pouring themselves into a historical chamber of "echoes" (Bakhtin, 1981), offering small but supple sound bites of wisdom: "when you can accept a situation for what it is, you will learn peace." Kisha, in her own way, leans over to Maya who is not in the room, responding to the echo of history and culture, re-voicing as it were the digital presences of embodied womanhood which, for her, symbolizes "a beautiful reality"—a reality she soon hopes to see in person.

The term *soon* (even more so than *reality*) in the exchange reveals much. It immediately signals the very real distances that sociolinguistically collapse between digital and embodied spaces. However, the digital, in this case, allows for a type of meaningful transaction—even intimate conversation—between two physically distant friends. On its surface, that conversation is distinct, played out on a stage of distinguishably digital dialects and spelled out in the script of distinctly digital diacritics. So we have not overlooked that Kisha tips her hand when she reveals that digital spaces are not the same as physical ones. Although the digital space offers a place for intimacy and friendly interaction, the embodied space—a presence that is missing—is yet longed for, as digital spaces have a way of simultaneously creating and collapsing distances (Kirkland, 2009). However, our point here is that the performance of spaces/realities overlaps and departs at once in very important ways around larger linguistic and physical boundaries that locate themselves on a stage of similarities (as opposed to differences) where surface distinctions are merely prompts.

VERNACULAR LITERACIES, DIGNITY, AND RESISTANCE

Taken together, the text messaging and social networking exchanges in our work raise important questions about literacy in the lives of contemporary urban youth communities. In both of these examples, space (where the action of writing and reading takes place and how that place is experienced) and modality (in what fashion and in what medium the experience of writing and reading is delivered and received) intersect with experiences of being Black and Brown youth in the 21st century in ways we must contend with as teachers and researchers.

We find de Certeau's (1984) notion of the *scriptural economy* particularly helpful as a backdrop to understanding the purpose and educational value of vernacular literacies. De Certeau theorizes that the everyday power of "writing" (comprised of a blank space, a text, and a social purpose) has been subsumed by institutions (such as schools and courts) and capitalist class structures to create and sustain inequities. This economy functions through writing individuals and groups into being through systems of recorded text with clear, dominating social purposes. As in the case of Maya and Kisha, such systems of recorded texts fall along deep lines of history and spaces in which languages of critique and counter cultural expression have incubated since the dawn of time.

History, of course, is not the only social element at play in the arranging of scriptural economies. Important to this work is the micro-institutional level of schools, where such textual records include cumulative files of academic and social evaluation, report cards, and demographic summaries of race/ethnicity and language proficiency. In this way, de Certeau's scriptural economy maintains its power by defining who is literate, educated, and potentially productive given the set of institutional records, thereby reinforcing classed, racialized, and language-based power inequities. We maintain that in schools, what counts as legitimate literacy, either at the institutional level or the individual level of student-produced writing (essays, tests, and so forth), also participates in this economy as students' school writing is regulated, evaluated, and translated into the systems of power that determine their worth and advancement.

Vernacular literacies resist this dominant scriptural economy of print by creating spaces, texts, and social purposes that contradict those that school promotes and demands. They are not always new forms of literacy, but mutating forms born in servitude and incorporating centuries of oral tradition and embodied space. In essence, they are what Bakhtin (1981) called *centrifugal forces* pulling against the centralizing (or *centripetal*) forces of the traditional DAE print-on-paper literacy most often legitimated in classrooms. If DAE and its assorted intellectual paraphernalia enforced a deep-seated sociocultural hierarchy, vernacular literacies have long worked to disassemble that hierarchy. As described in the text messages exchanged between Paris and Rochelle, vernacular literacies fold together alternative ruled-governed sequences of texts with emerging fields of discourse to express a new scriptural identity that performs new and old literate acts together. In consolidating modes, these acts are neither sufficiently oral nor written. The oral/written dichotomy long exercised to make legitimate dominant scriptural economies over alternative ones loses breath in the wind of deep analysis of youth texts. These texts absorb in a fine Bakhtinian way oral and written discourses.

Through these discourses—what we are calling vernacular literacies— youth critique the conventions, genres, and mediums of dominant school literacy by blurring the oral, the written and the otherwise symbolic. They also utilize digital and real spaces in ways schools rarely do. In the example offered by Kirkland and his research participants, the known world of "the Women's Voices showcase" is extended to the space of virtual conversation. The local context of the "city" in which Maya lived and vacationed is also collapsed here. Further, the themes present in the young women's exchange are very real (embodied), yet they occur on a virtual platform in a setting that is more or less viewed as artificial and contrived (Miller, 2002). Since the power of Maya's and Keisha's exchange arises in part from its oral and embodied qualities, the logic goes that the act of becoming written and digitally published will inevitably sap that power. However, in their virtual chat room, the two women put to use oral language in a written context. The digital space in which their text is produced draws as well on other linguistic products, such as AAL, that were created in contexts which embody the young women's physical and cultural identities.

Although we acknowledge that these literacies in no way eclipse the power or access of the scriptural economy of school literacies, we also submit that the ability to express linguistic, ethnic, and countercultural identities across literacy spaces is a vital skill and one that should be fostered in classrooms. Without the ability to preserve, practice, and enhance their vernacular literacies, students who are native the borderlands—that "liminal state between worlds, in between realities, in between systems of knowledge, in between symbology systems" (Anzaldua in Lunsford, 2004, p. 50)—between digital/embodied spaces and oral/written languages will continue to be left behind peers who are indigenous to institutional norms, who fall on the right side of institutional boundaries, and who too often seem more successful performing traditional school literacies.

Not unlike some of their more academically "successful" counterparts, the youth in our work, all students of color and all from working poor communities, were writing all the time. They were "verbal artists" attempting to inscribe their place in a "contradictory and multi-languaged world" (Bakhtin, 1981). Yet much of this writing happened with little meaningful connection to the other important writing that happens in schools. The Englishes and other languages of these young people waited for such meaningful connection. So, too, did the spaces they inhabited through cellular phones and in online communities.

Vernacular literacies as they express language and identity across youth canvases have the potential to help us understand and teach. They challenge what, where, and how writing is accomplished for the ultimate purpose of helping youth find dignity and self in the face of school and social structures that often do not adequately listen to ethnically and linguistically marginalized youth. Such literacies are integral in "crafting the humble prose of living," where ethnic, youth, and artistic communities exist in the echoes of words (Dyson, 2005). In the "Critical Perspective" section we offer a

practical discussion of how teachers can join the work of vernacular literacies through the learning they promote in their classrooms.

CRITICAL PERSPECTIVE

As we have demonstrated throughout this chapter, writing is changing. As
Lunsford (2007) recently put it, "Where writing once meant *print* text—
black marks on white paper, left to right and top to bottom—today 'writing' is in full Technicolor; it is nonlinear and alive with sounds, voices, and
images of all kinds" (p. xiii). Our classrooms must learn from vernacular
literacies to push against the oral/written and digital/embodied dichotomies
in ways that contemporary writing expects and demands. This will mean
crafting classroom literacy experiences that include Englishes and other languages. This will mean opening up digital spaces for school literacy work.
This will mean extending a hand into youth space and into communities
of color and inviting critical classroom dialogue about audience, purpose,
language, and power through the written word. We see several places in
English and language and literacy classrooms where vernacular literacies
should be included in meaningful ways that honor youth and their communities while simultaneously honoring the realities of contemporary literacies. These are spaces that can push our pedagogies and curricula to change
in the ways writing and culture are changing.

Literature work, the backbone of many English classrooms, is laden
with the rich literary history of vernacular languages as they lived and live in
the achievements and struggles of cultural communities. AAL, for example,
is the linguistic medium through which life is experienced and conveyed in
countless texts, including two books often studied in high schools, Zora
Neal Hurston's *Their Eyes Were Watching God* (1937/1998) and Alice
Walker's *The Color Purple* (1982) (see Rickford & Rickford, 2000, for a
brief literary history of AAL). In both works, understanding the features
of AAL, from grammar to phonology to larger rhetorical traditions of signifying and toasting, is crucial to comprehending the worlds and themes
of Black American experience expressed through the books. We propose,
as Jordan (1985) did in her eloquent essay "Nobody Mean More to Me
Than You, and the Future Life Of Willie Jordan"—about teaching AAL
and Black discourse through *The Color Purple*—that revealing, extending,
and utilizing the AAL knowledge and broader cultural knowledge of students is crucial in the study of such literary works. Further, the evolution of
new forms of digital literacy as seen in the examples we have analyzed in
this chapter coupled with the evolution of spoken word and rap have given
youth expanding cultural spaces and purposes to enact their ethnic and linguistic identities through Black and Brown discourses. The classroom study

of such literary classics (and many, many others) should be joined with an analysis of the vernacular literacies of students. Their text messages, Twitter exchanges, rap lyrics, and spoken-word pieces, then, become texts to study alongside those of authors in discussions of the history of Englishes, historic oppression and segregation, and historic and continuing achievement through the voicing of AAL, other Englishes and languages, and the cultural traditions of youth and their communities.

Lessons utilizing the strategy of contrastive analysis (Godley et al., 2006) will be helpful where examples of vernacular literacies, literature, and various dominant and modified Englishes can be placed side-by-side in discussions of structure, language variation, speech communities, audience, and purpose. These lessons invite vernacular literacies to the table not as gimmicks to pull youth to the more important literacies, but as level players in a critical dialogue about why language varies and how literacy happens in the contemporary world.

It is clear that any pedagogy that embraces vernacular literacies through the study of the literature of the past and present must also embrace contemporary spaces and forms of writing. That is, as teachers we must be willing not only to study published and youth writing that challenges the oral/written and digital/embodied dichotomies, but we must also offer opportunities to create such writing in the classroom. The fact is that "vernacular literatures," which represent "new forms of academic texts," are increasingly being put to use in colleges and universities to explore what Ahmad (2007) calls "the living and organic nature of language" (p. 32). Being sensitive to the living impulse of the rhetorical situation—the nuances and complexities of writings and writing spaces—we suggest that teachers promote organic or naturalist writing pedagogies that offer students choices to compose in linguistic codes that are primarily spoken rather than written and in spaces that are fundamentally digital as opposed to embodied.

Using classic and contemporary literature and the vernacular literacies of youth to help students successfully navigate the discursive borderlands in ways that maintain their ethnic, linguistic, and artistic dignity while providing access to broadened literacies cannot happen if teachers do not have the knowledge of the structures and histories of vernacular language varieties, the structures and histories of digital spaces and conventions, and the intellectual history of the literacy oral/written and digital/embodied dichotomies. This is where the work of researchers and teacher educators must come in. We are hopeful that this chapter may help in this regard, but more research looking to understand how urban youth understand and use these literacies in the current moment can offer needed knowledge to both teachers and teacher educators. Teacher educators, for our part, must become conversant in the complex linguistic and ethnic identity work of vernacular literacies. All of us involved in language and literacy work with urban youth must foster the ability to read, write, and participate in writing in the present moment as we ask youth to join us in other important forms of writing and knowing. We seek a place where youth and their teachers can span both shores of the borderlands at once, challenging and participating in dominant forms of literacy even as they seek to change them. A place where vernacular literacies meet school literacies as the consciousness of all of the verbal artists—youth and teachers and researchers—come to understand each other and evolve together toward a more equitable linguistic and literate future.

REFERENCES

Ahmad, D. (2007). *Rotten English: A Literary Anthology*. New York: W.W. Norton & Company.

Alim, H. S. (2006). *Roc the mic right: The language of hip hop culture*. New York: Routledge.

Alvermann, D. E. (2008). Why bother theorizing adolescents' online literacies for classroom practice and research? *Journal of Adolescent & Adult Literacy, 52*, 8–19.

Anzaldúa, G. (1999). *Borderlands/La frontera: The new mestiza*. San Francisco: Aunt Lute Books. (Original work published 1987)

Baca, D. (2008). *Mestiz@ scripts, digital migrations and the territories of writing*. New York: Palgrave Macmillan.

Bakhtin, M. M. (1981). Discourse in the novel. In M. Holquist (Ed.), *The dialogic imagination: Four essays* (pp. 257–422). Austin: University of Texas Press.

Collins, J., & Blot, R. (2003). *Literacy and literacies: Texts, power, and identity*. Cambridge, UK: Cambridge University Press.

de Certeau, M. (1984). *The practice of everyday life*. Berkeley: University of California Press.

Duke, N. K., & Purcell-Gates, V. (2003). Genres at home and at school: Bridging the known to the new. *The Reading Teacher, 57*(1), 30–37.

Dyson, A. H. (2005). Crafting "the humble prose of living": Rethinking oral/written relations in the echoes of spoken word. *English Education, 37*, 149–164.

Farred, G. (2003). *What's my name: Black vernacular intellectuals*. Minneapolis: University of Minnesota Press.

Fisher, M. (2005). From the coffee house to the school house: The promise of spoken work poetry in school contexts. *English Education 37*(2), 115–131.

Gee, J. P. (1996). *Social linguistic and literacies: Ideology in discourses* (2nd ed.). Bristol, PA: Taylor and Francis.

Godley, A., Sweetland, J., Wheeler, R., Minnici, A., & Carpenter, B. (2006). Preparing teachers for dialectally diverse classrooms. *Educational Researcher, 35*, 8, 30–38.

Green, L. (2002). *African American English: A linguistic introduction*. Cambridge, UK: Cambridge University Press.

Heath, S. B. (1983). *Ways with words*. New York: Cambridge University Press.

Hill, M. L. (2009). *Beats, rhymes and classroom life: Hip-hop pedagogy and the politics of identity.* New York: Teachers College Press.

Hull, G. (2003). Youth culture and digital media: New literacies for new times. *Research in the Teaching of English, 38,* 229–233.

Hurston, Z. N. (1998). *Their eyes were watching God.* New York: Harper Collins. (Original work published 1937)

Jordan, J. (1985). *Call: Political Essay.* Boston: South End.

Kirkland, D. (2007). The power of their texts: Using hip hop to help urban students meet NCTE/IRA national standards for the English language arts. In K. Jackson & S. Vavra (Eds.), *Closing the Gap* (pp. 129–145). Charlotte, NC: Information Age Publishing.

Kirkland, D. (2008). The rose that grew from concrete: Postmodern blackness and new English education. *English Journal, 97*(5), 69–75.

Kirkland, D. (2009). Researching and teaching literacy in the digital dimension. *Research in the Teaching of English, 44*(1), 8–22.

Kirkland, D. (in press). 4 colored girls who considered social networking when suicide wasn't enuf: Exploring the literate lives of young Black women in online social communities. In D. Alvermann (Ed.), *Adolescents' Online Literacies: Connecting Classrooms, Media, and Paradigms.* New York: Peter Lang.

Knobel, M., & Lankshear, C. (2008). Remix: The art and craft of endless hybridization. *Journal of Adolescent & Adult Literacy, 52*(1), 22–33.

Lunsford, A. (2004). Towards a mestiza rhetoric: Gloria Anzaldúa on composition and postcoloniality. In A. Lunsford & Ouzgame L. (Eds.), *Crossing Borderlands: Composition and Postcolonial Studies* (pp. 33–66). Pittsburgh: University of Pittsburgh Press.

Lunsford, A. (2007). *Writing matters: Rhetoric in public and private lives.* Athens: University of Georgia Press.

Mahiri, J. (1998). *Shooting for excellence: African American youth and culture in new century schools.* Urbana: National Council of the Teachers of English & New York: Teachers College Press.

Miller, C. R. (2002). "Writing in a Culture of Simulation: *Ethos* Online." In P. Coppock (Ed.), *The Semiotics of Writing: Transdisciplinary Perspectives on the Technology of Writing* (pp. 253–279). Semiotic and Cognitive Studies. Turnhout, Belgium: Brepols.

Morgan, J. (2000). *When chickenheads come home to roost: A Hip-Hop feminist breaks it down.* New York: Simon and Schuster.

Moss, B. J. (2003). *A community text arises: A literate text and a literacy tradition in African American churches.* Cresskill, NJ: Hampton Press.

Paris, D. (2009). "They're in my culture, they speak the same way": African American language in multiethnic high schools. *Harvard Educational Review, 79,* 3, 428–447.

Paris, D. (2010). Texting identities: Lessons for classrooms from multiethnic youth space. *English Education, 42,* 3, 278–292.

Perry, K. H. (2009). Genres, contexts, and literacy practices: Literacy brokering among Sudanese refugee families. *Reading Research Quarterly, 44*(3), 256–276.

Richardson, E. (2003). *African American literacies.* New York: Routledge.

Rickford, J., & Rickford, R. (2000). *Spoken soul: The story of black English*. New York: John Wiley and Sons.

Shange, N. (1977). *For colored girls who considered suicide/When the rainbow is enuf*. New York: Scribner.

Smitherman, G. (1977). *Talkin and testifyin: The language of Black America*. Detroit: Wayne State University Press.

Smitherman, G. (1999). *Talkin that talk: African American language and culture*. New York: Routledge.

Street, B. (1984). *Literacy in theory and practice*. New York: Cambridge University Press.

Walker, A. (1982). *The color purple*. Orlando, FL: Harcourt.

West, K. C. (2008). Weblogs and literary response: Socially situated identities and hybrid social languages in English class blogs. *Journal of Adolescent and Adult Literacy, 51*(7), 588–598.

Wertsch, J. V. (1991). *Voices of the mind: A sociocultural approach to mediated action*. Cambridge, MA: Harvard University Press.

Conclusion

Reflections on Urban Education

Valerie Kinloch, Sonia Nieto, and Peter Smagorinsky

Where We've Been and Need to Go: Concluding Thoughts on Education in Urban Settings

Valerie Kinloch

The 10 chapters that comprise this book take up various and significant cases that highlight both the promise and potential of working with children, youth, and adults, particularly of color, in urban settings, and the urgency of this work in these critical educative, economic, and political times in which we live. From asking that we revisit popular and often outdated notions of education, achievement, and literacy to insisting that we revolutionize the ways in which we work with, come to know and re-know, and come to learn with and from our students, their families, and their local communities, the chapters and their contributors describe current literacy work and literacy challenges that involve an array of participants. They include children and youth, families and community members, teachers and teacher educators, as well as administrators and researchers in urban communities across the United States. Taken together, these chapters teach and remind us that critical, transformative literacy teaching, research, and advocacy are only critical and transformative when they really seek to advance educational research, practice, and policy for the sake of our students *and* because of our students. To do anything less is to disregard the very lives of those with whom we work, those who challenge us, daily, to consider "new perspectives and ways of acting in the world" (see Smagorinsky, in this Conclusion). We cannot do anything less than critical, our work cannot be anything other than transformative, and our teaching, research, and advocacy efforts cannot be anything other than relevant. We all have "a key role to play in the education of . . . children" (see Nieto, in this Conclusion).

Even more so, the chapters here have raised more questions for me, questions that I hope we will continue to address as a field. These include: What does it mean to be committed to culturally relevant teaching *and* to acknowledge, as Smagorinsky writes, that "every child's potential is channeled culturally"? Why do some educational experts and policymakers continue to rely on traditional meanings of literacy, success, and achievement when such meanings have long excluded the lived experiences of people of color and of poor people across the Diaspora? Might a discourse of care in relation to our teaching and research initiatives and directed toward our students, their families, and ourselves, lead to a heightened respect for the multiple language and literacy practices that already comprise a large part of the landscape within urban communities? With this questions come challenges related to, among other things, respecting and including in our curriculum, family and community literacies, as well as redesigning teacher education programs in ways where teachers, especially from nonminority and nonurban backgrounds, are trained to work with a variety of students, families, and communities (see Nieto; see also Kinloch, 2011; Ladson-Billings, 1995). Undoubtedly, I believe that the chapters in this book get us on our feet and into communities, classrooms, and other spaces where children, youth, and adults are not asking these questions, by living out their meanings.

To further contemplate these questions and challenges, I close this book by turning our attention to insights provided by two renowned scholars in language and literacy studies, Professors Sonia Nieto and Peter Smagorinsky. I asked them to reflect on pressing issues in urban education in order for us all to take stock of where we've been (as a field) and where we might go. It is my hope that their insights, paired with the insights from the contributors to this book, further ignite a fire within us to continue, or begin, to engage in critical, transformative, and radically revolutionary work within urban communities, specifically, and within the various other communities where our work is needed.

Critical Insights

Sonia Nieto

My first presentation at the American Educational Research Association (AERA) conference was in 1980, and it was based, as is often the case with young scholars, on the research I did for my doctoral dissertation. The research focused on the role of Puerto Rican families in curriculum development, and it documented work I had done in two Puerto Rican communities in the Northeast.

I was then, and am still, firmly committed to the idea that families have a key role to play in the education of their children, particularly families who are marginalized by the public schools. I was on a panel with three others, each presenting his or her research, and a respondent. I don't recall much of what the respondent said that day except for one comment that still stings and angers me: that Puerto Rican families living in poverty probably have very little to contribute to the education of their children, particularly in curriculum development. After all, he said, what do they know about curriculum?

It is this kind of attitude that still pervades much of the research on the education of students of color in U.S. schools. Yet, as the authors of this powerful text document, it is precisely by engaging with Latino, African American, Native American, and Asian American families that teachers can connect students with school in meaningful ways. But teachers sometimes find it difficult to do so because too many of them enter the profession without a clear idea of the significance of family and community outreach, or of how to engage families in the education of their children. This is usually not the fault of the teachers but rather the result of teacher education and professional development programs that give short shrift to this issue. However, given their own middle-class, nonurban, and nonminority backgrounds, it is also the case that the school and life experiences of many teachers have not prepared them to work with families that are different from themselves. As a consequence, teachers may have a vision of parent involvement—parents as homework helpers, field trip assistants, and cake sale organizers—that is both outdated and irrelevant for many of the families of the children they teach.

The contributors to *Urban Literacies* address this gap by focusing specifically on language and literacy practices in urban communities. They provide readers—teachers, teacher educators, researchers, and professional developers—with practical strategies, firmly grounded in critical perspectives on literacy, for engaging with students and their families in respectful and affirming ways. They also make it clear, however, that working with families is not always easy or fluid. Although engaging with families in authentic ways is always worthwhile in the end, getting there may be full of unexpected tensions and misunderstandings. It takes repeated attempts, a humble attitude, and a willingness to become learners of both their students and of their communities for teachers to become successful at working with families of disempowered youth.

What the editor and contributors of this text show us is that nothing will improve the education of urban students, or to use the current jargon, eliminate the "achievement gap" (a gap often created and exacerbated by unjust and unequal societal and school conditions and contexts) until there is a concerted effort to give teachers and schools the financial and moral resources they need to accomplish the job. This includes a concomitant will and shared belief that 1) children of color and all children living in poverty can be academically successful; 2) a thorough knowledge and deep respect for students and their communities on the part of teacher educators, administrators, and teachers can go a long way in improving student learning; and 3) teachers and other educators have a crucial—indeed, often a life-or-death role—to play in the literacy learning of young people who are too often dismissed or disparaged in our society.

Educational deficiencies are generally defined as emanating from students rather than from the system that is supposed to serve them. The authors of this text ask us, in myriad ways, to reject the notion that students are to blame for the brutal outcomes and massive failure of urban schools, and instead to accept our responsibility to turn the situation around.

Critical Insights

Peter Smagorinsky

In the mid-1980s, I visited my parents in New Jersey and had a conversation with their next-door neighbor, who was an elementary school principal in nearby Trenton. Trenton schools, like those in many urban systems, served students who were largely living in poverty; most students of means or potential were siphoned off by independent schools, or were swept away by White flight to other school systems. In the 2 years in which I worked in the Trenton schools in the 1970s—as both a substitute teacher and a high school hall monitor—I experienced the disaffection that most students felt toward formal education. The schools had many challenges that were quite similar to those facing urban educators today: high incidences of poverty, life trajectories headed more toward the streets than higher education, tremendous pressure from peers to reject public institutions such as schools, and scholastic emphases on facts and formalities that had little to do with students' lives.

At the time of my conversation with the Trenton principal, I was an early-career teacher outside Chicago, and so asked him about the schools and how he approached the challenges of urban education. His response was surprisingly simple: "You can't get these kids to learn anything until they've first mastered the conventions of formal English. That task was foremost in his school: to get Black kids to talk more like White kids. After that, an education was possible, but not before."

I found this conversation to be remarkable at the time, even at a point when I was teaching mostly affluent White kids in a suburban system and had not yet read extensively about the sorts of issues that the authors in this collection raise so impressively. What remains troubling to me is that in the decades since—in spite of a wealth of new knowledge about communicative competence, cultural ways of knowing, culturally relevant instruction, the richness of linguistic variety, the infusion of the "standard" form of a language with vitality from its derivatives, and much else—the beliefs of the principal not only remain in play, but have become institutionalized in public policy as part of the current emphasis on assessment through standardized tests, and the standardized curricula that feed into them.

Standardization is a simple solution to a complex web of challenges. And yet, what the authors in this collection demonstrate, empirically and persuasively, is that the world of standardization is a fool's paradise. The volume is replete with documentation of the richness of cultural ways of knowing and poses a formidable challenge to the conventional thinking that guides current policymaking. The collective work of the contributors shows conclusively that there is no standard or norm that provides the best destination for all people; indeed, the authors show that any social group benefits from attention to its variations in terms of the new possibilities that become available from new perspectives and ways of acting in the world.

The authors accomplish this feat without resorting to anarchy or acceptance of any value. Rather, they argue a point that I believe needs to become part of the education of anyone who undertakes teaching as a career: that every child has potential, that every child's potential is channeled culturally, that the dominant culture's sense of appropriate destiny may not be best for every child including those of its own, and that education serves everyone best by bringing out the best in everyone. This argument, I believe, should be strongly considered by policymakers as they establish the context in which teachers learn to teach and children learn to learn through their establishment of how school effectiveness is determined and how education is thus promoted.

REFERENCES

Kinloch, V. (2011). Crossing boundaries, studying diversity: Lessons from preservice teachers and urban youth. In A. Ball & C. Tyson (Eds.), *Studying diversity in teacher education* (pp. 149–166). Lanham, MD: Rowman & Littlefield.

Ladson-Billings, G. (1995). But that's just good teaching! The case for culturally relevant pedagogy. *Theory into Practice, 34*(3), 159–165.

Afterword

What If . . .

JoBeth Allen

> I been reading books my whole life, but I was doing it in a "school" kinda way. . . . It wasn't until I started readin' real knowledge that I realized that some books got the truth in them. You can use that truth to grow, to school other people in the community, to, like, make the world better. Now I'm not just a student, I'm like a young scholar in training. (Rashad, patron of Rasul's bookstore)

Like the insightful Rashad, many of us as educators have been reading books about education our whole lives. Maybe you felt like Rashad when you read *Urban Literacies*, like the book had some truth in it, that these truths could help you grow, that they could maybe even make the world better. That's how I felt—like a young scholar of urban education in training. I began to imagine. What if . . .

What if pre-service (and in-service) teachers walked the neighborhoods, talked with the families, learned the social and political issues, and documented the cultural resources in urban communities? How might teacher education be more relevant if it started with "knowledge of the vast cultural and linguistic norms present in dynamic urban settings"? What if professional development became a problem posing space "where colleagues engage in collective problem solving and as a polyphonic space where multiple perspectives are not simply tolerated, but honored and respected"?

What if every school had the opportunity to partner with college or community groups like Poetry for the People, and kids with college or community partners focused on issues in the community such as racial profiling?

And speaking of partners, what if school librarians partnered with and ordered from local Black or Latin@ or women's bookstores? What if school libraries operated like Rasul's bookstore, as a *literacy counterpublic* where students could "acquire oppositional formations of knowledge, challenge majoritarian narratives about the canon, and reimagine the purposes and functions of literacy within their everyday lives"?

What if literature discussions were more like book clubs and less like recall exams culled from teachers' editions? What if teachers recognized the importance of students operating with double consciousness, scaffolded discussions to draw on racialized experiences and perspectives, and worked toward dialogue and critique? How would learning change if students could "question power and contest static constructions of knowledge" in school texts? What if teachers solicited parents' stories and encouraged students to tell stories related to the ones they read? How can we encourage students to explore both connections and counternarratives with school literature?

What if we recognized students as "verbal artists" with "the ability to express linguistic, ethnic, and countercultural identities across literacy spaces"? What if we studied cultural movements such as hip-hop, not to develop simplistic strategies for engaging students in the "real" academics, but as the foundation for a curriculum that deeply values and incorporates cultural values? What if teachers and teacher educators studied and became "conversant in the complex linguistic and ethnic identity work of vernacular literacies"? What if teachers and students brought in texts in multiple languages and Englishes, analyzed their purposes and audiences, and created texts where students could both showcase and expand vernacular literacies? What if students wrote multigenre pieces incorporating tweets, rap, social networking posts, or text messages on investigations of issues such as global warming, affordable housing, or AIDS?

And what if we created these dynamic, community-connected, critical classrooms not just for some students but for all, including those who are or have been incarcerated? What if students who have rich out-of-school experiences with theatre, poetry, and other arts were invited to lead similar school performances? What would it mean to students on the margins to create, revise, interpret, and make language their own, to question and re-story the narratives imposed on them by the media?

What if.

About the Editor and Contributors

JoBeth Allen conducts collaborative action research with teachers on educational equity and social justice in relation to literacy teaching and learning. A professor of language and literacy education at the University of Georgia, she co-directs the Red Clay Writing Project. Her most recent books are *Creating Welcoming Schools: A Practical Guide to Home-School Partnerships with Diverse Families*, and *Literacy in the Welcoming Classroom: Creating Family-School Partnerships that Support Student Learning*.

Arnetha F. Ball, professor at Stanford University and president-elect of the American Educational Research Association (AERA), has worked as a classroom teacher, speech pathologist, consultant, educational administrator, and teacher educator. Her research focuses on oral language and written literacies for culturally and linguistically diverse populations, and on the preparation of teachers to work with students who are poor, members of racially or ethnically marginalized groups, and speakers of first languages other than mainstream or academic English.

Stephanie Power Carter is a former high school teacher and is currently an associate professor of English education at Indiana University-Bloomington. Her work includes various fields: literacy and secondary education; sociolinguistics; Black feminist theory; research on silence; social and cultural aspects of education; qualitative inquiry and ethnography; critical discourse analysis; and Black women's literature.

Jamal Cooks is associate professor at San Francisco State University, the Department of Secondary Education. He taught middle and high school social studies and English at the junior college level. He earned his B.A. from University of California at Berkeley and a M.A. in social studies curriculum development from the University of Michigan. His dissertation, completed at the University of Michigan, is titled *Explicit Instruction, Assumed Skills, or Something in the Middle: Expository Writing Development in Different Learning Environments with High School Freshmen.*

Anne Haas Dyson is a former teacher of young children and currently a professor at the University of Illinois at Urbana-Champaign. She studies the childhood cultures and literacy learning of young schoolchildren. Among her publications are *Social Worlds of Children Learning to Write in an Urban Primary School*, which was awarded the David Russell Award for Distinguished Research from NCTE, *Writing Superheroes*, and *The Brothers and Sisters Learn to Write: Popular Literacies in Childhood and School Cultures.* She recently coauthored two books with Celia Genishi, *On the Case* and *Children, Language, and Literacy: Diverse Learners in Diverse Times.*

Lucila D. Ek is assistant professor in the Department of Bicultural-Bilingual Studies at the University of Texas at San Antonio. She received her Ph.D. in urban schooling from the University of California at Los Angeles. Her research focuses on language, literacy, and identity in Chicana/o and Latina/o communities. Her work has been published in journals such as *Anthropology and Education Quarterly*, the *Bilingual Research Journal, High School Journal*, and the *International Journal of Bilingualism and Bilingual Education*.

Colleen Fairbanks's work focuses on the intersection of literacy, pedagogy, and the social contexts in which teachers and students work. This effort has spanned classroom-based research focused on critical teaching and students' lives; long-term research that followed a group of working-class, ethnically diverse girls through middle school and high school; and an examination of teachers' co-construction of knowledge as they collaborate to grow professionally.

Celia Genishi is a professor of education and the coordinator of the Program in Early Childhood in the Department of Curriculum and Teaching at Teachers College, Columbia University. She is coauthor (with A. H. Dyson) of *Children, Language, and Literacy: Diverse Learners in Diverse Times* and *Language Assessment in the Early Years*; (with M. Almy) of *Ways of Studying Children*; editor of *Ways of Assessing Children and Curriculum*; coeditor (with A. L. Goodwin) of *Diversities in Early Childhood Education: Rethinking and Doing*, and coauthor (with A. H. Dyson) of *The Need for Story: Cultural Diversity in Classroom and Community*. She is a 2010 fellow of the American Educational Research Association (AERA).

Juan C. Guerra, associate professor of English, is currently serving as associate dean and director of the Graduate Opportunities and Minority Achievement Program in the Graduate School at the University of Washington (UW) in Seattle. He has taught courses on literacy, ethnography, composition theory and pedagogy, as well as language variation and language policy. Dr. Guerra earned his Ph.D. in the Language, Literacy, and Rhetoric Program in the English Department at the University of Illinois at Chicago (UIC).

Marcelle M. Haddix is assistant professor of English education in the Reading and Language Arts Center at Syracuse University. Her work centers on literacy, language, and culture in K–12 and teacher education. She has published in various journals, including *Research in the Teaching of English,* and is the recipient of the 2010 Promising Researcher Award from the National Council of Teachers of English (NCTE).

Marc Lamont Hill is associate professor at Teachers College. His work covers topics such as hip-hop culture, politics, sexuality, education, and religion, and has appeared in numerous journals, magazines, books, and anthologies. He is author of *Beats, Rhymes, and Classroom Life.*

Korina Jocson is assistant professor of education in arts & sciences at Washington University in St. Louis. Her research and teaching interests include literacy, youth, and cultural studies in education. Her work examines the changing nature of literacies and media technologies across educational contexts. She is author of *Youth Poets: Empowering Literacies in and out of Schools.*

Jung Kim is assistant professor of reading and literacy at Lewis University in Romeoville, Illinois. She has worked in urban education as a high school teacher, literacy coach, and consultant. Her primary research revolves around issues of equity and urban education, particularly in examining how notions of teaching and learning can be redefined in the creation of dynamic classrooms. Her current work looks at the potential of using elements of popular culture, such as hip-hop music and graphic novels, with students to create a more viable and relevant curriculum.

Valerie Kinloch is associate professor in literacy studies at The Ohio State University, coeditor of the NCTE/Routledge Book Series in Literacy, and director of the Cultivating New Voices Among Scholars of Color Program (CNV). Her research examines the literacy learning of youth and adults in and out of school. Her most recent book is, *Harlem on Our Minds: Place, Race, and the Literacies of Urban Youth*. She received the 2010 Scholars of Color Early Career Award from AERA and the 2010 OSU Dean's Inspiration Award.

David E. Kirkland is assistant professor of English education at New York University's Steinhardt School of Culture, Education, and Human Development, Department of Teaching and Learning. His research focuses on urban youth popular culture, language and literacy, digital identities, and urban teacher education. He received the 2008 AERA Division G Outstanding Dissertation Award.

Kafi D. Kumasi is assistant professor in the School of Library and Information Science at Wayne State University. Her work centers on school library media issues, particularly social and cultural aspects of adolescent literacy instruction and programming. She will be instrumental in bringing the school's planned certificate in Urban Librarianship to fruition.

Carol D. Lee is professor of education and social policy at Northwestern University and past president of AERA. Her work focuses on urban education, cultural supports for literacy, classroom discourse, and instructional design. The design principles that undergird her research involve drawing on forms of cultural capital, especially that of community language practices.

Margarita Machado-Casas is assistant professor at Wayne State University in the College of Education, Division of Bicultural-Bilingual Studies. She completed her Ph.D. at University of North Carolina, Chapel Hill, and a postdoctoral fellowship at Frank Potter Graham (FPG) Child Development Institute at University of North Carolina, Chapel Hill. Her research focuses on migrant, indigenous, and Latino education; transnational communities; biliteracy; bilingual education; and minority agency.

Guillermo Malavé is a lecturer at The University of Texas, Austin, offering courses on diversity issues relevant for developing cultural competent practices in education, social work, and so forth, that provide services to Hispanic/Latina/o populations. Previously, he worked in social work and had supervisory positions in which he provided direct services to Hispanic, Spanish-speaking families in Puerto Rico. His current research projects involve parental involvement in schools and the socialization of children, focusing on Mexican-descent children and parents.

Carmen M. Martínez-Roldán earned her doctorate in language, reading, and culture from the University of Arizona, and her M.A. in curriculum and instruction from the University of Puerto Rico. Her work examines young English language learners' reading comprehension processes as they read expository texts, focusing on how the structure of the texts and the language of reading events mediate their development of scientific concepts.

Sonia Nieto is professor emerita of language, literacy, and culture, University of Massachusetts, Amherst. She has written widely on multicultural education, teacher education, and the education of students of culturally and linguistically diverse backgrounds. She has taught at all levels from elementary school to graduate school, and she has been recognized for her research, advocacy, and service with many awards, including four honorary degrees.

Django Paris is assistant professor of English at Arizona State University. He is also on faculty at the Bread Loaf School of English in Vermont. Before entering the academy, he spent six years as an English teacher in California, Arizona, and the Dominican Republic. His research has appeared in *Harvard Educational Review, English Education,* and *Journal of Language, Identity, and Education,* and is forthcoming in the *International Journal of Qualitative Studies in Education.*

Detra Price-Dennis is assistant professor of language and literacy in the School of Education at the University of Texas at Austin. As a teacher educator, her work examines transformative literacy pedagogies that seek to create and sustain equitable learning environments. Her research interests also include critical perspectives on children's and young adult literature.

Mary Alexandra Rojas received her doctorate in English education from Teachers College, Columbia University. She has taught English literature at the secondary level in the Los Angeles Unified School District in California as well as English methods for pre- and inservice teachers, M.A. students at Teachers College. Her research interests are focused on U.S. Latino literature, high school English curriculum, and feminists poststructuralist theories.

Patricia Sánchez is associate professor in the Department of Bicultural-Bilingual Studies at the University of Texas, San Antonio. She uses a sociocultural lens to examine globalization, transnationalism, immigrant students and families, teacher preparation, and critical research methodologies. Her work has appeared in *The Urban Review, Linguistics and Education, New Directions for Youth Development, Social Justice,* and *Bilingual Research Journal.*

Peter Smagorinsky is professor of English education at the University of Georgia. When chair of the NCTE Research Foundation in 2000, he helped to found the Cultivating New Voices Among Scholars of Color (CNV) grant program, and served as its first director.

Howard L. Smith is associate professor of bilingual education and biliteracy at the University of Texas, San Antonio. Dr. Smith conducts research in teacher preparation, dual-language programs, and biliteracy development. His article, "Cartitas de Cariño: Little Notes to Say You Care," was coauthored with Dr. Mari Cortez and will appear in the *Language Arts Journal.*

Mariana Souto-Manning is associate professor of curriculum and teaching at Teachers College, Columbia University. She is the author of *Freire, Teaching, and Learning: Culture Circles across Contexts,* and *Teachers Act Up!: Creating Multicultural Learning Communities through Theatre.* She received the 2010 AERA Division K (Teaching and Teacher Education) Early Career Research Award.

Maisha T. Winn is associate professor in the Division of Educational Studies at Emory University. Currently, she is examining the role of literacy in the lives of incarcerated and formerly incarcerated youth. Her research interests include sociocultural theories of learning, historicizing literacy, and the intersection of language, literacy, and the school-to-prison pipeline.

Index